D0108513

Studies in Music

780
G 869s
1976

AMS PRESS
NEW YORK

JOHANNES BRAHMS

STUDIES IN MUSIC

BY VARIOUS AUTHORS

REPRINTED FROM 'THE MUSICIAN'

AND EDITED

BY

ROBIN GREY

LONDON

SIMPKIN, MARSHALL, HAMILTON,

KENT AND CO., LIMITED

1901

Library of Congress Cataloging in Publication Data

Grey, Robin.
    Studies in music.

        Reprint of the 1901 ed. published by Simpkin,
    Marshall, Hamilton, Kent, London under title: Studies
    in music by various authors reprinted from The Musician.
        CONTENTS: Spitta, P. Johannes Brahms.—Legge, R.H.
    Letters from Brahms to Schumann.—Widor, C.M. John
    Sebastian Bach and the organ. [etc.]
        1. Music—Addresses, essays, lectures. I. The
    Musician (English) II. Title.
    ML55.G84   1976   780'.8   74-24092
    ISBN 0-404-12937-4

Reprinted from an original copy in the collections
of the University of Virginia Library

From the edition of 1901, London
First AMS edition published in 1976
Manufactured in the United States of America

AMS PRESS, INC.
NEW YORK, N.Y.

TO MY FRIEND

CHARLES T. GATTY

Contents

Johannes Brahms

PHILIPP SPITTA

I

'IF you wish to move a thing you must not stand upon it,' Robert Schumann once said, and he meant to convey that the creative artist must rise above the condition of emotional excitement which contains the germ of the work of art. 'Roland in a fury cannot write verse; a loving heart says least about it.'

It is natural to think of Schumann when speaking of Brahms. I here apply what he said of Art to the Science of history. The growth and development of facts and personal details cannot be set forth in mid-stream, so to speak. Any one who has, for more than thirty years, followed with sympathetic interest every step taken by Brahms as a composer may be fully informed of such details; but he will hardly venture to pronounce any explicit historical opinion on the man. It is not un-necessary to insist on this. Theories of evolution are so popular in these days that no sooner has any conspicuous personality appeared on the scene than men are busy trying to fit him into the great connected scheme of

A

things, as they say. But since contemporaries are not called upon for such a task, this ends in useless or mischievous speculations.

Mischievous especially in regard to Art. The artist lives for the present; and the musician, whose work perishes with the instant, does so in a twofold sense and measure. He must be apprehended at the moment in which he produces his work. He asks that it should be enjoyed there and then, not with a comparing and wandering reference to what may exist before or after it, but as though there were at that instant nothing else in the world. When we note the way in which the public pronounces on new works of Art we can but wonder what there is in them that gives these folks pleasure; often it would seem that it lies in disparaging criticism rather than in open-minded receptiveness. Brahms has suffered all the more from this historical dilettantism because the peculiarities of his art seem to rouse its animadversion.

But it is quite another matter when we honestly endeavour to discover what it is that gives rise to the peculiar impression made by a work of art. It will at least not be denied that this demands an æsthetic training, and the comparing power given by its expanding and refining action on the mind. It is impossible to give the portrait of an artistic individuality in words without calling up some familiar figures to throw light on it. Still, premature depreciation is a mistake. The contemporaries of a great artist can do no more than learn to understand his individuality. This they have a right to do; it is their duty to themselves. Everything beyond this is no concern of theirs; they may leave it to posterity. Posterity will pronounce how far the artist's power has had a procreative influence, and that is the only point which deserves consideration from history. For beauty is infinitely multiform; the utmost diversity may walk hand-in-hand in peace and harmony.

I speak of Brahms as a great artist, and I assert that this opinion will meet with general acceptance, though not undisputed by many. He is not one of those who can rouse vehement displays of feeling; in this respect he is the direct opposite to Richard Wagner. On his first appearance it was curiosity that moved the public, and that soon died out. For many years he remained mute and was almost forgotten. During the sixties the number of his admirers gradually and very quietly multi-plied; he himself seemed to shun everything that could attract attention. He wrote no Opera, no Oratorio, no Symphony; only songs, chamber-music, serenades. He never advertised his work: when once it was published he left it to its fate. He had held no appointment at the head of any well-known Institution or Society, he did not covet the laurels of the virtuoso. In later years he brought himself to be occasionally more conciliatory to the world at large; but essentially his attitude remained always the same.

His earliest compositions reveal the man. He was twenty when he began publishing his work. Till then he had been silently ripening; he had felt little external stimulus; his native town was anything rather than a high-class musical centre. He had to find the best of his inspiration in himself; nevertheless, as the son of an orchestral-player, he early learned the technique of the executant. In some aspects his musical youth resembled Beethoven's.

It is impossible to say that the young composer was a follower of any particular master. All the evidence that critics have adduced seems to me purely superficial. The discovery of certain resemblances is not sufficient.

They show less lack of independence in Brahms than perhaps in any other composer ; he did not avoid them at a later date, nay, he deliberately adopted them in the fullest consciousness of his powers. His first sonatas and songs reveal perfect familiarity with everything in German music before his time, so far as such complete knowledge was then accessible. But, even then, the suggestions he derived had received a stamp of individuality. At that early age these works indicate a mental effort full of remarkable energy and purpose, and a precocious maturity which is none the less astonishing because it made no outward display but was marked by modest reserve. Throughout his life Brahms had the power of assimilating everything that came in his way ; this was one of his most marked peculiarities. No musician was more well read in his art or more constantly disposed to appropriate all that was new, especially all newly discovered treasures of the past. His passion for learning wandered, indeed, into every field, and resulted in a rich and most original culture of mind, for his knowledge was not mere acquirement, but became a living and fruitful thing.

The strangest thing that is, even now, said about Brahms is that he is a follower of Schumann. They are as totally unlike as two artists with a common view of art can possibly be. It was, indeed, Brahms's striking independence that first attracted Schumann's admiration ; and then the mastery he discerned in Brahms, so early ripe, for which he himself had been forced to toil so much longer. To recognise the justness of Schumann's opinion we must remember what the standard of form-sense was among the composers of the middle of this century. Brahms himself subsequently accustomed us to a far higher type of completeness of form ; his early works are not to be compared with his own later achieve-

ments, but with those of the masters of his youth—
Schumann's, for instance, or Gade's.

The leading characteristics of Brahms's music are all
plainly visible in his first ten works: A manliness that
is almost brusque, a dislike for purely emotional music,
stern conciseness in the melodic matter, a delight in
organic structure, particularly by the use of strict polyphony, combining with the freer style of Beethoven to
produce entirely new results. The serious underlying
feeling, a sense of depth, exquisite beauty of sentiment
shrouded under a dignified reserve; again, a spirit of
contradiction, a determination to combine what nature
seemed to have set asunder, and the fancy for working
out organically plastic elements to their highest end
while making enjoyment more complete by a close
interweaving of ideas.

Composers who have come before the world with
distinctly marked features from the first, have not un-
frequently produced but little. This was not to be
our experience of Brahms, though there was a time
when he seemed to be doing little. At the beginning
of the sixties his friends began to wonder what he would
indeed achieve. Many believed—for Brahms never spoke
of his schemes—that he was cheating himself with dreams
of impossible innovations. He, meanwhile, had made his
plans. With the exception of *Rinaldo*, he never over-
stepped the limits he had laid down for himself by 1865;
even his greatest Choral works were foreshadowed in the
'Funeral Hymn,' in his first Motets and in other works,
just as the Serenades were the very evident preludes to
his later Symphonies. Such self-contained individualities
as his never feel the craving for new worlds to conquer.
They find enough to do in the old home, and never are
misled by cant phrases about 'exhausted forms of art.'
Time has shown that Brahms was right. The fount of

his invention flowed inexhaustible and with unflagging strength within these limits of form.

In most composers it is easy to point to the class of work in which their genius shows to the best advantage. No such favourite form can be named for Brahms. The songs stand beside the Symphonies and Overtures, the chamber - music beside the 'Funeral Hymn' and the *Triumphlied*, the *a capella* compositions beside the Concertos or *Rinaldo*. In all we see the indivisible identity of the composer, and those who would estimate that, must not overlook one of his works—more than a hundred in all.

II

Such a complete comprehension of all the forms and means of musical expression during the last century as we find in Brahms, and their application in the forms of composition he affected, is really stupendous, and, in its way, quite unprecedented. Any one who fancies that he worked on the lines of Haydn, Mozart, or Beethoven, with occasional reference to Sebastian Bach, knows little of Brahms.

In the first place, we find him enriching tonality by a reversion to the methods of the sixteenth century. These methods had never entirely died out, but they lurked *incognito*, and might be thankful if, when detected, they were so much as endured. Brahms is the first great composer for above a century who consciously and intentionally wrote melody in the Dorian mode and brought out the characteristic expression which dwells in it. The reader is referred to the songs No. 8, Op. 14, and No. 6, Op. 48. There the strength and richness of his harmony is fed by his adopting a characteristic use of the octave. Many very striking effects may be directly referred to this. The diminished lowest tone in the minor scale was

regarded by the older writers as an admissible note in
the diatonic scale. They did not use it as a tonic by
reason of the unmelodic tritonic interval which was forced
upon the bass. In our day, when harmonic rather than
melodic progression is looked for, this detail is not regarded.
The D major chord in the key of C sharp minor, which
we now regard as inadmissible, is thus justified (Op. 46,
No. 1, bar 34). In the major key this flattened lower
note is the bass of the chord of the major third, which has
a grand effect known to all who are familiar with old
vocal music ; we find it used in Brahms's *Marien-lieder* in
four parts (Op. 22), to mention one of many instances.
The sharpening of minor thirds and sixths was regarded
by the older writers as a passing sharpening of the note
whose value in the key was not changed. This is not
now the general practice : chromatic raising or lowering of
a note entails new harmonic relations. But if we attempt
to revive and emphasise the use of the old scheme of
tonality we obtain a twofold source of harmonies which is
fertile in modulatory effects. How fully Brahms understood
this every one knows who has studied his compositions
with attention to this point. The immediate transition
from the major and minor thirds is often introduced as
it is in much earlier music. That the minor and major
scales, starting from the same note, are closely allied
keys, is a feeling that has never died out, and in Schubert
we often need to remember this to enable us to understand his endless resource in modulation. Still I know
of no instance in his works where it is so conspicuously
asserted that C and C sharp can be treated as the same
note, as in Song 5, Op. 7, by Brahms. A treatise might
be written on this subject.

Then, as to rhythm, I say nothing of his various
use of bar measures $\frac{3}{4} + \frac{2}{4}$, $\frac{3}{4} + \frac{4}{4}$, and the like. The
lengthening of the measure in the cadenza is a revival of

an old practice. The *Hemiolia*, the playing of a common-time bar against a triple-time bar, had almost fallen into desuetude till Brahms brought it into repute again. Among the earlier masters, indeed, we find that a phrase is sometimes lengthened by the value of one or two beats, and yet continues its progress in accordance with the prevailing measure. (*See* Schütz, *Werke* VIII., p. 69 ; X., p. 58.) Brahms makes use of this figure of rhythm in Op. 107, No. 3. In the part songs of the older masters, various rhythms are used in combination, and in the latest of our composers we find the same practice. Such a structure as the song *Es weht um mich Narcissenduft* is certainly a singular production in our age. The voice sings in $\frac{4}{4}$ time, the right hand plays in $\frac{3}{2}$, while the left hand plays in $\frac{6}{4}$, but the bar is counted as two crotchets.

If we go on from the elements of form to form itself, we see the types of modern art mingling everywhere with those of a bygone time. Schumann had already seriously studied and revised the Canon, which had sunk to the level of an amusing exercise ; Brahms interested himself in its stricter construction and used it in a greater variety of forms. The extension and diminution of the melody again, that is to say, the lengthening of the strain by doubling the value of the notes, or shortening it by diminishing their value, which was such an important element of form in the fifteenth and sixteenth centuries, came to light again for the first time with all its innate musical vitality when Brahms took it up, and even in his earliest works (for instance, Op. 3, No. 2) showed how thoroughly he understood it. The same is to be said of the method of inversion, the derivation of a new melody from the former by reversing the intervals. When the use of such 'artifices'—as they were called with an amazing misapprehension of the very essence of music—had from time to time been admitted, they had always been restricted to what was termed a *Gelehrten Satz*; that is to say, they were worked out as school exercises and formed no part of the artist's living work. But with Brahms they pervade all his music, and find a place as much in the pianoforte sonata and the simple ballad as in the grand choral pieces with orchestral accompaniments.

The *basso ostinato* with the styles pertaining to it—the *Passacaglia* and the *Ciaccona*—resume their significance for the first time since Bach's time, and their intrinsic importance is enhanced by the support of the symphonic orchestra.

The old Variation form, above all, is brought out from the treasures of the old composers, and glorified in his hands. Brahms's variations are something quite different from what had been commonly known by that name. Their prototype is Bach's *Aria* with thirty variations, and that work is an elaboration of the form known as the *Passacaglia*. In this the determining idea is not the addition of figures or of various accompaniments to the theme or melody, but the persistent identity of the bass. This continues the same through all the variations; upon that a free treatment is worked out—not, however, excluding an occasional reference to the original melody. Beethoven so far adhered to the usually accepted form, as to restrict the supremacy of the bass to alternate use with variations in the melody, and Schumann followed his example. This form was not adopted by other great masters, and even Beethoven and Schumann only used it fitfully. Brahms, so rich in inventive combinations, stands nearer to Bach than to Beethoven, but has much of Beethoven's freer style of treatment. Augmentation or diminution of the phrases forming the theme are a manner of variation never used by Beethoven, and employed by Brahms only in the variations in the two first Sonatas, and in the independent 'Air with Variations' (Op. 9). In this it is often surprisingly ingenious, but he must have thought the process incompatible with his strict sense of form, just as he gave up changes of key from one variation to the next, which Schumann often used, though Beethoven allowed himself only once (Op. 34).

In the second variation in Op. 9 we find, on the other hand, what important pre-eminence he assigns to the bass; and in the tenth variation of the same set he even uses it as the melody in the upper part. Then he derives a subject from the diminution to half or quarter notes of the opening of the theme; this is worked out to fill up the required measure, while the essential harmonies are maintained in the same succession, so that the theme, or part of it, is reflected, as it were, to and fro, from two or four mirrors. This first work of his with variations was written on a theme by Schumann, and dedicated to Clara Schumann, and Brahms therefore introduced some other musical ideas of theirs as a mark of respect.

Similar ingenious adaptations of borrowed materials often occur in his works. A brilliant instance of ingenious and artistic combination is to be seen in the ninth variation, which seems to introduce a whole piece of Schumann's with a slight alteration (out of *Bunte Blätter*, Op. 99, No. 5) in the middle part, heard through the compressed thema-melody. How thoroughly he had thought out the spirit of the Variation is seen in the fact that he is fond of interchanging the modulatory relations of the two phrases of the theme. The place where this generally occurs is at the beginning of the second part; but also in the second half of the first part. The digressions, more or less important, which he admits are always so chosen that the effect of the newly introduced key approximately answers to that produced

by the original key of the preceding or following phrase.
Even the cadenzas appear altered from this point of
view.

It is impossible, from description, to form even a faint
idea of the wealth of fancy, of inventive power, of vigorous
vitality that lies in Brahms's variations. I cannot, indeed,
conceive of any more subtle or more thoughtful treatment of this form of music than that of Brahms—for
instance, in the Variations for the Piano, on a theme
of Handel (Op. 24). The danger, as it seems to me, is
that the true form of variations should be lost sight of,
which consisted originally in the persistent embellishment
of an air. The bass of a simply harmonised thema-
melody has not, as a rule, any very distinctive character.
And when it happens that the theme is a mere popular
and insignificant tune, the result is a series of movements
that have nothing in common with it but the constant
number of bars and the regular alternation of the original
key with those of the two dominants. This is the case
in the Paganini Variations (Op. 35); and also, it must
be said, in Beethoven's Thirty-three Variations on a waltz
by Diabelli.

In close relationship to the Variation form, we had in
the seventeenth century the Suite, both being essentially
species of Clavier music. Of the set of dances which
constituted a Suite, the first was the theme; the others
were variations on it, each in its own rhythm. Traces
of this connected form survived into the eighteenth
century, till Bach finally severed the parts. His Suites
having come into favour again in our time, some modern
composers have felt prompted to imitate him; but their
Suites are not *Suites*. When they are not Sonatas, or a
simplified form of Symphony, they are Serenades. Brahms
has altogether neglected the Suite. Though in his second
Sonata the *Scherzo* is developed like a last variation from

the *Andante* (with variations), it is one of the ingenious
ideas of which his early works are full. There is no
intentional reference to any old form ; but dance melodies,
as such, he has constantly composed, of the kind so
much in vogue at the time of the Vienna masters.
Dances, all of the same type, are arranged in series of
any number and variety. Then the same thing occurred
as in the time of the Suite. The dances of which they
were made up had at first been conceived of as practically
dance tunes ; but by degrees they were more and more
idealised, and it would never occur to any one to dance
to one of Bach's *Courantes*.

Schubert's waltzes could still be played for dancing to ;
not so most of Brahms. Brahms won for the waltz its
restoration to a place in the higher ranks of music.
Treated at first as pianoforte music, the waltz was still
further idealised by being used for singing. A similar
process was gone through by Hungarian dance and vocal
measures. Brahms did not invent these, but he added so
much that was original and important that his ' Hungarian
Dances ' may almost be regarded as original compositions.
Every one knows how marked his influence has been on
contemporary composers through this class of work.

III

Brahms drank deep of the fount of the Past. At the
same time it cannot be said that his music has any
tendency to archaism. This could only mean that by
the use of such antiquated methods of expression as now
seem strange to us, he gave it a superficial charm which
was to have a poetical effect and suggest a feeling. Since
this is often really done in these days, both in music
and poetry, I should wish to say emphatically that
Brahms's method and inspiration seem to me to have

nothing whatever in common with this realistic tendency. Everything that he derived from the old composers has become part of himself, and he has amalgamated it with his own thoroughly individual musical utterance. This is full of new expressions, new idioms, so to speak ; but he uses them solely for the presentment of the inmost core of his idea. In the *Marien-lieder* how exactly he has hit on the innocent, reserved and maidenly austerity of sentiment which is the fundamental tone of the poem. In the *Volkslieder*, for four voices, the treatment varies with the character of the words and the melody. If the old feeling predominates, Brahms adopts the method of treatment which naturally fits it ; modern sentiments he sets in the modern style. He always goes to the heart of the matter.

That Brahms at all times gave his earnest attention to the *Volkslied*, the music of the people, we see even in his earliest works ; and from what has been said it is evident that this would be the case. His own melodic inventiveness was fed on it, and alike on sacred and on secular music. He was also fond of setting the words of popular songs to original music, words of every degree of antiquity ; their simple originality of conception and sentiment was evidently a strong incitement to his fertile inventiveness. The revived taste for the songs of the people has had this effect on several composers, and many beautiful and original things have been written in that simple form. Think only of Weber, for instance. But many efforts of this kind also betray the inability of the composer to free himself from the trammels of the man of culture. Such hybrids may occasionally be pleasing, but are quite unsatisfactory.

Brahms, whose too self-revealing style must often be blamed, is artless in his treatment of the *Volkslied*. It never occurs to him to alter the verse, to substitute elegant phraseology for rough, strange, or even tasteless expressions; he loves it in its natural state. And he reflects the feeling he finds in this simple poetry with unsurpassable truth. I know nothing more impressive in severity of expression than the 'Funeral Hymn,' a setting of a sixteenth-century hymn, *Nun lasst uns den Leib begraben.* The simple monotonous dirge moves on like a funeral march with inexorable, almost indifferent, solemnity, like implacable Fate. The instruments that accompany the choir are reduced in number and kind to what are strictly necessary; their character is a mixture of the piercing and the grave. In the *trio* we have no feeble lament, no heartrending emotion, but the consolation of perfect confidence in the release from the anguish of life. The melody is strictly 'popular' in style, and every note seems chiselled.

And in his setting of *Volkslieder* for a single voice we find the same compact structure, which seems to evolve fresh meaning with every verse, so that we feel as if we could go on singing such a strain for ever.

Since the time of the great Austrian composers, symphonic and dramatic song has established itself side by side with the verse song. A fourth class of song was produced by Zumsteeg and Löwe: the character-lyric *Ballade.* Brahms, too, wrote *Balladen*; but *character* in Löwe's sense of the word—what we may call pictorial treatment—was not to his mind. He always scrupulously avoided dramatic song-writing; it has, indeed, never found much favour with German composers. Weber was its chief exponent; Mozart has left us a few fine examples, and Marschner some of great merit in his *Bilder des Orients*, especially the new series (Op. 140).

Brahms has shown how great an attraction song-writing had for him in nearly two hundred songs and ballads. When he began, Schumann stood supreme, and after him, with inferior power but quite peculiar tenderness, Robert Franz. He has little in common with either. The delightful use of the Phrygian mode, as treated by Franz, must be recorded to his honour; he was the first in this field; Brahms affected the Dorian in preference. Certain little touches in his melodies faintly remind us of the songs of 1820-30, when as yet Schumann was not, and Schubert had not yet penetrated throughout Northern Germany. I fancy that Brahms in his childhood and youth must have been under the influence of that type of song music, and derived from it an impression which is heard at intervals in his work all his life through. Personal feeling is often associated with certain musical phrases and cadences, and they remain dear to us as memories of our childhood, even when they seem old-fashioned to younger generations. The evident pleasure with which Brahms derives suggestions from such poets as Flemming, Hölty, and Voss arises no doubt from that cause.

The romantic vein of Schumann's songs finds no response in him. In contrast with the magical web and overgrowth, the airy, broken character of Schumann's pianoforte parts, Brahms gives us a far more closely woven accompaniment. It is in the representation of the moods of Nature that the difference is most marked. Compare Schumann's setting of Eichendorff's *Dämmerung will die Flügel spreiten* with Brahms's setting of Goethe's words *Dämmerung senkte sich von oben*, or their two compositions to the words *Aus der Heimath hinter den Blitzen roth* and *Es war als hätte der Himmel die Erde still geküsst.*

However, Brahms set but few of Eichendorff's verses. Schumann's great delight in plunging — losing his human individuality—in the placid waters of a pantheistic sense of nature was not shared by Brahms. He has given very simple colouring to the two last-named songs, but a firm, clear outline; to him the actual *tune* is the most important point; Schumann merely weaves it in dreamily with the instrumental texture. On the other hand Brahms, better than any other composer, has hit upon the very spirit of Eichendorff's freshness, as of a mountain spring, and of his placid melancholy in his *Romanze* (or elegiac lyrics). Here human joy and sorrow stand in the foreground, and his first aim in song-writing is to represent human feeling. The sympathy of Nature serves only as a foil; in that sense indeed he treats it with the finest effect. In Hölty's *Mainacht*, Schack's *Abenddämmerung*, Klaus Groth's *Regenlied*, Allmer's *Feldeinsamkeit*, and such songs as *Es kehrt die dunkle Schwalbe; Mit Geheimnissvollen Düften; Unbewegte lauer Luft; Ich sass zu deinen Füssen; Ueber die Haide hallet mein Schritt; Mein Herz ist schwer, mein Auge wacht,* we see the relation of the two factors in his mind. Songs like *An eine Aeolsharfe* or *Die Meere* (from the Duets, Op. 20) are exceptional with him.

The part attributed to the accompaniment in Brahms's song-writing is the result of this relation, which we may call normal, without disputing his occasional reversion to other methods. Brahms treats the accompaniment, considered in its elements, with greater simplicity than Schumann, or even Franz, who substitutes a firm use of the middle parts for Schumann's capricious polyphony. It should always be subordinate; this does not hinder it from being sometimes very elaborate, from somewhat overpowering the voice by fulness of tone, and being extremely difficult to play. But the melody and the bass are always the unfailing mainstay of the composition. In Brahms we find once more the fundamental bass. There are not a few of his songs for which the bass alone is a sufficient accompaniment, more especially when it is the foundation of harmonies in broken chords; the right hand then plays the full chord or the melody itself, which he is fond of supporting with thirds and sixths. The figures of his accompaniments are often highly ingenious, but he frequently contents himself with the simplest materials. He has found some of his forms of accompaniment in the stores of the old composers, as, for instance, the familiar rocking, onward motion frequent in Bach; but he avoids imitating Bach's polyphonic treatment of solo vocal music. *Sommerfäden* (Op. 72) is a clever exception. Again, in the preliminary symphony and interludes he often gives the melody to the bass; this was a very general practice in Bach's and Handel's time in cases when only the bass was written out below the voice part, but which had been entirely abandoned in our century. When the *Ritornell* was supported by other instruments, the old composers gave it an altered aspect by weaving in the voices, and thus at the same time giving a pleasing addition to the vocal part of the composition. We see, from certain compositions by Brahms (Op. 69, 1 ; Op. 85, 3 ; Op. 86, 1), that he did not overlook this treatment.

And what applies to his songs is yet more clearly marked in his duets. Not only is the three-part structure much more decisively handled than by Mendelssohn and his lesser imitators, but the bass has an independent theme; and this brings us to polyphonic passages, which have no parallel in our century; we must look for them in Steffani's and Handel's chamber duets.

The first five Books contain chiefly verse songs. Then suddenly their character is changed, and we have songs of broader structure, in which instrumental forms are brought into play. This is Schubert's realm. And Brahms resembles him in so far that he does not introduce us to dramatic situations or psychological processes.

B

He seizes on lyric situations without exception, even in those poems which, like Herr von Falkenstein's song and some others, have a dialogue form. He is stricter than Schubert—often so free-handed that he did not hesitate to introduce passages of recitative. As I have already remarked, he gives us no *character* music in the strictest sense, such as we find in Löwe's *Balladen*, and more fully developed in the Oratorio. The imagery demanded by the poem has, indeed, its due effect on the treatment, but it does not supply the groundwork ; the images are but reflected from the shore in the mirror of the current. They add to its charm ; but even if they were absent the stream would flow on all the same, and the strength of its vitality remains unbroken by them. That vitality is far more essentially musical than in any other hands since the time of Beethoven.

Hence Brahms has no love of sentimentality, not even in instrumental music, where it is universally admitted. Though he has set popular ditties of the most various nationalities, he does not therefore imitate their national music. Now and again he may borrow a strain, but his first aim is to write music that expresses his own individuality. If it were not so we should find in the *Liebeslieder* waltz tunes in the Russian, Polish, and Servian styles, or Turkish, Persian, Malayan ; *Die Kränze* (Op. 46, 1) would be Greek, and the thoroughly German music to *Es träumte mir ich sei Dir theuer* would be Spanish.

Among the symphonic songs—I allow myself to use the term for the sake of brevity—the fifteen *Romanzen* from Tieck's *Magelone* are pre-eminently brilliant. The question as to whether solo vocal music is possible in our day in such a broadly composite form is here emphatically answered in the affirmative. The man who could write these could also compose songs of the *Aria* type in sacred music and oratorio, with orchestral accompaniment. This, indeed, Brahms never did ; but in the *Rinaldo* we find *arias* of great perfection. He here had the right class of words to work on, without which such composition is impossible. He was probably led to choose Tieck's poem chiefly because it was well suited for song-writing in a broad style. As regards these two types of song then, there, so far as Brahms is concerned, the matter rests. A composer who so wholly devotes himself to lyric settings must be conscious of his strength in the invention of melody. The strength, indeed, was there ; no one can mistake that who does not confound melody with a mere facile tunefulness. Brahms is rarely pleasing. He has not even Schumann's heartfelt quality ; on the other hand, no composer can compare with him in peculiarly *distingué* elegance.

His warmth is in reserve ; his tenderness is shy of coming forward, and is apt to restrict itself to the briefest possible expression. This is quite North-German ; the man is North-German from head to foot. But long-suppressed feeling, when at last it finds its way, is apt to break down all barriers. When Brahms, the Hamburger, settled in Vienna, he did so, perhaps, in the expectation that the glow of southern emotion might thaw his northern reserve and reconcile the antagonisms of his nature. And this may, in some degree, have been the result ; but a nature, hewn as his was out of one piece of wood, cannot be taken apart and put together again. His calm verges on the sublime ; his passion is frenzy. So harmonious a concord of rapturous feeling with beatific, undesiring contentment as we find in perfection in the song *Wir wandelten, wir zwei zusammen* is rare indeed with him. And there are works by Brahms in which coldness and fervency are intermingled in a way that gives the hearer a quite uncanny impression.

Our greatest song-writers, Weber and Schubert, Mendelssohn and Schumann, all had a certain youthfulness of spirit. They died young, or in the prime of life. Brahms (still living when this was written) writes in a key of lyric manhood, and is, so far, a new figure; only Beethoven might have compared with him in this respect if he had composed songs less rarely. I do not know whether any one has hitherto noted that all but a very few of Brahms's songs, after Op. 32, are men's songs, and should never be sung but by men. In youth the sexes are more closely allied, softer and less strongly marked ; Schubert's *In Grün will ich mich kleiden*, and *Wo ein treues Herz in Liebe vergeht* sound quite appropriate from a girl's lips. In riper years the contrast is greater, the expression of feeling is more unlike, and its utterance more difficult. Sung by a woman, the song *O Nachtigall, dein süsser Schall* loses half its meaning ; its passion lies deeper down and shakes the foundations of one's being. And this, which is true even of *Mainacht* and the *Magelone* series, holds good in the strongest and widest sense of Op. 57 and the succeeding collections. Not tears, but drops of blood befit these songs.

Youth rides the higher waves of feeling with delight ; it hails the Spring with happy shouts, and bewails lost joys in an ecstasy of grief. Geibel was a singer of youth. Brahms has set but few of his verses, though he made great use of his fellow-countrymen of north-west Germany, Hebbel, Storm, Klaus Groth, Schack, and others. He has conceived Geibel's *Nun wollen Berg und Thal wieder blühn* in quite a different sense from that intended by the poet. In his setting of the Spring song, *Mit geheimnissvollen Düften*, we do not hear the lark's carol of the youthful soul, which Geibel preserved even in his old age, and whose desires and griefs, as Uhland says, 'Heaven graciously smiling swiftly effaces.' The song *Es kehrt*

die dunkle Schwalbe is unsurpassed in feeling, and none
but those who have felt in their soul the bitter disillusion-
ment of life can respond to such tones as we hear in
Schack's *Herbstgefühl,* Candidus' *Schwermuth,* or Lemcke's
Verzagen. And from the lips of such a one alone can
we understand such bitterly ironical reflections as the
Hirngespinnste der Menschen and the *Fetzen goldner
Liebesträume.* These utterances are a world removed
from mere *blasé* heart-sickness. It is with solemn calm
that Brahms depicts the imperceptible decline from the
heights of life to the haven which shelters and hides all.
The refreshing strains from the Psalter of the Father of
Love console us for the scorn of man.

It is self-evident that such a nature has a stern hand
for the erotic vein. Mozart's and Goethe's sensuality
is more guileless and mirthful. But if, in order to understand *Figaro,* or the *Römische Elegien,* we take into due
consideration the spirit of their time, we cannot refuse to
give due importance to the prevalent views of life when
studying so powerful a personality as Brahms. By him,
as by the earlier masters, erotic feeling is purified by the
strictest artistic treatment, and weighted with solid
musical matter. Here and there we may wish a touch
altered, but the whole impression is healthy. If anybody
doubts this he must surely learn to know better if he
looks at the little songs in the *Volkslied* style which
Brahms composed all his life through. Nothing can
surpass the innocence, freshness, and sincerity of his compositions, many of which might become popular in the
most literal sense, and will, no doubt, in process of time.
No skill in execution is needed to reveal them as little
gems of musical art.

In his other, and more especially in his grander songs,
the case is different. Indeed, I think it would be
extremely difficult to do justice to them in the perfor-

mance. The melodies have none of the soft and flowing character of Schubert's; they are full of sharp jerks and angles, even when no artistic reason requires it. And we find occasionally almost instrumental passages which the singer must understand as such, so as not to make them too conspicuous. The human voice being endowed by nature with limited compass and power, the composer must take the greater care to husband it. Quite small intervals here answer to strong inward emotions, and intervals of no great difficulty of intonation may suggest a serious distortion of the line of beauty. An appeal to Bach in confirmation of a contrary view is futile. With Bach the vocal melody is not predominant, it is wedded to instrumental melodies of equal importance, which limit its function, and to which it must give way. This is not the case with Brahms. He may possibly have wandered unconsciously now and again into Bach's methods, having so deeply studied and assimilated his art; in other cases a cry of passion may be intended because it responded to the composer's nature. A noteworthy and favourite feature is the tritonic interval; and its counterpart, the diminished fifth, occurs most frequently in the cadenza which so often surprises us by its novelty and power.

The accompaniments too are extremely difficult; nor is it so much the variety of figure-writing that strikes us as so remarkable, as the amazingly multifarious rhythm and the novelty of the harmonies. Both, no doubt, may enhance the general effect, but they also may divert the attention more than they ought from the melody itself. This, it seems to me, sometimes is the case; and it strikes me that the performer should aim rather at minimising these effects than at making the most of them. At any rate Brahms, as a song-writer, has certain secrets of style to which the key does not lie in everybody's hands.

The earlier schools of music possessed a highly developed class of vocal chamber-music, which gradually died out in the last century. The song, its mortal foe, had conquered it. Brahms has written several quartets for the voice with pianoforte accompaniment. It does not seem to me correct to speak of these in a breath with Schumann's *Spanisches Liederspiel, Spanische Liebeslieder* or *Minnespiel*—settings of poems by Rückert, works in which the quartet of voices only occasionally appears. They are, in fact, and essentially, a new thing, into which Brahms infused his noblest art and soul, his warmest and inmost feelings. Cheerfulness and grace are predominant in them. The first series (Op. 31), the *Zigeunerlieder*, and the two series of *Liebeslieder* in waltz form are drawing-room music — entertainment music — of the choicest type. These last may be performed with or without the voice parts, and in some of them it is difficult to say which the composer originally intended. The infinitely various charm that pervades these little pieces, full as they are of flower-like inventiveness, is enhanced by the gleam of humour that shines in them all. The idea of setting every kind and type of love-sentiment to be sung in waltz-form, proves a lofty superiority to them all, which is the speciality of this composer, and reminds us of Goethe as a poet.

The quartet called *Fragen* (Op. 64, 3) is a masterpiece of humour in a broader style. Brahms would not have been the man he was, if he had not utilised this newly developed form for more serious ends. The songs *An die Heimath, Spätherbst,* and *Abendlied,* and more especially the later works *Sehnsucht* and *Nächtens,* are deeply felt monologues in solitude. The four voices and the pianist are simply instruments through which the artist gives utterance to his personal emotions.

Unaccompanied vocal part-music did not need to be

re-created in our century ; it was already in existence. But—though the fact seems almost forgotten—it now appears as an amplified and refined form of the male chorus for four voices. It is to this, and not to any reversion to the flowers of vocal-music in the sixteenth century, that we owe its revival. Its musical value and its sphere of feeling were at the same time extended. Brahms stands distinctly apart from Mendelssohn and his school by having tried to infuse the style and technique of old vocal music into the form he found at hand. A wider foundation was thus secured, and I think it probable that vocal part-music may flourish upon it more rapidly than of old, for after its first bloom it had almost immediately begun to wither away. That the old diatonic style should be reinstated is of course not to be imagined : it is enough to admit that it was the inevitable starting-point. Singers who in our day are accustomed to use their voices in harmony can be required to do many things which their colleagues would have found very faulty in style three hundred years ago, when nothing was recognised but a combination of melodic strains. How far this may be carried is beyond our power of foresight. The artist must know how far he can venture without damaging his own work. I am far from saying that purity of intonation is not often a matter of greater difficulty in Brahms's music than is at all necessary. Still, when we cast into the scale the increased meaning which he infused into vocal music it must surely sink in his favour. Highly trained vocalists will gladly undertake the enharmonic difficulties in *Darthula's Grabgesang*, for instance, for the sake of enjoying the whole, which seems indeed to sound with wonderful effect from beyond the ages. It is easily seen, from the structure of the old models, why Brahms would not limit himself to ordinary four-part writing. In one

of his later works (Op. 104) Brahms has shown with what
facility he writes for six parts. He seems to take little
interest in quartets for male voices, and to prefer writing
them for a female choir; and for this again he has
ventured to develop six parts.

IV

Polyphonic writing may be learned; but what cannot
be learned is to conceive of a work in polyphonic form and
to invent it so originally. Schumann had this now rare
gift, but he utilised it only in instrumental compositions.
He never felt prompted to elaborate it in polyphonic vocal
music.

Brahms also had the gift, I will not venture to say in
a still higher degree; but at any rate he did not allow
his energy to shrink from the difficult problem which
Schumann had set aside. To solve it after the manner of
Cherubini and Mozart was to him impossible. They had
drawn their inspiration from Palestrina; Bach had inter-
vened from the point of view of the North German
Protestant.

Bach's polyphony is not originally vocal; it is only
adapted to the voice. He had a right to treat it so; if
church music were to be the aim and end of all his work
this could only be possible on the basis of organ music,
which was at that time the only admitted type in the
Protestant Church. Times have changed. Protestant
Church music is a thing of the past; Bach survives. No
one can surpass him; let each one try how he may be
his equal.

This is now the situation. How to find a way out no
historian can tell; nothing can alter it but the achievement of the artist. Those who refuse to renounce the
inheritance of the sixteenth century are confronted with

a twofold difficulty ; for how can any use be made o
it when Bach seems to have converted it to anothe
standard ?

The attitude of our living composers plainly betray:
their embarrassment. The Catholics, so far as they have
gone in the reform of church music, know not what tc
make of it. The line taken by Winterfeld and Grell o
Berlin treats the Catholic ideal as absolutely irreconcilabl(
with Bach's methods. Brahms tries to bridge over the gul:
between the Reformation period and Bach, and between
him and the writers since Beethoven. This is the light
in which I see his Motets, the 'German Requiem,' and
the *Triumphlied*; time will show whether I am right.

The liturgy of the church gave him no fulcrum ; but
his sacred music is not therefore aimless and vague. The
foundation on which it rests is the religious sense of the
people, as revealed in Luther's Bible and in their spiritual
songs for centuries past. He enriched his store of ideas
from that source as he did from the secular *Volkslied*, and
he has treated each with equally frank simplicity. We
have nothing to do with the question as to how far the
revelations of the Bible or the services of the church
affected his personal belief. They were essential facts to
him, as the expression of the beliefs and the emotions of
the people.

I cannot help regarding the sacred songs for women's
voices with Latin words as studies. They are extraordinarily clever, not free from forced effects, and besides,
do not display the real essence of Brahms's nature in any
marked degree. Even in the earliest German Motets :
Es ist das Heil uns kommen and *Schaffe in mir, Gott, her
ein reines Herz* (for five voices), he does not reveal that
high pitch of skill which the difficulty of the task demands.
All after this are admirable. The writer has composed
them in his own style, which never reminds us of

Palestrina, or Eccard, or Bach, or of any one but Brahms, and which moves with elastic freedom and dignity in the eight-part *Fest- und Gedenksprüchen.* Only the introduction of the Chorale *Mit Fried' und Freud' ich fahr' dahin* at the end of the beautiful Motet, *Warum ist das Licht gegeben den Muhseligen,* is a sort of homage to Bach which is no part of the main idea of the composition. A chorale thus borrowed to form part of an original work can only be regarded as emblematical of the Evangelical congregation. Bach could do this because his works were used in Divine worship. This is not the case with Brahms. He knew this as well as we know it; and therefore I speak of it as a homage to Bach.

His smaller choral works with accompaniment, namely, the 'Funeral Hymn,' an *Ave Maria* with a small orchestra; a 'Sacred Song,' by Flemming, with the organ part; and the 23rd Psalm, with organ, lead up to the 'German Requiem,' which, nevertheless, on its first appearance, seemed to the world a perfect revelation. Even those who looked for the greatest wonders from Brahms had not expected this eagle's flight. All the intensest rays of the fire that had been kindled in the artist's genius by contact with what was highest and grandest is here focussed into a single point.

The Requiem bears much the same relation to Brahms's smaller choral compositions as his grander vocal pieces do to his ballads. Beethoven's symphonic writing is absorbed into the ideality, so far as form and disposition of instruments is concerned. The lyrical treatment of the Requiem is of the Oratorio type, so far as that in most of the movements it is founded on the popular ideas and images of Death and Life everlasting. On the other hand, these have not so deep an effect on the musical setting as they would have had with Handel. The composition is worked out more decidedly on the lines of pure music, and thus has an affinity with Bach's mode of work. So here again we find something new in point of style.

What is also new is that the 'German Requiem' consists exclusively of choral movements. Brahms has shown elsewhere that he is capable of great compositions for a solo voice. In the Requiem there are but three brief solo passages combining with the choir so as to enhance its effect by contrast. Only the most superficial view can regard Cherubini's Requiem as its prototype. That is essentially adapted to the Catholic liturgy; its whole feeling is subordinate to that, and depends on the various vividly imagined impressions produced by the function of a mass for the dead.

Brahms calls his work 'A German Requiem,' and thus sufficiently indicates that it should only be remotely compared with the Church Service for the Dead. After the Franco-German War it was considered on various occasions suitable for performance at memorial services for those who were killed. To me this does not seem a happy choice. The sort of music suited to such occasions may be found in the famous march in Handel's *Saul*, or the opening chorus in *Judas Maccabæus*. If the audience is already possessed by strongly marked and emotional ideas, the only music they can take in is such as recognises, expands, and transfigures them. The music of the 'German Requiem' sinks in too deep, and soars too high. Only a spirit free from the burthen of sorrow can keep up with it. Nor even then is it easy to follow without fatigue. It is Brahms's cruelty that keeps the listener so long at such a high-strung pitch of agitation.

He is seen in even a more ruthless frame in the *Triumphlied* (for eight voice-parts and an orchestra), with which he hailed the victory of the German armies in 1872. Manly sorrow is the ruling idea of the Requiem;

in this it is heroic joy. Still, none but a nature of bronze is capable of sympathetically enjoying the colossal structure of this matchless monument of sound, and of never finding its ponderous structure somewhat a burthen. Brahms ignored the fact that the mass of music-loving Germans are not exclusively Spartans.

Since the *Triumphlied* consists only of three movements, while the Requiem has seven, this is characterised by a comparatively greater diversity of feeling. The lyrical treatment is in some parts identical, but in the Requiem the images it clothes are more various. The composer has, indeed, made the familiar Bible-words of the first two choral numbers more vividly real by his admirable choice of musical expression ; the leading subject of the first is a modification of the National Hymn, as a form of homage to the monarch as victor ; in the second the chorale-tune *Nun danket alle Gott*, coming in like a peal of church bells, suggests a solemn thanksgiving. But the images thus suggested would not be sufficiently vivid to the mass of hearers. It is the ecstatic vision, in the third movement, of the hero on a white horse riding into the open gates of Heaven, that carries away all who have ears to hear, by its irresistible power of imagery. This chorus is most instructive as to Brahms's apprehension of the Bible, from which he himself selected the words both for the ' Requiem ' and the *Triumphlied*. It is to him the Book of the people, a narrative that he is setting to music. To those who insist on a mystical interpretation of the Revelation of St. John it may not be satisfactory ; they will not have understood the composer.

Brahms has not written any third choral work on so grand a scale. But he has given us four smaller compositions which may be regarded as religious. Still it is only in the ' Rhapsody ' on Goethe's *Harzreise im Winter* that the religious element is the love enjoined by

Christianity; nor is the work so strictly speaking choral. The leading motive is the solo for an alto voice which discourses in a finely worked-out form, of the hate of men, and the love which the Almighty Father pours from a thousand springs for all who thirst. The male chorus, which comes in at the end, serves only as a soft, warm background, above which the solo phrases move gently on, full of sublime comfort.

The other compositions are Greek in feeling—a wide gulf parts the gods in bliss from hapless Man. Brahms, struck, as it would seem, by the contrast, immediately followed up his Rhapsody with a setting of Holderlin's *Schicksalslied*, and he subsequently composed music to Goethe's *Parzenlied*. Here we see the gods dwelling in the heavens, in childlike bliss, gazing on budding life with calm, clear eyes, while Man, thrust out of heaven, falls in stormy unrest into the dark abyss, like water over a precipice. The gods are the egoistic aristocratic race who make use of men and then cast them forth, refusing their just demands. The music corresponds to the different sentiments of the words. In the *Schicksalslied* it is more thoughtful and melancholy; when the chorus ceases from depicting the overthrow of suffering humanity, the picture of the realms of the blest is put before our longing eyes, high up in the clear empyrean whither no voice of man can reach.

Of the song of the Parcæ, *Als Tantalus vom goldnen Stuhle fiel*, Iphigenia says, 'They suffered with their noble friend; their heart was furious, and their song terrible.' It is gloomy wrath that here uplifts its threatening voice. This composition comes down on the hearer with crushing force. It is not till the end that a vein of deep pity steals in with a forecast of the sufferings of the coming race of Tantalus.

The third of these works is Schiller's Elegy, *Auch das*

Schöne muss sterben. In the Requiem we were told
'Death is swallowed up in Victory.' The Greek idea
was that the gods themselves must bow to Fate. To the
Christian all tears are wiped away beyond the grave, and
everlasting joys are his; the Hellenic mind perpetuates
in Beauty only all that has been noble and grand ; what
is common vanishes into the limbo of shadows. The
threads of which the 'Elegy' are woven were spun from
the glory and the mysterious melancholy of the ancient
Greek world.

We perceive at once that the style of music is totally
different in these, so to speak, antique compositions and
in those of a Christian type. The deep imagery of Polyphony was not adapted to their spirit ; we find a more
homophonic treatment in broader masses, and a certain
simplicity prevails throughout. They bear witness as
much to the composer's penetrating power as to his large
comprehension. But their small number, as compared
with his Christian sacred music, plainly shows that he
felt most at home when working from the point of view
of his own people.

V

I have already said that Brahms was no lover of
the romantic or picturesque in writing for instruments.
Schumann's delightful pianoforte *pictures* with names to
them have few parallels in Brahms's work—the *Andante*
of the Sonata in F minor, and the *Balladen* for the
pianoforte. I do not mean to say that poetical imagery
does not occasionally enliven his instrumental music with
its tinted lights. A perfectly lucid musical vitality,
sufficient always to itself, is to be found only in Mozart ;
Haydn and Beethoven are more open to poetical influences, Beethoven very much more so than Haydn.

It may be said of Brahms that he stands, to a certain
extent, at Beethoven's point of view, but with even greater
reserve: he has never allowed himself to produce such a
piece of *programme* music as the 'Pastoral Symphony,'
the 'Thanksgiving for Recovery,' or even an overture such
as those to *Egmont* and to *Coriolanus*, which derive a
distinct romantic character from their purpose. At the
same time he frequently arrives at the same result from
his singular selection of particular musical material—a
horn-trio, a clarinet-quintet, violins with the mute—and
different kinds of tone-value intended to produce a
definite impression. Still, all this is comparatively rare
with him.

What he strove after from the first with all his might
was organic unity of structure on a strict musical basis.
He neglected none of the forms used by the Austrian
masters ; he even found a place for the forgotten *Rondo*.
For his larger works he took the form of the four-
movement Sonata or Symphony, giving to each movement
the same *rôle* as to character and construction as it had
filled in the hands of Haydn, Mozart, and Beethoven.
The musical critics of the day call him reactionary.
There could be no stranger accusation. No one objects
to the fact that songs are still composed. This form of
music has existed for five hundred years; in spite of
occasional changes it has always remained fundamentally
the same; and though hundreds of thousands of songs
have been written, it is not yet exhausted. And if this
is true of such a narrow and restricted form, why should
it be impossible in the broadest conceivable symphonic
forms, which afford an immeasurably wider field for
individual development? Some say that Brahms has
shown that there was *still* something new to be said in
these forms. But we need not say *still*; this will always
be the case so long as our music exists; for these forms

are the outcome of its inmost essence, and their main features cannot be imagined as more perfect. Even those composers who believe that they have broken through them and so achieved a stroke for freedom, nevertheless make use of them in order to produce that very effect of enhanced freedom. They cannot do otherwise so long as balance and contrast[1] exist in the art of music; only they come off worse than a composer who enters consciously into the inheritance of the past with the deliberate purpose of employing it in the service of beauty to the best of his power; and there are many gates into the sanctuary.

Weber and Schubert, Schumann and Gade have in many ways weakened the strong fabric founded by Beethoven, and are certainly minor masters in the science of musical construction. They try to make up for this degeneracy by other delightful characteristics, and no one to whom music is more than a mathematical exercise will be so pedantic as to hold them cheap by reason of their weaker points. Still, it is a mistake to assume that their caprices point the way to greater aims. The foundations must remain the same, though each may build on them according to his needs. Others will come after Brahms whose work will differ again from his. His efforts are directed to concentration and to welding together in immutable strength all the means at the command of music.

From the first, Brahms set himself the highest possible standard, and cautiously tested his powers for each task he attempted. His works are not all of equal merit; it must always be so in human effort; but nothing that he published is insignificant. He evidently had a very high respect for certain kinds of work. He did not try his hand on a Symphony till long after he had reached the

[1] *Satz und Gegensatz*, the opposition of subject and episode.

summit of his power; the pianoforte Sonata he never touched again after his first youthful attempts. Very numerous, on the contrary, are the pieces of chamber music in which the piano is combined with other instruments. He scarcely altered his style of writing for the piano after his first compositions for that instrument.

That he did not assimilate Schumann's manner is greatly to the advantage of his chamber-music. Schumann's polyphonic use of the pianoforte makes the co-operation of the other instruments extremely difficult; they are reduced to a more subordinate position than befits them. If the normal structure for the pianoforte is in two parts, all the more must this be the case when other instruments are introduced. In these conditions the general principle must be adhered to, followed by Bach in his well-known Violin Sonatas. It must, of course, be allowable to add to these two principal parts supplementary harmonies founded on the theory of figured bass; and, moreover, these harmonies may be broken or ornamented. Both in his Violin and his Violoncello Sonatas, and in his trios Brahms from the first fully understood this. The former are written in three parts (in the freer sense here set forth), and the latter are sometimes in four parts, and sometimes antiphonal, the concerted instruments working together against the pianoforte.

The C minor trio is almost entirely written in this antiphonal manner; the C major trio, written four years before, is in three parts. It is instructive to compare them from this point of view, and it would always seem as though the composer had intended to mark the contrast. In the C major trio only the *Andante* with variations is antiphonal, but so decidedly as to show a predetermined plan. The strings, instruments, and the piano have two separate themes, which appear in contrapuntal

combination, and are then alternately *varied*; at the close
both are varied together. It is an idea worthy of Bach.

When the piano has more than two instruments with
it, the relations are altered, and antiphonal treatment is
the principle throughout. Mozart remains the unsurpassed model in this style of writing. Brahms, we see,
started on another road. He may have reflected that the
power of the pianoforte is far greater than that of the
harpsichord of Mozart's time, and has gained a preponder-
ating strength as against the combined instruments. In
his first two pianoforte quartets and the quintet the
proportions observed might almost be called orchestral
so far as that the piano fills the part which, in an orchestra,
is assigned to the strings—it gives out the principal
matter and subject : the other instruments come in to
add strength and fulness, appearing now and then as
solo players, and more rarely, in alternating groups.

This manner of writing is not precisely the same as
Schumann's, which gives the pianoforte a yet more important *rôle*. It is a new thing ; and at a later time does
not seem to have fully satisfied the master himself. In
his third pianoforte quartet he goes back to Mozart's
methods, or rather he has adapted them to the altered
conditions of tone material.

Mozart's music always gives an impression of natural
spontaneity and growth ; it seems as though he had
never had to work, hence the pure Elysian rapture it
conveys to the heart of the hearer. Beethoven knows
that he shall infallibly conquer ; we follow him with a
proud anticipation of triumph. Brahms labours in a
Cyclopean forge, served by mighty powers ; but they are
often rebellious and need coercion by a master will. He
is always imperious, and the hearer submits, though not
always willingly. Though the third pianoforte quartet
suggests this reflection, it is for one reason only. Its

predecessors and the pianoforte quintet, and even the first sestets for strings, show a wealth of ideas which we might almost call extravagant, if extravagance were possible in so thrifty a manager. In the third quartet, as it would seem, he intends to show that he can do something different, quite different. In the leading ideas he restricts himself to the narrowest measure; nay, he goes so far as to prohibit himself in the first movement any long episode, and instead of it he twice introduces a short series of figures on a subject of eight bars. He here proves himself as inexhaustible in the development of the thematic material as he is in the invention of melody in the other concerted pieces; it is always one of his strongest characteristics. Indeed, he trusts to it so confidently that he sometimes overlooks the fact that there is in the natural constitution of the idea a limit to the use that can be made of it. We come upon passages where the materials are, indeed, coherent thematically, but yet do not convince the hearer of their intrinsic connection. They cannot, to be sure, be torn asunder, but we see the rivets and feel that force must have been used.

It has always struck me as remarkable that Brahms, whenever he had seized on a new class of work, always did so with a double grip, as it were, from two sides at once. He would write two Serenades, two pianoforte quartets, two stringed quartets, two Symphonies, two Overtures, one immediately after the other. In this there evidently lies a purpose. It has been said that every finished work of art leaves in the artist a remnant of dissatisfaction, and that this constitutes the germ of his next production. This cannot be altogether the case with Brahms, for the two examples are, in his case, always alike as to form and the employment of his materials. No one can say that either is better than its fellow; it is only quite different. It almost seems as though on each occasion his conception divided spontaneously into two halves, each of which was worked up with renewed energy. When the excitement of the first inspiration is past, and he has assured possession of the idea, he takes matters easily. Such a notion would not occur to us if it were not for other enigmatical features. How is it that an artist, to whom the representation of structures of perfect unity is a supreme consideration, so often wilfully ignores the simplest means to that end? The whole structure of a sonata movement depends on the treatment of the principal second subject. This our master knows full well and invents one accordingly. But the demon prompts him to disfigure his own offspring. He takes a melody which, when it floated along on gently rolling waves, enchanted every hearer by its beauty, and he gives it a restless, difficult accompaniment, full of crossing rhythm which in the first instance is sure of but one result, that, namely, of attracting attention. It is as though he were embarrassed by his own beauty. The whole force of the subject is lost and the general effect is monotonous, which it ought not to be, and closely examined, really is not. On the other hand it sometimes happens that the accessory subjects are suddenly lost, and the hearer finds it difficult to preserve a sense of the connecting fundamental feeling.

In speaking of his vocal music, it has been already said that Brahms's temperament made him liable to lose his sense of proportion under the stress of passion. He errs in this direction more frequently in his chamber music for strings alone than when he is writing for the piano and strings. With the great Austrian composers —excepting in some late works by Beethoven—even where there is the utmost display of power, there is

always a perceptible reserve of force which is not usually
called out. Of this the hearer is conscious, and it gives
him a sense of calm enjoyment. Brahms often urges
the performers to the utmost limit of their strength and
yet fails to fill up the presentment of his idea. Such
passages are more frequent in the working-out sections.
If we listen to them with closed eyes, or think of them
as the utterance of human organs, we try to imagine
the state in which men must be for such tones to befit
its expression, and what their look and behaviour would
be. Can this even be spoken of as beautiful?—Does this
seem a strange verdict? But 'man is the measure of
all things,' says Protagoras.

One of the mysterious features is the indifference
shown by Brahms in the matter of tone-quality. The
pianoforte quintet was first written for strings, then
he remodelled the material as it now stands, but also
worked it up as a Sonata for two pianos. The variations
on a theme of Haydn's appeared written for the orchestra,
and at the same time for two pianos, with no indication
as to which they were originally composed for. Some
of the variations seem best suited to one purpose and
some to the other. 'He is a Spiritualist,' it will be said;
'what he cares for is the germ of the invention. But
there is no such thing in music as Invention, and a
mercy it is that it should be so.'

Brahms himself proves this proposition to be false.
He can show creative genius in his effects of tone. All
his works bear witness to this, from the serenades, the
first pianoforte concerto, and the choral works for female
voices with harps and horns, to the quintet for
clarionets. He is always equal to the demand. At
times he cares but little for general sweetness of effect
and the consequent softening down of tone-qualities;
things easily learned by other composers who might think

themselves splendidly endowed if they had but one-tenth of his genius.

All this, it must be understood, is not intended to detract from his merit, only to define his individuality. And it would be altogether wrong to imagine that these singularities are to be found in all his works. They appear and disappear, and become rarer in his later compositions. The golden harvest of chamber music produced in the last five years[1] indicates a mature development of the equalisation of his powers, which is not wholly the outcome of advancing years, since his vital energy and delight in creative work are as strong in the man of fifty-nine as ever they have been. They are the result also of indefatigable striving for the highest ideals.

Brahms has written four Concertos. He has, if somewhat tardily, fulfilled our expectations. He has produced and revived the *Concerto Grosso* of the older writers, which seemed to have sent out its last offshoot in Beethoven's inappropriately named *Triple Concerto* (Op. 102). Violin and violoncello play together against the orchestra. Though admirable in structure and full of important and beautiful thoughts, this work seems to me not quite happy in the treatment of the solo instruments. The passage writing especially is too much like piano writing. The case is far different with regard to the violin Concerto (Op. 77), a brilliant work of manly and dignified construction, requiring, no doubt, a manly player for the solo. The violinist who attempts it must have studied, not only Beethoven, but Bach; it is not merely a piece of dazzling virtuoso work, elegant and insinuating. In the middle movement the solo instrument is, indeed, too much deposed from the leading part that tradition very rightly assigns to it.

[1] This was published in 1892.

The two others are pianoforte Concertos. The practice of the older composers, which was to write their Concertos for themselves to play, is the natural course, and must always obtain as far as circumstances allow. In a Concerto the solo instrument must put forth all its highest powers of execution, and how that is to be achieved can be perfectly known only to a composer who has mastered the instrument. Brahms was not a piano virtuoso ; he had neither time nor taste for such special training. Still he was a powerful player. He had a technique of his own, and was inventive within its peculiar limits. Its character is more apt to impress the strong executant than the delicate player. A full grasp, wide extensions, bold intervals, great agility and endurance in playing passages in thirds, sixths, and octaves, perfect independence both of hands and fingers, even in the most varied polyphonic passages of cross rhythm, are some of the special requirements. His Variations on a Theme by Paganini, five books of Studies for the Pianoforte on compositions by Chopin, Weber, and Bach, and many passages in the Eight Pieces for the Piano (Op. 76), and the two Rhapsodies (Op. 79) leave us in amazement as to what he could do. He displays this technique on the grandest scale in the Concertos, and is consequently very interesting to the executant. But he is not, for all that, a popular composer, and chiefly for these reasons.

Brahms's pianoforte Concertos have been called Symphonies with the piano. This they are not. The special characteristics which constitute the peculiarity of the Concerto form, which Mendelssohn and Schumann, and sometimes Weber, made light of, was, by Brahms, strictly respected. The Symphony form is combined by these composers with that of the older Italian Chamber Concerto. The newer Concerto form, as it was left by

Mozart, is a model of pure and intelligent musical proportion; it is stamped in the happiest degree with the idea of two equal but differently endowed powers playing in concert, and at the same time shows such elastic cohesion that it always yields pliantly to the free play of the solo instrument, which, to produce the desired result, must have an improvised effect. Brahms was far too competent an artist not to perceive how far Mozart's and Beethoven's Concerto form transcends the *fantasia*-like type of their immediate predecessors. But he deviates from the Vienna masters in another particular. Their Concertos are constantly faithful to the leading purpose of a cheerful and brilliant entertainment. Solemn feeling has no place in them, excepting as a shadow to enhance the sense of gladness. Even romantic composers adhered to this view of the Concerto. Brahms was the first to transfer the feeling, but not the form, of the Symphony to the Concerto. The solo player has to enter into that feeling, and as a matter of course must keep his own in the background. To me this seems a means of adding depth to the form, and of enriching it as it goes on; and I fully admit that I regard the Concerto in D minor (Op. 15) as an admirable work of its creator's; all the more wonderful because he achieved this bold flight while still quite young. It leaves an impression of gloomy majesty rising to sublime solemnity, and it is not till the last movement that human feeling smiles kindly on us.

The Concerto in B major (Op. 83), written nearly a quarter of a century later, is dressed in brighter hues. The outburst of irrepressible force that characterises the two first movements subsides in the two last to a soothing calm and gentle grace. The introduction of a fourth movement is accounted for by the Symphony-like structure. So long as the standard idea of the Concerto is the development in alternation of the different modes of expression of *Solo* and *Tutti* a fourth movement is superfluous. This which Brahms has given us is extremely beautiful, but he does not convince me of the necessity of exceeding three in number.

When Brahms had once overcome his reluctance to attempt orchestral composition, he threw himself into it with such perseverance that one decade of his life may be fairly termed *Symphonic*. During the nine years from 1877 he produced four Symphonies, two Concertos, and two grand Overtures. The two first Symphonies display that contrast of treatment which is so often found in Brahms; they must be regarded as a pair, grown up from one deeply buried root. Any one who desires to know the character of the man, epitomised, as it were, should hear and study these compositions.

The opening movement of the first stands like a mountain-top wrapped in clouds, and is worked out with terrific power almost entirely on a single motive of three notes. A comparison with the first movement of Beethoven's C Minor Symphony is here suggested solely to emphasise the peculiar character of the younger master. The *Andante* is an image of sublime fervency and noble ecstasy; in the *Allegretto* we find the serious grace which no other German master had in the same degree, Gluck perhaps excepted. The *Finale* is led up to by an exciting and fanciful introduction, a mixture of wild vehemence with a vein of solemn festivity; the *Finale* itself is a song of triumph of culminating power, such as we shall find nowhere else, perhaps, but in the sixth movement of the 'German Requiem.'

The contrasting counterpart, the second Symphony, sparkles like spring sunshine, now in the romantic freshness of the forest, and now on the firm open way; or again it flows round vague and graceful figures; the

emotional *Adagio* alone is a striking departure from
the fundamental sentiment. In speaking of the close
I cannot refrain from dwelling here on the extraordinary
beauty of Brahms's treatment of the *Coda*. Beethoven
was the first to give to the *Coda* the peculiar charm of
reminiscence. Brahms here does this with even greater
emphasis, for the contrast with what has gone before
is, in many places, even more marked. We are amazed
to find the theme that has grown familiar still capable
of so much new and captivating witchery. Whatever
distress the artist's vehemence and recklessness may
have caused the hearer he is now at once forgiven, and
leaves us reconciled and happy.

The two last Symphonies are the ripe and satisfying
fruit that the master has produced from the fertile depths
of his most original individuality. It is idle to compare
them ; and it is a purely personal reflection when I say
that to me the Symphony in E minor contains all the
finest work that Brahms can have to give in this branch
of his art, and that the *Andante*, above all, has not its
match in the whole realm of Symphony-writing. Those
who, judging from his Serenades, doubted of his vocation
for the Symphony, and who were not at once converted
by the first two, must have abandoned all hesitancy, for
the two last Symphonies and the overtures allow of no
doubt that Brahms was a born and most original master
of this form, who achieved his vocation by severe toil.
Where he will stand in permanent esteem and influence
with relation to his precursors—the great and the greatest
—the future must decide. We of to-day may rejoice
in possessing him.

How conspicuously Brahms stands apart from the
commoner run of contemporary composers—indeed, in
emphatic contrast to them and to their immediate
predecessors—must be sufficiently evident. We live in

an age of literary composers. Brahms is no *littérateur.* Nor has much been written about him, and I fancy that this gratifies rather than offends him.

The contrast is especially marked by the fact that he has written no Oratorio, and yet more, that he has nothing to say in Opera. One work alone, *Rinaldo,* has any touch of the first; and the almost dramatic introduction to it may suggest the opera. He himself is said to think highly of this work ; and it seems not impossible that he should yet feel impelled to the drama. Still, the attraction cannot be overwhelmingly strong, or he would not have lived to be near sixty without yielding to it.

We do not, however, demand this of him. As we see him, he stands forth as one who has most faithfully guarded and added to the hereditary treasure of German music. Against this, at least, posterity will have nothing to say.

[The above analysis of the life-work of Johannes Brahms, written by the late Philipp Spitta, has been pronounced by Herr Joachim to be the soundest criticism that has yet appeared upon the master's compositions.]

Letters from Brahms to Schumann

ROBIN H. LEGGE

[Most of the information in the following article and the letters themselves are derived from a *Feuilleton* by La Mara published in the *Neue Freie Presse*.]

A FEW years ago Eduard Hanslick published, under the title 'From Robert Schumann's Last Days,' four letters from Schumann to Brahms.[1] The following are extracts from Brahms's replies; they require but little explanation :—

In the FIRST, dated from Hanover, 16th November 1853, Brahms thanks Schumann for his now famous greeting (after their meeting at Düsseldorf in the autumn of 1853) in the article 'Neue Bahnen': 'One who should claim the mastership by no gradual development, but burst upon us fully equipped, as Minerva sprang from the brain of Jupiter.' Brahms wrote :—

I.—'You have rendered me so unspeakably happy that I cannot even attempt to thank you in mere words. May Heaven grant that my works may prove to you soon how

---

[1] These the translator regrets he has not been able to procure.

your affection and kindness have inspirited me. The praise which you have publicly uttered concerning me will have stirred up the public expectation to so inordinate a degree, that I do not know how I can answer it at all. I must exercise great care, at any rate in the selection of my works for publication. I am not thinking of issuing any one of my trios, and have chosen for Ops. 1 and 2 the sonatas in C and F sharp minor; for Op. 3 the songs ; and for Op. 4 the E flat minor *Scherzo*. You will naturally understand that I am trying hard to bring as little shame as possible upon you. I delayed for so long before writing to tell you that I had sent the four works to Breitkopf, that I might be in a position to give you the result of your letter of recommendation. From your last letter to Joachim we learned this result, so now I have but to add that, following your advice, I intend to start in the course of the next day or two—probably to-morrow—for Leipzig.

'Further, I would tell you that I have written out my F minor Sonata, and materially altered its *Finale*. I have also improved the violin sonata. Let me thank you a thousand times for the portrait you sent me, and for the letter you wrote to my father. You have thus made two good folk very happy.' [The F minor sonata referred to is Brahms's Op. 5.]

II.—The SECOND letter is not only of more interest to the musical world in general, but also of more importance, since in it Brahms mentions a sonata for violin and pianoforte in A minor, which has disappeared. La Mara declares that Brahms destroyed it. But the fact of its having once existed is of interest, since it proves Brahms to have had in his youthful mind a combination of instruments which he did not use again for thirty years. The first of his published violin Sonatas is that in G (Op. 78). In place of the A minor violin Sonata that for pianoforte alone in F minor was substituted as Op. 5. Brahms's second letter is as follows, its date, 29th November 1853 :—

'Mynheer Domine!

'You must forgive me for this merry mode of addressing you, since you have made me immensely happy. I have nothing but the best to tell you. Thanks to your warm recommendation, I have met with a reception in Leipzig beyond all expectation and far beyond my deserts. Härtels declared their great pleasure in accepting my first attempts for publication. [These are Op. 1 to Op. 4.]

'Senff has Op. 5, the *Sonata in A minor for violin and pianoforte*; Op. 6, Six Songs.

'May I place your wife's name upon my second work? I hardly dare venture to ask it, yet I am very anxious to give you some little mark of my esteem and gratitude. I hope to receive some copies of my first works before Christmas. . . .'

III.—In December of the same year Brahms again wrote from Hamburg :—

'Herewith I take the liberty of sending you your first foster-children, which indeed have you to thank for their existence in the world at large. I am particularly anxious to know if they may still look for the same forbearance and affection from you as before. To me they look much too ordinary and proper in their new dress—ay, almost Philistine! I cannot accustom myself yet to look at these innocent children of nature in such decent apparel. I am delighted at the prospect of seeing you in Hanover that I may have the opportunity of telling you that my parents and I have to thank you and Joachim for the happiest moments in our lives.'

Between the third and FOURTH letters an interval of a year has elapsed, the date of the latter being 2nd December 1854. The letter is written from Hamburg.

The variations referred to are those known as Op. 9,
dedicated to Mme. Schumann.

' How can I describe my delight at your letter ? You
have so often made me happy by mentioning me in your
letters to your wife. And now you have written a letter
to me. This is the first, and I cherish it accordingly. I
expect to return in a few days to Düsseldorf, a place I
love. Your quite exaggerated praise of my variations
gives me pleasure, that you should think them worthy of
praise. Since the Spring I have been diligently studying
your works. . . . I have been during nearly the whole
of the year at Düsseldorf, and shall never forget how I
learned to honour and love you and your charming wife.
Hitherto I have never looked so brightly and surely
into the future as now, nor believed that so glorious a
future could be. . . .'

V.—The FIFTH letter was written from Düsseldorf on
the 30th December 1854.

' I could write you a great deal about our Christmas,
how Joachim's news made us happy, how we spoke
during the whole evening of you, while your wife
wept silently. We are full of the hope of seeing you
among us again. Somehow you always change what
would be days of double sadness into days of joy. On
the first holiday your wife kept Christmas. She will
doubtless have told you how beautifully Marie and
Joachim played your A minor Sonata, and Elsie the
Kinderscenen, and how happy she made me with a set
of Jean Paul's works. I had little hope of acquiring
them, at any rate, for many years. Joachim received the
scores of your symphonies, a copy of which your wife had
already given me. On Christmas Eve I came back here
—how long a time it seems since I parted from your wife !
I had become so accustomed to her surroundings, I had
spent the whole summer so delightfully near her, and

learned so to admire and love her, that everything seemed empty until I could see her again. I brought many lovely things away from Hamburg, including the full score of Gluck's *Alceste* in the old Italian edition of 1776, from Ave,[1] your first letter to me, and several from your wife. For one charming word in your last letter—the little word ' du '—I have to thank you heartily. Your wife also uses it when speaking to me. It is to me the highest token of your goodwill, and I will always strive to deserve it.

' I have much to write about to you, dearest friend, but it would, I suppose, only be a repetition of what your wife has already told you. . . .'

VI.—The SIXTH letter, written in January 1855, also from Düsseldorf, is of special interest, since in its post-script it mentions another work by Brahms, which has entirely disappeared. The first of Brahms's symphonies known to the world is that in C minor (Op. 68), produced in 1876. Here Brahms speaks of one composed upwards of twenty years previously. What has become of it? Even La Mara is silent on the point. The work mentioned in the beginning of the letter which Schumann had dedi-cated to Brahms, was the Concert-Allegro in D minor, published as Op. 134. The letter is as follows:—

' I must thank you myself for the great happiness you have given me by dedicating to me your lovely work. How happy I am to see my name in print! . . . I am always thinking with pleasure of the few short hours which I was allowed to spend with you; they were delightful, but vanished all too quickly. I cannot tell your wife enough about them. It makes me doubly happy to think on the way in which you received me. . . . Jenny Lind's letter I think you would like in the original. The handwriting is, I suppose, what you wish, and what is written I need not first copy out.

[1] Ave-Lallement was a musical friend of Brahms.

D

'Bargiel's[1] new work we are sending with this note. It
will doubtless give you as much pleasure as it gave us.
It, his Op. 9, is a great advance on his Op. 8. Both are
dedicated to your wife. That is what I would like to do
—to alternate between your wife's name and Joachim's
until I had courage enough to add yours. That is not
likely to happen yet.' [The postscript is]: 'Do you
remember urging me on last winter to write an overture
to *Romeo*? In the summer I tried my hand on a
symphony, the first movement of which I have already
orchestrated, while the second and third are composed.
(In D minor 6–4, slow.)'

VII.—No. SEVEN is dated Düsseldorf, February 1855.
'I am sending you herewith the two things you ask for:
a neckband and the *Signale*. For the former I alone am
answerable, since, as your wife is in Berlin, I had to
choose. I hope it is right and not too high. I also send
last year's *Signale*, a few numbers of which are missing, as
we have not taken sufficient care of them. I will send
them regularly in future.

'I am now able to assure you positively that Arnold
received the proofs of your *Gesänge der Frühe*. His delay
in publishing the work must be due to some other cause.

'How did the long walk with me agree with you?
Well, I hope. I often think of that lovely day: rarely
have I been so happy. I have calmed your wife's
anxiety and my letter gladdened her. . . .'

The sonata mentioned in No. EIGHT was also dedicated
to Mme. Schumann. The title is dated Düsseldorf,
March 1855.

VIII.—'You will have wondered that I wrote of an
F sharp minor sonata, which should have gone to you
with my letter, but went not. I quite forgot to enclose it,
so send it now with the songs and choruses of *Maria*

---

[1] Bargiel was Mme. Schumann's step-brother.

Stuart. . . . Your wife has just written so happily about your letter. She will send you the most beautiful music-paper. I suppose I was too hasty—only ladies can do things quickly and well, as well as tenderly.'

IX.—The NINTH letter is dated two months later, from the same place :—

'I must thank you for remembering me on the 7th May. Your handsome present and the charming words you wrote in the book are delightful. The day was beautiful, such as one rarely sees. Your dear wife knows fully how to make matters go well. The ladies understand that better than we do.

'Portraits of mother and sister and you surprised me. In the afternoon Joachim came, and we hope he means to stay. A short time ago I heard your overture to the *Braut von Messina* in Hamburg, as you already know. It and *Manfred* (the former a deeply earnest work) affected me strongly ; and I wished all the evening that you were with me to hear them, too, and to see the pleasure your work gave.

'For a long time I had wished to hear *Manfred* or *Faust*: I still hope we may hear this latter, the greatest of all, together. Only your prolonged silence, which made us anxious, restrained me from writing sooner to offer you my thanks. Take them now for your beautiful souvenir of the 7th May 1855.'

The wish, expressed in this last letter, to hear *Faust* in Schumann's company was never fulfilled. Schumann never again left Endenich alive. His intellect became darkened more and more until death released him on the 29th July 1856. Forty years later his darling wife followed him, and now his beloved Johannes has also been called, so that of the three it may be said, as in Brahms's glorious *Schicksalslied*, 'Sie wandeln droben im Licht!'

John Sebastian Bach

and the Organ

C. M. WIDOR

'IF in the eyes of our generation, Beethoven resembles a Greek statue, Bach must accordingly assume the form of one of those Egyptian sphinxes, whose masterly gaze embraces the vast plains of the desert.' This comparison is pictorial, but hardly accurate.

Bach is a sphinx, thanks to the greatness of his proportions, if you will, but not by his nature. He is undeniably the most powerful of all musicians. On reading the almost incredible catalogue of his works, while thumbing those forty huge in-folios, or scrutinising one of those pages on which the slightest sketch seems to owe its existence to long premeditation and strong will, and in which a deep and original idea can always be traced, one is unwittingly overcome by a sense of fear. But, on the other hand, was there ever a less enigmatic thinker?

Yes indeed, this immense figure soars above all that surrounds it; but its straight look, its frank and luminous eyes are not those of a sphinx. They belong rather to the statue of common sense.

An eminent virtuoso confessed to me recently that he would have felt very ill at ease if he had had to dine alone with Beethoven. 'But with old Father Bach, I am sure I should make myself quite at home! I can fancy myself full of confidence smoking a pipe with my elbows on the table, chatting with him upon a thousand interesting questions, with a pewter of beer before us, as in the good old times.'

This brings one into closer contact with the real Bach.

He was a good citizen, an excellent father, as the local clergyman would say, a devoted friend endowed with a sociable nature and blessed with rare artistic modesty. When asked to explain the cause of his greatness, he would say, 'I have worked a great deal, and whoever works as hard as I, will undoubtedly achieve the same result.' He never missed an opportunity of hearing the compositions of others—he had a high opinion of Handel, was much interested in the work of Couperin, and, ensconced in a dark corner of the church, spent three months listening to Buxtehude, the famous organist of Sainte-Marie de Lubeck, though he had only been granted three weeks' vacation. He was an excellent man. No human brain ever contained a more wonderful mechanism ; no healthier or better equipoised brain was ever contained in a healthier body. He mastered his nervous system better than any other musician. The barbarisms of Gœrner did indeed upset him on one occasion when he flung his wig at the head of that unfortunate accompanist, saying, 'Go, you are but a cobbler!' This is one of the rare displays of anger ever quoted against him, for, thanks to the enormous vitality of his organism, he was patient by sheer strength of will and the natural kindliness of his disposition.

See him with his pupils. During the first year he kept them to exercises ; such as tierces, trills, scales, changes of fingering and all sorts of combinations to obtain an even action of the hand.   He supervised everything, and, with the utmost attention, he judged the clearness and neatness of their touch.   If one of them lost courage, he, in the fulness of his heart, would write a short composition in which he would disguise the very difficulties that had overawed the beginner.

At eighteen he was organist of the new church of Arnstadt, and he had then studied the works of the great harpsichordists of his time :—

Froberger [1615 (?)-1667], the protégé of the Emperor Ferdinand III., who had sent him to study in Rome under Frescobaldi.

Fischer, the *Kapellmeister* of the Margrave of Bade.

Johannes Caspar Kerl, the rival of Froberger, and like him a pensioner of Ferdinand, and a pupil of Carissimi in Rome.

Pachelbel [1653-1706], who was at first assistant organist at Saint-Etienne in Vienna, and eventually organist at Eisenach, Erfurt, Stuttgart, and Nuremberg.

Buxtehude [1637-1707], the famous organist of Lubeck.

Bruhns, his pupil.

Böhm, organist of Saint John of Lünebourg.

It was through Froberger and Caspar Kerl that Bach first became acquainted with Frescobaldi and the Italian school ; the 'symphonic form' was first revealed to him in the Suites played by Zell's French orchestra, which interested him keenly ; but he received the greatest and most enduring impression of his youth from the striking personality of Buxtehude, who imparted to him the ancient and purest German tradition.

Reinken one day heard Bach commenting for half an hour upon the Chorale *An Wasserflüssen Babylons*, and in his joy the old man threw his arms round his neck, exclaiming : ' I thought I had witnessed the death of this great art, but thanks to you it is now assured of a new and vigorous life.'

Bach handed down this tradition to his two sons, Wilhelm Friedemann and Philip Emmanuel, musicians of recognised merit, and to a whole plethora of brilliant pupils as :—

Johannes Caspar Vogler, a virtuoso more appreciated by Mattheson than Bach himself : he was organist at Weimar. His preludes in the shape of chorals, written for two keys and pedal, have been preserved.

Homilius of Dresden, a composer of church music.

Transchel of Dresden, a famous player on the harpsichord.

Goldberg of Königsberg, author of the selections called *Bagatelles for ladies*, and so difficult that no one could play them (his favourite amusement was to play all sorts of music, upside down, and read from right to left).

Krebs, the organist at Altenbourg, a player of great merit and a most prolific composer.

Altnikol, the organist at Hamburg, his son-in-law.

Agricola, composer to the King of Prussia, whose theoretical productions won him fame.

Müthel of Riga.

Kirnberger, court musician at Berlin, who ' loved that art with sincere and passionate enthusiasm,' said Forkel. ' Not only did he make us familiar with Bach's method of teaching composition, but the musical world is indebted to him for the first logical system of harmony, derived from the works of his master—the first of these teachings is contained in his book *Kunst des reinen Satzes* ; the second in *Gründsätze zum Gebrauch der Harmonie*. He rendered eminent services to art by means of other writings as well as by his compositions. His harpsichord works are charming. Princess Amelia of Prussia was his pupil.'

Kittel, the organist at Erfurt. He was the only pupil of Bach living in the days when Forkel, himself an organist and Musical Director at the University of Göthingen, wrote his book entitled: *The Life, Talents, and Works of John Sebastian Bach* (1802).

Forkel was on intimate terms with Wilhelm Friede-mann and Philip Emmanuel Bach, Agricola, Kirnberger and several other great pupils of the great master. He worked (so we are told by M. Felix Grenier in his translation) with Schicht, a man of education and a distinguished harmonist, who afterwards became *Cantor* of the church of Saint Thomas. It was in collaboration with him that he undertook the publication of Bach's com-positions for the organ and the harpsichord to which he so often refers in his book. Forkel had collected a musical library: thanks to it and to the one at the Göthingen University, he was enabled to lay hands on a vast amount of matter for his *History of Music*, that was to consist of six volumes, only two of which, however, were published.

The last volume was to have contained the documents that Forkel possessed upon Bach and his work, but he foresaw the impossibility of finishing this huge encyclo-pædia of music, and it would seem that he published his pamphlet on the life and work of Bach lest he should be deprived by death of the opportunity of addressing to the memory of this great man, a sincere and well-deserved tribute of respect and of gratitude.

Kittel [1732-1802] was Rinck's master, and the pupil relates that his teacher always concluded his conversa-tions on Bach by the following words: *Ein sehr frommer Mann,*—'he was an excellent man.'

The learned Fétis of Brussels, while initiating me in the mysteries of fugue and counterpoint, has often spoken to me of Rinck, whom he had known, of Kittel his musical father, and of their great ancestor, Sebastian Bach.

When Rinck was asked why he neglected the study of fugues he was wont to say : ' Bach is a colossus, who towers over the musical world : you can only hope to follow him at a distance in his own ground, for he has exhausted everything, and is inimitable in what he has achieved. I have always thought that, in order to compose something worthy of attention and approval, one must seek it in quite another sphere of thought.'

Poor Rinck !

It is only Bach the organist that we have to study in this work. M. André Pirro having conscientiously analysed the special work of the great master, I have merely to consider the technique of the virtuoso.

This is the way in which Bach played the harpsichord. ' His five fingers bent so that their extremities fell perpendicularly on the keyboard, above which they formed a parallel line ever ready to obey. The finger did not rise perpendicularly on leaving the touch, but rather glided back towards the palm of the hand ; in the transition from one touch to another, this very gliding imparted to the next finger the exact strength of pressure that had been put into force by the preceding finger ; hence a great evenness and a touch that was neither thick nor harsh.' It is Philip Emmanuel that has given us this description.

Bach had a small hand ; the motion of his fingers was barely perceptible, as the first phalanges were the only ones that moved. His hand preserved the rounded shape, even in the execution of the most difficult passages ; the fingers were barely raised above the keyboard, just a shade more than in the playing a shake. As soon as a finger had been used, he brought it back to its proper position. The remainder of his body took no part whatever in the work. It is only those whose hands are not sufficiently nimble that need to exert their whole frame when playing.

Nowadays we do not play the harpsichord, and the piano which has replaced it with great advantage requires methods and means that were hitherto unknown. No change has occurred in the art of playing the organ for the past two centuries. Perhaps the system of Bach's pedalling differed somewhat from ours ; there is no doubt that in his youth, when the stops of the pedals were very short, he made much more use of toe than of heel. But he soon perceived the necessity of improving the key of the pedal organ, either by increasing its size or by lengthening the pedals to their present dimensions. When seated at the organ, he leaned his body slightly forward.

He played with admirable rhythm, an ensemble that was absolutely polyphonic, and with marvellous clearness. He did not play fast, but remained master of himself and of the time, so to speak. The effect produced was of incomparable dignity and grandeur.

His contemporaries waxed enthusiastic over his exquisite art of combining his stops and his original and unexpected way of dealing with them. Forkel adds that nothing connected with his art could possibly escape his notice. He studied with great care the acoustic effects in the churches where he had to play. During his visit to Berlin, in 1747, he was brought to the Opera House, and saw at a glance its qualities and defects in connection with music. On being shown the adjacent *foyer*, he looked at the ceiling and declared, without any further examination, that the architect had built, perhaps unknown to himself, a 'thing of great merit.'

The *foyer* was in the shape of a parallelogram ; and by standing in a corner with one's nose against the wall, one need only pronounce a few words in order to be distinctly heard by some one standing in the same position in the corner diagonally opposite, though no one else in the room could hear a word that was being said.

When distinguished strangers asked Bach to play the organ, he generally chose a subject and proceeded to treat it in every shape and form, sometimes playing for over an hour without an interruption. He first took the theme as a prelude and a fugue on the foundation-stops of the great organ; then he enjoyed varying his stops, in a series of episodes composed of two, three, or four parts. Then came a Chorale, the melody of which was intercepted by fragments of the original subject. He concluded with a fugue on the full organ, in which he treated his theme either alone or in conjunction with a number of counter-themes grafted upon the original motive.

When trying a new instrument, he began by pulling out all the stops and playing the great organ with all its combinations, 'just to test the lungs of the organ,' as he used to say. He then proceeded to make a minute examination of each of its parts. When he had completed it, he would give full vent to his inspiration.

It was then he really showed himself to be the prince of virtuosos upon the organ and the clavichord, as he was christened one day by his colleague Sorge, the organist of Lobenstein.

No, the art of playing the organ has not changed since the days of John Sebastian Bach; but our organs are infinitely better than those of last century. Go and hear them at Saint Sulpice or at Notre Dame in Paris, or at Saint Ouen, in Rouen.

In the old instruments the reed-pipes were only used as basses to strengthen the pedals, or as minor stops, cremonas, and oboes; our profuse wealth of clarions, bombardes, and trumpets was then quite unknown. *Organo pleno* did not mean a full artillery of four, eight, sixteen, or thirty-two feet, but merely the combination of a few principals and mixtures with a sub-bass and a bourdon. As to the means of graduating the intensity of one particular sound, they were not even known to exist.

I have stated elsewhere that the swell-box was invented towards the end of last century : Handel had great admiration for this English invention, and the Abbé Vogler recommended it years afterwards to the German makers. Nowadays our instruments have become, in the opinion of the uninitiated, as expressive as a whole orchestra.

This is a grave mistake : I repeat that the *expression* introduced into the modern organ can only be subjective ; it is due to mechanism and can never be spontaneous. While the orchestral instruments (both wind and string), the piano and the voice can only shine by the spontaneity of the tone and the suddenness of the stroke, the organ, encompassed by its primitive majesty, speaks as a philosopher. It is the only instrument that can continuously expand the same volume of sound, and thus create the religious idea through the thought of infinity.

A good organist will only make use of his expressive means—in an architectural way, that is—by treating them as lines and plans ;

As *lines*, when he passes slowly from *piano* to *forte* on an imperceptible incline, by a constant progression without stops or jolts.

As *plans*, when seizing the opportunity afforded by a pause or rest, he suddenly closes his swell-box between a *forte* and a *piano*.

To try and reproduce the expressive accents of a treble string or a human voice is better suited to the accordion than to the organ.

The chief characteristic of the organ is its greatness—that is to say, its strength and will. Every illogical alteration in the intensity of sound, every shade that cannot be expressed or translated by a straight line, constitutes an outrage upon art, a crime of high treason.

So all those who treat the organ as an accordion, who play arpeggios, slur their notes, or are rhythmically unsound, should be branded criminals, and held up to public scorn. On the organ, as in the orchestra, everything should be accurately realisable; the uniformity of feet and hands is absolutely necessary, whether you are beginning the note or finishing it. All sounds placed by the composer under the same perpendicular should begin and end together, obeying the *bâton* of the same leader. We still see here and there unfortunate organists who let their feet drag upon the pedals, and who forget them there long after the piece has been played.

They remind me of that old viola player at the Opera, who used regularly to fall asleep at the fourth act, and was charitably awakened by his companions at the end of the play. It was a tradition, but when a new manager was appointed the tradition had to cease, for he insisted that the sleeping musician should not be awakened. One night *Le Prophète* was being played, and the old man went on dreaming as usual, notwithstanding the loud din of the symphony, the wreck of the palace, blown up by dynamite, and the noise made by the public leaving the theatre. When he opened his eyes he was in the dark, thought himself in hell, like Orpheus; and, in trying to get out, he fell head forward on to the kettledrums, and smashed them. The next day he was pensioned off.

I should like to know what an orchestral leader would say if, after his last beat, his third trombone dared to hold a note? From what savage land did this barbarous custom find its way amongst us? It was prevalent amongst us some years ago—in fact, it was really epidemic.

They are indeed guilty, those organists who do not link closely together the four voices of polyphony, the tenor and soprano, the alto and the bass. Take Bach's gigantic work, and you will not find in it more than two or three passages, two or three bars, that exceed the limits of the hands' extension. But, admire the art of the sublime creator; a moment before or a moment after these passages pauses occur, which clearly afford the time to open and close the sixteen-foot pedal, so as to play with the help of the pedals tied notes that could not possibly be played on the manual alone. Save these two or three exceptions, which are fully justified by the music of the voices, the whole of Bach's work is admirably written, both in this and every other sense.

I now wish, by way of parenthesis, to say something about articulation. The hammer of the piano strikes a chord ten times per second, and our ear can easily recognise the ten separate strokes, the sound dying immediately; but on the organ we must allow for a silence equal in duration to the sound between each repetition, if we wish clearly to distinguish these repetitions in a quick movement, or even in a moderate one. This is the formula that I suggest :—Every articulated note loses half of its value.

The rests should have the value of a semi-quaver.

If we are dealing with the long periods in slow movements, we must of course be guided by the spirit and not by the letter of this law. In the following example

it would of course be ridiculous to curtail by one-half the value of the dotted minim.

This, I think, is the way the bar should be played:

Execution:

giving the same value to the other rests.

Detached notes cannot be allowed on the organ. Each detached note becomes a *staccato*, like that of bow-instruments—that is to say, a series of equal sounds separated by equal silences. Detachment should be effected by holding the fingers as near the keyboard as possible, the wrist being slightly contracted.

Example:

Execution:

When two chords contain the same note, it should be tied and not articulated.

Example:

Execution:

When enumerating the different outrages committed upon art, I referred to the unsoundness of rhythm.

What is rhythm?

It is the constant manipulation of the will at each periodical recurrence of the strong beat. Rhythm alone

will command a hearing ; and, on the organ, every accent,
every effect depends upon rhythm. Much as you may
lean the whole weight of your shoulders upon the keyboard, you will obtain nothing from it. But just postpone
the attack of a chord for one-tenth of a second, prolong
it ever so little, and you will soon see what an effect is
produced. On a keyboard devoid of expression, and
without touching any mechanism, and with all stops
open, you obtain a *crescendo* by the mere increase of
duration given progressively, to chords or detached notes.
Playing the organ really means playing with chrono-
metrical quantities.

Woe be to you if your movement is not possessed of
absolute regularity, if your will does not manifest itself
with energy at each respiration of the musical phrase,
at each break, or if you unconsciously allow yourself to
' urge.'

Would you like a lesson in rhythm ? Listen to those
huge engines pulling tons of goods, admire that formidable piston beat, marking each repetition of the strong
beat, slowly but pitilessly : it is like the very stroke of
fatality ; it makes one shudder.

Avoid every useless movement, every displacement of
the body, if you wish to remain master of yourself. A
good organist sits upright on his bench, slightly leaning
towards his keyboard, never resting his feet upon the
frame of the pedals, but letting them lightly touch the
notes, the heels being, so to speak, riveted together, and
the knees likewise.

Nature has provided us with two very useful com-
passes ; with both heels tight together, the maximum of
separation between the points will give us the fifth ; and
with the two knees placed in the same position, this
maximum should produce the octave. It is only by
training in this way that we can ever hope to attain

precision : the calves touching, the feet constantly coming together again.

The foot should never strike the pedal perpendicularly, but with a forward movement, just touching the note as near as possible an inch or two from the black key.

Considering the state of perfection which the present builders have reached, we are almost dazzled by the amount of wealth they offer us, and tempted to wander from the straight road. We must not forget, however, that all music depends upon the quartet, whether it be on the organ, in an orchestra, or a choir. That is really the foundation of the language. Our quartet on the organ is composed of the limpid and noble sonorousness of the eight-foot pipes. The *basso continuo* of some organists who fall asleep on their sixteen-foot pedals is fast becoming a public nuisance. We would go mad if we had to listen to a Symphony in which the double basses played without interruption from the first to the last note. Plain-song itself loses its eloquence with such an interpretation, and yet it seems better adapted than any other form of art to a uniform bass, considering the apparent monotony of its structure narrowly confined within the limits of the octave. But this apparent monotony only exists in the opinion of those who have no eyes to see, and whose ears cannot hear.

Plain-song is complex of its nature ; like Janus,[1] it has two faces. To understand it we must listen to it from a musical and a literary point of view. This is the synthesis which, in later years, the school of 'decadent' poets or musicians has endeavoured to revive.

The superb accent of the basses, when the organ

---

[1] Take the most beautiful type of plain-song, the admirable *Te Deum*, for instance. Vocalise it, sing it without words : accents, beauty, grandeur, everything disappears. Translate it, sing the same music with a French or German text, and it becomes ridiculous. If the Catholic Church had not insisted upon Latin being the liturgic language, plain-song would have ceased to exist.

E

answers the choir, must comment upon the text, sustain
it in its flights, and not vulgarise it by continued and
unintelligent abuse.

The organ is a wind instrument; it wants to breathe.
The musical phrase, like its literary sister, has its commas,
its full stops, and its new paragraphs. The organ must
vary its plans, as the orator must change his intonations.
Is there anything more insupportable than an improvisation with four parts, proceeding monochromatically,
lamely, without a will of its own, without a pause, a
contrast, or any form of construction, having no beginning,
no middle, no end?

All the old type of organ of Bach contains those sound
properties that suit plain-song, and harmonises wonderfully with the polyphony of the sixteenth-century masters.

Plain-song was implanted almost in every country; it
came originally from Athens, Rome, and Jerusalem, was
handed down to us in the Middle Ages, and was carefully
cultivated in the sunny domain of counterpoint, of which
Palestrina was the sole guardian. We should preserve it
for our grandchildren just as we received it from the
old masters. The plan adopted by the Paris Conservatoire
during the last fifty years will be continued; plain-song
will be commented upon by means of flowery counter-
points in the soprano or the bass, or it will be accompanied
in severe counterpoint, note against note, as is the use of
the Church.

Several great French builders have wilfully ignored the
old style of registers, and in this they are wrong. It is
a great pity!

Last July, at Notre-Dame, where Cavaillé-Coll had
just completed the restoration of the superb organ, we
admired the sonorous and diverse series of these combination stops, producing with the ' Pedal,' a fundamental of
thirty-two feet, at the Bombardon a fundamental of sixteen

feet, at the Grand Choir one of eight. It is impossible to describe the effect produced by the Chorales of the great Sebastian Bach with these crystalline and sonorous strains repercussed under those admirable arches.

This is no more the time for organ cataclysms, thunder-tremors, goat-bleatings, called *vox humana*, and all such children's rattles. At the inauguration of the organ at X, Mr. Z. produced a storm which he would have done well to precede by a few flashes of genius !

We owe the great progress that French art has made in our times to Cavaillé-Coll and his masterpieces, which lend themselves to all the manifestations of thought, whether past or present.[1]

Thanks to Cavaillé-Coll, people are beginning to study Bach. Do you know that sixty years ago you could not have found in all Paris two virtuosos who knew the fugue in B minor? With the exception of the conscientious Boëly, of Saint-Germain l'Auxerrois, I know of none ; and the published compositions of those times tell us what the ideal of that period was—a nameless ideal.

But one day some of the 'young,' more inquisitive than their elders, began to turn over the dusty books of the great Sebastian ; they found the matter somewhat dry, but interesting—at least so far as its execution was concerned. There was something to be learned in it. Soon they were greatly surprised, while working their fingers, to find that their hearts were struck. So they took pleasure in running through the book of chorals, and when they reached the cantatas their enthusiasm knew no bounds.

I shall never forget, when leading the *Concordia*, the hours we spent in teaching the admirable series of lyric works, which we crowned by the ' Matthew Passion ' at the Conservatoire.

---

[1] I should like our organ-builders to adopt the use of an uniform model of pedals going up to G, like the manuals.

It is only fair to our elders to state that in Germany Bach was forsaken for a long time. All honour is due to Mendelssohn, who, on the 29th of March 1829, conducted, at the Sing-Akademie of Berlin, the Matthew Passion, a prodigious work which had been sleeping in a pigeonhole for over a hundred years. It was heard for the first time at Leipzig on the Good Friday of 1729.

In 1840 Mendelssohn gave an organ recital at the Church of Saint Thomas, in Leipzig, to raise funds for a monument to Bach. He played on the same instrument that Bach had used, and the following was the programme:—

1° Fugue in E flat.
2° Improvisation on themes of Bach.
3° Prelude and Fugue in A minor.
4° Passacaglia.
5° Pastorale, Toccata.
6° Fantasia on Chorales.

On the 4th of April 1841, he again conducted the Matthew Passion in the same church, and at the very spot where Bach had conducted it 112 years before.

Lastly, on the 23rd March 1843, he gave a grand symphonic concert :—

1° Suite d'orchestre (ouverture, arioso, gavotte, trio, bourrée et gigue).
2° Motett en double chœur a capella.
3° Concerto pour clavecin (harpsichord) — Mendelssohn played the solo.
4° Air de la Passion (Ich will bei meinem Jesu wachen).
5° Fantaisie sur un thème de Bach (Mendelssohn).
6° Cantate.
7° Prélude pour violon (F. David).
8° Sanctus (Mass in B minor).

The subscription was a great success, and the monument had just been finished.

After the concert Mendelssohn unveiled the bust of the master of masters.

A Contemporary
Criticism of Bach

J. S. SHEDLOCK

JOHANN ADOLPH SCHEIBE, son of the famous organ-
builder, Johann Scheibe, was born at Leipzig in the year
1708. Like many another musician, he commenced by
studying law, yet finally devoted himself wholly to music.
In the year 1737 (March 5) he founded a weekly musical
paper, *Der critische Musikus*, which lasted for over a year.
Although, as we are about to relate, Scheibe fell into bad
repute through attacking Bach, he was a thoughtful and
intelligent musician, and wrote many excellent articles.
He it was who anticipated Gluck's idea with regard to
the overture of an opera. On May 14, 1737, a letter,
professing to come from a musician on his travels, was
published in Scheibe's paper, and in it occurred the
following passage :—

'Mr. ——, of ——, is really the most distinguished
among the musicians. He is an extraordinary performer,
both on the clavier and on the organ ; and at the present
time he has only met with one worthy of being named as
a rival. Several times have I heard this great man play.
His dexterity is astonishing, and one can scarcely conceive
how it is possible for him to draw in and stretch out his

hands and feet in so exceptional and nimble a manner, and also to make the widest leaps without striking a single wrong note, and further, without, by such violent movement, disfiguring the body. This great man would be the wonder of all nations if he had a more pleasing style, and if he did not spoil his compositions by bombast and intricacies, and by excess of art hide their beauty. As he measures by his own fingers, his pieces are fearfully difficult to play, for he expects vocalists and instrumentalists to accomplish with their throats and instruments what he can do on the clavier. This, however, is impossible. All ornaments, all small grace - notes, and everything which by rule musicians understand how to play, he writes out in full, and thus not only are his pieces deprived of the beauty of harmony, but it is totally impossible to distinguish the melody. All the parts are alike as regards difficulty, and no single one stands out as principal part. In short, he is in music what formerly Herr v. Lohenstein was in poetry. Bombast has drawn both away from the natural in art, from the sublime to the obscure. The heavy labour is admired, yet the exceptional trouble taken, being contrary to reason, profits nothing.'

'(Der Herr —— ist endlich in —— der Vornehmste unter den Musikanten. Er ist ein ausserordentlicher Künstler auf dem Clavier und auf der Orgel; und er hat zur Zeit nur einen angetroffen, mit welchem er um den Vorzug streiten kann. Ich habe diesen grossen Mann unterschiedene Male spielen hören. Man erstaunet bey seiner Fertigkeit, und man kann kaum begreifen, wie es möglich ist, dass er seine Finger und seine Füsse so sonderbar und so behend in einander schrenken, ausdehnen, und damit die weitesten Sprünge machen kann, ohne einen einzigen falschen Ton einzumischen, oder durch eine so heftige Bewegung den Körper zu verstellen.

'Dieser grosse Mann würde die Bewunderung ganzer
Nationen sein, wenn er mehr Annehmlichkeit hätte, und
wenn er nicht seinen Stücken, durch ein schwültiges und
verworrenes Wesen das Natürliche entzöge, und ihre
Schönheit durch allzugrosse Kunst verdunkelte. Weil
er nach seinen Fingern urtheilet, so sind seine Stücke
überaus schwer zu spielen ; denn er verlangt, die Sänger
und Instrumentalisten sollen durch ihre Kehle und In-
strumente eben das machen, was er auf dem Claviere
spielen kann. Dieses aber ist unmöglich. Alle Manieren,
alle kleine Auszierungen, und alles, was man unter der
Methode zu spielen versteht, drücket er mit eigentlichen
Noten aus, und das entzieht seinen Stücken nicht nur die
Schönheit der Harmonie, sondern es machet auch den
Gesang durchaus unvernehmlich.

'Kurz: er ist in der Musik dasjenige, was ehemals der
Herr von Lohenstein in der Poesie war. Die Schwültig-
keit hat beyde von dem Natürlichen auf das Künstliche,
und von dem Erhabenen aufs Dunkele geführet ; und
man bewundert an beyden die beschwerliche Arbeit und
eine ausnehmende Mühe, die doch vergebens angewandt
ist, weil sie wider die Vernunft streitet.')

This was meant for no other than Johann Sebastian
Bach, but a champion soon appeared to defend the
worthy Cantor. The latter could, of course, well afford
to laugh at such feeble attacks, yet it was well that
some one should come forward to expose the narrow-
mindedness, not to say impudence, of this criticism.
Such a one was Magister Johann Abraham Birnbaum,
who published a pamphlet entitled ' Unpartheyische,
Anmerckungen über eine bedenkliche Stelle in dem
sechsten Stücke des critischen Musikus.'[1] The author
was Professor of Rhetoric at Leipzig University, a friend

[1] Impartial comments on a doubtful passage in the 6th Number of the
Critischer Musicus.

of Bach's, and, further, one who showed taste as a performer on the clavier. Birnbaum finds fault with both the praise and the blame of the critic. His reply, though reasonable, can scarcely rank as brilliant ; it is indeed verbose. The critic objected to Bach's style of writing ; Birnbaum, like all serious musicians of the present day, admired it. Anon. finds Bach confused, Birnbaum does not. The latter remarks that if Anon. is speaking honestly, then surely *his* thoughts must be confused, whereby, of course, he is prevented from dis- covering the truth ; it is unnecessary to notice the reply in detail. There is, however, one little passage of interest. With regard to the charge of writing out ornaments and grace-notes, Birnbaum remarks as follows :—' Either the author points this out as a peculiarity of the composer's, or he looks upon it as a decided fault. If the former, he makes a huge blunder. The Court-composer is neither the first nor the only one who does this. From among many composers whose names I could cite, I mention only Grigny and Du Mage, who in their *Livres d'orgue* have made use of this method. If the latter, I can see no reason why it should be thus named.' The name of Grigny is interesting, in that Bach, in his young days, when he was at Celle, copied out a Suite in A by this composer, who, about the year 1700, seems to have been organist of Rheims Cathedral. A De Mage is mentioned by Fétis, who was a pupil of Marchand, and of whom— according to this authority—a book of organ pieces appeared in 1753.

Two months later (March 1738) came a reply from Scheibe, who expresses surprise that so much notice should have been taken of the remarks on Bach, which appeared by chance in the *Critischer Musicus*, and which, moreover, were written, as he asserts, by a foreign hand (aus einer fremden Feder). He does not feel actually

called upon to answer Magister Birnbaum's comments,
yet for his own honour and that of all other honest-
minded musicians, he will do so. Scheibe thinks that
possibly Bach himself may have had a hand in drawing
up the Birnbaum pamphlet, which was indeed dedicated
to the composer. Anyhow, he says:—'The *Herr
Hofcompositeur* distributed it with great glee among his
friends and acquaintances on the 8th of January of this
year' (*i.e.* 1738). Birnbaum had complained of certain
terms used in the passage in the letter referring to Bach,
and so now Scheibe complains of Birnbaum's title,
'Impartial Comments': he considers them extremely
partial, since they were written specially to protect and
exalt the writer's friend. The reply is long, and there
are many complaints in it of Birnbaum's insincerity,
ignorance, and spite; of real argument there is, however,
little. Scheibe makes merry over the fact that so
excellently drawn was the portrait of the person meant,
yet not mentioned by name, that it was at once recognised by Bach himself and his friends. Although denying
the authorship of the letter, Scheibe declares that the
passage in question was meant for Bach, and, further,
that he endorses the views expressed therein.

There is an interesting reference to Handel. In the
original letter it was stated that Bach had only met with
one musician worthy to be considered a rival as performer
on the organ or clavier. Who this can be, says Birnbaum
—with more zeal, perhaps, than judgment—is unknown
to me and to many others; and he challenges his
opponent to name the man. If, continues he, Scheibe
refers to a certain great master of music living in a
foreign country, 'I can only refer to the testimony of
some impartial connoisseurs of music, who, on their
travels, have had the good fortune to hear this great
man, and who, while highly praising his uncommon skill,

have declared unreservedly, and in all sincerity, that
"There is only one Bach in the world, no one else
can be compared with him."' Scheibe replies that the
correspondent was in reality opposing to Bach the great
Handel himself; also that all connoisseurs are so impressed by the performances of the latter, that they
scarcely know which of the two is to be preferred.
Scheibe also quotes the 'impartial' judgment of some
very intelligent and true connoisseurs of music who have
heard both these great men. 'Mr. Handel,' say they,
'plays in a more touching, pleasing manner; Mr. Bach
with more art and wonder-creating effect.' Further, they
declare that as they listen to each in turn they think him
the greater.

Here Scheibe certainly scores; Birnbaum, by pretend-
ing that Handel was not fit to be compared with Bach,
was scarcely displaying the quality of impartiality. The
opinion expressed by Scheibe agrees with all that one
has read about Handel's wonderful playing.

Scheibe alludes to Kuhnau. To assert that Bach had
failings is simply to assert that which Birnbaum himself
acknowledges, viz., that no man is perfect. And then he
goes on to remark :—'The famous Kuhnau, the worthy
predecessor of Bach in the Leipzig Cantorate, was a
learned man, thoroughly well experienced in all matters
relating to the theory and practice of music, and one
who in his day was held in high esteem. Yet, notwithstanding all his great merits, how badly did he come off
when he undertook to set an operetta (*Singspiel*) to music
and to produce it on the stage!'

The writer of the letter complains that Bach spoilt the
beauty of his music by excess of art (durch allzugrosse
Kunst), for writing of this kind is contrary to the nature
of true art. Birnbaum maintains that the greatest art
(die allergrösste Kunst) cannot spoil the beauty of a

thing. Scheibe, in reply, begs him to note the difference between art that is *allzugrosse* and *die allergrösste* : the latter he declares to be true art, the former not. This appears as an editor's note to Birnbaum's pamphlet. Yet Scheibe, in his formal answer, begins discussing about *allzugrosse* art, and Birnbaum, in his reply, naturally complains that he has not been fairly dealt with.

It would be tedious to set out in full the *pros* and *cons* of any of the points touched upon by Birnbaum and Scheibe. The above short illustrations must serve to show that after all it was mainly a war of words. Birnbaum evidently felt the greatness of his friend's music, but to prove it was quite another matter. In the dedication to Bach of his second pamphlet ('Vertheidigung seiner unparteyischen Anmerkungen'), Birnbaum declares that his object in writing is to defend the unjustly belittled fame of the master. He hopes that his defence may prove successful ; yet he adds :—

'Where prejudicial opinions, and the obstinate assertion of them, prevent the truth from gaining access to the hearts of our opponents, is it possible to hope that even the most intelligent refutations will bring them to other thoughts? I fear, and not without cause, that the pains which I have taken in this defence, to convert my opponent to sounder opinions with regard to the perfections with which your Honour is endowed, will be utterly in vain. I shall, however, count myself sufficiently rewarded if my just zeal for your Honour is esteemed in any way worthy of your approval.'

Who was the author of the letter which gave rise to such heated discussion ? This question is again introduced into the defence. Birnbaum expressly says : 'It is well known that he (Scheibe) is the author of this letter (dass dieser Brief von ihm selbst aufgesetzt ist) ; that it is the fruit of his desire for vengeance.' Birnbaum informs us of this thirst for vengeance. 'Ought the *Hofcompositeur*,' he says, 'to be blamed if he declared him (Scheibe) an unjust and incompetent judge—the man who, not so very many years ago, at a competition for an organist's post here in Leipzig, could not find the answer to a fugue subject, to say nothing of developing it properly.' So then Scheibe had a grievance, and as Spitta—to the best of my knowledge—makes no mention of this competition, in which Bach himself was umpire, an extract from *Der critische Musikus* will perhaps be welcome. It forms, indeed, a comment on the very passage just quoted from Birnbaum's defence. It is only fair to hear *alteram partem*. This is what Scheibe says :—

'All Leipzig well knows that during the last nine or ten years, no post of organist has been vacant for which I should have cared, or been able, to become candidate. But if reference is made to something which happened nine or ten years ago, it is true that, on the death of an organist at Leipzig, I was one of those who presented themselves for regular trial. Persons, however, of a certain importance who were present, can easily give the lie to the statement that I made such glaring faults. Yet why need I refute this charge in detail? Herr Bach, in Leipzig—if he will judge according to knowledge and conscience—will himself declare the contrary of Birnbaum's reproach. This celebrated man, at that former organists' competition, was appointed one of the umpires. I must, however, not be confused with another hero, who would not play (develop?) the theme placed before him by Capellmeister Bach, but, in place of it, one of his own selection ; or with him who, when a theme was given him, vanished out of sight.' If Scheibe's statement is a true one, then Birnbaum's attack seems scarcely fair. In ten years a man may learn much ; and, besides, at the time of the competition in question, Scheibe was only just over twenty years of age.

Birnbaum was not Bach's only champion. Lorenz Christopf Mizler, born in 1711, was a pupil, and, as one may imagine, an ardent admirer of Bach, his master. He too, in 1736, thus even earlier than Scheibe, had started a musical paper, entitled *Neu-eröffnete Musikalische Bibliothek*, and in the 4th Part (April 1738) there is to be found a notice of Scheibe's paper which had appeared in the previous year. Reference is made to the No. 6, and Mizler says :—' The Editor may have spoken the truth to many against whom he had either a real, or merely imaginary, grievance ; he may have sought to avenge himself. I cannot possibly know, and the whole matter does not really concern me.' And then he advises those interested in musical disputes carefully to read the letter and also Birnbaum's 'Impartial Comments.' Later on (in 1740) there is a review of Birnbaum's second pamphlet. Mizler considers it a dirty business to discuss with such rough, narrow-minded opponents as the writer of the letter. He does not attribute it to Scheibe, who, he believes, has only lent his name to the *Critischer Musikus*.

Some years later (1746) we find another reference in Mizler's paper to the same matter. This time the writer is no less a personage than Christoph Gottlieb Schroeter, who long enjoyed the honour of having invented the pianoforte. He is writing about the *Critischer Musikus*, and of the famous No. 6 he says :—' Although on the 41st page (*i.e.* of the *Crit. Mus.*) it was stated that the letter had been written by a travelling musician to a Master of Music, with a request that it should be inserted, yet it soon became known that *Criticus* alone had concocted this over-smart satire.'

In the year 1745 Scheibe republished his *Critischer*

Musikus, with alterations, additions, etc.   In the preface he writes as follows :—

' I regret that one so celebrated as Herr Bach should have served as a cloak to cover, in a measure, the unseemly attacks and incivilities of some of my opponents ; and yet not one of them has been able to show that I have done injustice to this great man.   And if in one or other of my expressions I may in any way have offended him, the blame should be charged to my adversaries rather than to myself.   How easy it is in polemical writing, through some bold expression, to say more than one actually means !   It is impossible to believe that Herr Bach can really have taken offence at the so-called doubtful passage in No. 6, for it is sufficiently clear that it makes honourable, rather than harmful, mention of him.'

Scheibe, says Spitta (II. p. 733), confessed, later on, that the letter was a fiction, and that he was the author of it.   Bach's biographer does not, however, give the source whence he derived this interesting piece of information, which, indeed, forms a fitting close to our story.

César Franck

GUY DE ROPARTZ

Thus calmly, with his soul caught up to Heav'n,
The artist works . . . and all the rest is naught.

I SELECT these two lines, which M. Vincent d'Indy puts
into the mouth of Wilhelm in the second scene of the
Song of the Bell, for the heading of this brief article on
César Franck, because no artist ever wrote more calmly
than did he, no artist's soul was ever more caught-up and
consequently more careless of the chances of renown
and of fortune. He stands out from among his contemporaries like a man of some other age ; they are
sceptics, he was a believer ; they are self-advertising, he
worked in silence ; they seek glory, he was content to
await it ; they aim at an easily acquired reputation by
daring improvisations, he built enduring monuments amid
the calm of a retired life ; they shrink at nothing if only
they may attain : concession, compromise, meannesses
even, to all those they consent ; he unhesitatingly performed his mission without yielding, without counting
the cost, leaving us indeed the very finest possible
example of artistic uprightness.

But if, by the nobility of his character and the dignity of his life, he seems to belong to the Primitives, the excessive modernity of his work proclaims him the youngest of the French musicians of the last half of the century.

All true creators must be in advance of their time and must of necessity be misunderstood by their contemporaries: César Franck was no more of an exception to this rule than other great musicians have been; like them, he was misunderstood. And the admiration which I profess for his colossal work, an admiration which I shall express in the course of this article, would have been termed exaggerated by the majority but a few years ago: all this has changed to-day, and the hour is fast approaching when full justice shall be done to the composer of *Les Béatitudes*. The reaction in his favour had indeed set in some time before his death. The artists were the first to draw nigh the young artist, and a school of composers gathered round him which to-day forms the first rank of the musical world; the critics had recanted and, save for a few obstinate ones, a few deaf ones who will not give ear, all those whose part it is to communicate their artistic appreciations to the crowd by means of the newspaper had acknowledged his great merits. Then, one day at a festival organised by Pasdeloup by request of some of Franck's pupils, several of his works were applauded by the public who, in spite of the disadvantages of an inadequate execution, understood if not all—understood, as has been so well said by M. Adolphe Jullien, 'at least that all was beautiful'; and, ever since the memorable concert at the *Cirque d'Hiver*, January 1887, the opinion of what we agree to call the 'mass of the public' has coincided with that of the artists. The death of the artist was the finishing stroke. And now those very persons who ignored, or feigned to ignore, the existence of this incomparable musician, profess a boundless enthusiasm and are loudest in proclaiming Franck a man of genius. This marvellous reaction in Franck's favour is much like that which took place in favour of Berlioz on the day after his death. But if the two men were alike in being misunderstood, Franck had none of the rebellious spirit which characterised the composer of the *Damnation de Faust*. It is indeed by no means certain whether even he suffered acutely from the indifference, the injustice of the public. ' The master,' says M. Arthur Coquard in a remarkable notice of Franck, ' had formed an ideal atmosphere of his thoughts and affections, an atmosphere which his soul gladly inhaled, undisturbed by strange currents . . . his spirit delighted itself with its own ideal of art and philosophy. Wrapped in the contemplation of serene beauties such as these, his genius brought forth those great and sometimes sublime works of which we shall presently speak. No wonder that his work, conceived in the calm joy of ecstasy, without thought of public opinion, the artist's dream, lasted over the day of its performance and, soaring so high, lost sight of earth altogether. On the occasions—alas ! too few — when Franck came in touch with the public, he saw and heard nothing but the music, and if the execution struck him as adequate, he was the happiest of men. It was not that he despised the indifference of the public ; he *had not so much as a suspicion of it.*' . . . He had not the rebellious spirit of Berlioz, and yet he had a better right to rebel than Berlioz, for Berlioz was for ever repining against the injustice of fate. And on what score ? Merely this : that each and all his works were not, at first production, applauded with positive frenzy ! Whereas the musician who is convinced of his right to the title of *creator* should be content to wait until he has slowly

F

educated his public up to such a level as that at which they can appreciate him. One only wish is legitimate, which is that the execution of his works should be worthy of the works themselves. Whether or not the works, when given, gain the hearts of the people a little sooner or later, is a matter of little moment. The painter sees his picture as soon as it is completed. The musician has a right to view his work by means of orchestral performance. This right, never denied to Berlioz, was too often refused to Franck. Not only were his two operas never given in his lifetime, but he never so much as had the joy of hearing a complete performance of *Les Béatitudes*, that admirable Oratorio, unique not only among the compositions of to-day, but of all time— that work for which Franck so justly had a peculiar affection and by which he wished to be ultimately judged. This might indeed have given just cause for rebellious discontent, if such a mood had not been foreign to that serene soul. Franck was resigned.

The life of César Franck lies in his work: petty detail, racy anecdote, all this he would lack who would undertake to be his biographer. And it were an insult to the memory of one who so loved retirement to elaborate the unimportant details of his life. This is no place for posthumous research—there were little to glean if it were fitting to attempt it. But I will jot down a date or two in the interest of certain among my readers.

César Franck was born at Liége in Belgium on the 10th of December 1822. He studied first at the Conservatoire of that town, but, on the 2nd of October 1837, he entered that of Paris, studying counterpoint and fugue under Leborne and the piano under Zimmermann. In 1838 he took honours in fugue and the first prize for piano. This last was awarded him under the following exceptional circumstances which Ch. Darcoms thus relates in the *Figaro* :—' One of the youthful competitors, having played the piece set for competition with remarkable brilliancy, the usual piece set as a test for sight-reading was placed before him, and he at once set to work. After a few moments a general look of amazement ran through the room ; the pupil was reading the piece in another key, transposing as he went along, and this he accomplished without one false note. A perfect thunder of applause rewarded the successful performance of such a feat, and when the child reappeared it was to receive a special prize of so exceptional a nature that we think that it was never awarded before or since.' This anecdote testifies to the extraordinary musical aptitude with which Franck was endowed, and it is for this reason that I quote it. He completed his musical studies in 1842, having won the first prize for fugue in Berton's class in 1840, and the second prize in Benoist's organ class in 1842. His father wished him to follow the career of a *virtuoso*, but Franck preferred the comparative retirement of a teacher's life. The lessons by which he made his livelihood left him indeed but little leisure for composition, but so prodigious was his power of production that the total of his work is considerable. There was a period of great activity towards his twentieth year, a period to which, besides other works, we owe the trios, *Ruth*, and several melodies, but later his ardour relaxed somewhat, or rather, as the same Arthur Coquard above quoted says : ' He withdrew into himself, and sought a way in which he should walk. What inclines us to this theory is, that during the years of comparatively little productiveness, he composed first a fine mass and then a series of grand organ pieces, real symphonies, in which there is suddenly revealed a curious kinship with

the great Bach.' . . . We will treat of this organ music
later on.   It was about the year 1870 that he began that
series of powerful creations which followed one another
uninterruptedly from that time to that of his death.   As
in all such, each work is a distinct advance towards the
goal which he had set himself.   In 1872 he was appointed
Professor of the Organ at the Conservatoire (he had
naturalised himself a Frenchman in 1870), and he held
the post of organist at the Church of Ste. Clotilde.   It
was, I think, in 1886 that the Minister of Fine Arts
granted Franck the Legion of Honour, and it was upon
this occasion—the only official recognition which Franck
ever received—that I heard him pronounce the only
repining word that perhaps ever passed his lips.   When
I was congratulating him upon this honour, he replied
rather sadly : ' Yes, my friend, they honour me as a
Professor ! '   No doubt the thought then uppermost in
his mind was this, that in high places he was still ignored
as a composer.

But enough of these biographical notes, it is of Franck's
work that I wish to speak, and, in order to do so
methodically, let me begin by dividing this work into
classes.   I will discuss it in the following order : Oratorios,
chamber-music (trios, quintet, sonata, quartet), Symphonies (*symphonie, poèmes symphoniques*), church music
(organ pieces, mass, motets), and, finally, operatic music
—*Hulda, Ghisèle.*

.   .   .   .

César Franck composed four Oratorios : *Ruth, Rebecca,*
Rédemption, Les Béatitudes.   *Ruth* is one of the very
earliest works of the master and was first given at the
Paris Conservatoire in the year following that in which
Félicien David's *Désert* had been first heard.   It pleased
the public by its simplicity of construction, by its charming melodies, by the interesting orchestration.   It was a

success—the only success Franck had during the course of many years. The first part indeed—the departure of Naomi, and the devotion of her daughter-in-law Ruth, who declines to leave her—is of a touching melancholy. The second part includes many brilliant pages, such as the famous song of the Reapers, while the third rises to an even higher level of inspiration. But neither this work nor *Rebecca*—a brief biblical scene where the orchestral effects are already full of colour and the harmonies novel—gave any promise of *Rédemption* or of *Les Béatitudes.*

Rédemption was written in the days that immediately followed the Franco-Prussian war, and it was given for the first time in 1873 at the Odéon concerts, just founded by M. Edouard Colonne in collaboration with MM. Duquesnel and Hartmann. There is a wide gulf between *Ruth* and *Rédemption* ; for in the latter, Franck's mastery first asserts itself together with that mysticism which in *Les Béatitudes* is entirely revealed.

It has been objected by some that Franck's orchestration lacks colour, flags amid tame modulations and becomes monotonous owing to a certain lack of light and shade. I know that there are composers whose instrumentation swarms with picturesque detail and whose palette is more brilliant, more varied ; but I do not hesitate to affirm that one must hark back to the greatest masters of symphony to find any orchestration as solid, as well built up, as that of Franck. No man of our age has written orchestral quartets to equal his. In support of this assertion, let me quote an incident from my own experience which, since it deals with *Rédemption,* is appropriate. Two years ago I was preparing to produce this great work at the concerts of the Nancy Conservatoire. Prior to the full rehearsals, I, in accordance with my usual custom, insisted upon the strings going through their part of the score alone. There was not one among my instrumentalists who knew *Rédemption*, but I shall never forget the enthusiasm for my revered master's work which they expressed at the end of the rehearsal, moved solely by his superb handling of the string quartet: what other work written for full orchestra and voices could so triumphantly endure the test of being deprived of both wind and voices?

The short prelude to the first part, a prelude built up upon the motive of the angel's song and treated in strict canon, is a positive marvel. And surely no more fit opportunity will occur in which to point to the surprising skill with which César Franck handled this severe scholastic form of canon which was always dear to him, and of which we find admirable examples in nearly all his works.

Of course mastery of composition is the common heritage of all masters, but, in the case of Franck, we must not fail to notice that this mastery, which was his in the highest degree, is never practised for its own sake, but is always subservient to the musical idea of which, far from delaying, it hastens the development. Bach, the immortal Cantor, had a musical idiom equally complex, but he too never permitted complexity to stifle thought.

The prelude is followed by a full chorus of men, in contrast to the chorus of angels which follows. These are the angels for whose singing Franck has written such divine music, the same angels whom we shall meet later on in *Les Béatitudes*. M. Ernest Chausson says of them:—'These angels are not like those introduced by M. Maurice Bouchon into his Mass in D, who have rich blood and are swift to anger, who are girt with swords upon their thighs, and whom the reading of Rabelais would not amaze! Franck's angels are more subtle, now soaring and casting glances of pity upon earth, now drawing nigh to share in the sorrows of mankind. It may even be that they too have lived, that they too have tasted of grief. Their tenderness has in it something human.' It is the seraphic soul of the master himself who sings by their lips, that soul which we have seen serene and unruffled by everyday deceptions, but yet so full of altruism as to be moved by his neighbour's sufferings. I cannot refrain from reference to two more numbers in the first part of *Rédemption*—the air, namely, in which the archangel announces the birth of the Redeemer in the stable of Bethlehem, and the final chorus, where indeed the introductory *motiv* may be a little lacking in distinction, but which soon recovers and is certainly incomparably sonorous from beginning to end.

Between the two parts which make up the work, which we are now considering, there is a purely orchestral interlude known on concert-programmes as *Morceau symphonique de Rédemption*. In the few pages of which it consists, inspiration attains its highest point, but it was actually composed some years after the score, to replace another *entr'acte symphonique* which, not satisfying the master, figures only in first editions. This restless desire of doing better has produced a masterpiece. The melody upon which is constructed this admirable interlude, in which the archangel's song from the first part recurs, is one of the most exquisite musical ideas which we owe to Franck's inspired pen. And those who assert that Franck's inspiration fell short—an assertion which cannot be maintained by any who are at all familiar with his work—can certainly never have read the theme here so finely treated or they must have altered their opinion.

This piece, of which we cannot speak in terms sufficiently high, is inscribed :—'The joy of the world transformed and expanded by the words of Christ.' Centuries have indeed gone by, and men, redeemed by the birth of God made man, are once more assailed by doubt. Their sorrow for this is told in a chorus of poignant sadness. But now the angels return, the same who heralded the coming of the Messiah and who now bewail the sorrows, the sins of earth ; and the archangel calls men to repent, telling them that by their tears they can obtain God's pardon. The closing chorus does not perhaps begin very happily. The *motiv* is not sufficiently expressive. But no sooner does the strain of the angel's song reappear than inspiration begins to soar, developing as voice after voice joins in into a Finale of supreme magnificence. We soar with the music, carried higher and higher, leaving earth behind, and borne by the music to heaven itself.

Rédemption had sufficed to place Franck in the first rank of masters of oratorio. But Franck was the composer of *Les Béatitudes* also, and, great as is the beauty of the earlier work, it pales beside the splendour of this very cathedral of tone. How indeed can one hope to speak of it adequately, or in an article of limited length such as this find space for a complete analysis? It were impossible, and I set myself no such ambitious aim. I will confine myself to going through Franck's master-score with the reader, pointing as I go to those passages which strike me as especially deserving admiration.

I do not deny that, in choosing to give the form of oratorio to Christ's divine Sermon on the Mount, Franck set himself a difficult task, but we shall see how skilfully he avoided the obvious pitfall of monotony. Still I cannot but wonder how it was that so admirable a subject never suggested itself to any one before Franck, for it is an essentially musical one and lacks action, which is an essential point for oratorio. The subjects treated in oratorio are too often dramatic, and merely result in the production of theatrical pieces without staging or costume. Cannot music dispense with action and deal best with abstract ideas and sentiments? To my mind the ideal of an oratorio is a symphony with solos and choruses. And surely the Sermon on the Mount offers musicians all this. The more honour to Franck, who first proved it! It is indeed a question whether his chosen collaborator, who supplied the text, was quite competent to perform such a task. One had need to be an excessively indulgent critic to answer this in the affirmative. The scheme of each Beatitude is indeed not bad, but is it not worked out as obviously suggested by the divine words themselves? M. Colomb's verbal technique and his vocabulary are alike so inadequate that, apart from the score, the text is barely endurable reading.

There is a short prologue in which the Christ-*motiv* is first introduced, a *motiv* which recurs again and again in the course of the work, transformed, developed, combined in a hundred unexpected ways, with consummate art. This prologue produces the desired mood in the hearer. On the one hand is the old world, wretched, criminal, suffering, and dying of distress, and on the other the new doctrine which supplies man with a reason for his life, his pain. In this prologue the Christ-*motiv* deserves especial notice. It is sung by the violoncellos and tenors in an involved counterpoint which is a perfect marvel of elegance and expression ; nor must the exquisite snatch of the angel-choir be allowed to pass unheeded. Blessed is he who whispers hope to drooping hearts.

The First Beatitude : ' Blessed are the poor in spirit, for theirs is the kingdom of Heaven ! ' Men strain after material wealth, terrestrial happiness, worldly pleasure, but amid their joy there is sadness in their heart. ' Where,' they cry in desperation—' where can we find happiness ? '

Then Christ's voice makes itself heard: 'Blessed is the man who hath set his heart upon true riches, blessed is he to whom love opens the kingdom of Heaven!' And this strain is taken up by the chorus and developed to the magnificent Finale of this first part. This is surely the occasion in which to remark that, in this work, in which feeling never for one moment fails, the pages which depict the brutal enjoyments of man before his redemption through Christ never attain so high a level of beauty as those devoted to mystical joys. It is when Christ speaks, when the angels sing, that Franck's music soars highest. It is as though, his own soul never having been steeped in material joys, he were ill at ease in describing them.

The Second Beatitude : 'Blessed are the meek, for they shall inherit the earth!' The terrestrial chorus of this second part is written in an extremely modernised form of fugue, profoundly expressive. The response of the celestial choir : 'Meekness can alone make light the fetters which bind you,' is sung by soloists and full choir alternately, and at last Christ's voice speaks : 'Blessed are the meek,' etc. The whole number is of a purity quite unearthly.

The Third Beatitude : 'Blessed are they that weep, for they shall be comforted!' This third beatitude is more elaborate. The poet treats all griefs in succession. First, that of all men, for do not all men weep from the mere fact of living? Then the griefs of individuals, of the mother bereft of her child, of the motherless orphan, of the husband parted from his wife, of the slave groaning in chains, of philosophers vainly seeking truth, of exiles longing for home. For all these Franck has found phrases of intense bitterness, of poignant sadness. His compassionate heart was indeed moved by all human suffering, and the first part of this third beatitude is full

of human anguish. But now the voice of Christ is heard :
' Blessed are they that weep, for they shall be comforted !'
and the angel-choir takes up the words of the despairing,
and one by one transforms each phrase into one of
resignation, by means of grace and the divine words
which promise comfort to them that suffer. The pages
are brimming over with emotion, so that the most callous
could hardly listen with indifference.

The Fourth Beatitude : ' Blessed are they that hunger
and thirst after righteousness, for they shall be satisfied !'
I have already said that Franck succeeded in evading
the monotony, inherent to a poem which eight times
contrasts the human soul, its sadness and its doubts, with
the Redeemer's comforting voice. He did indeed understand how to vary the musical form, for, in this fourth
beatitude, the chorus is altogether silent. Mr. Ernest
Chausson writes as follows : ' This fourth beatitude
certainly surpasses all other French music in sublimity.
One would be obliged indeed to go back to the very first
classical masters to find so powerful an expression of the
soul's despair, its appeal to Divine Justice, its striving
after the ideal, after holiness.' And there is, I assure
you, no exaggeration in this appreciation by one of
Franck's best pupils. This fourth part opens with a
purely instrumental passage, the melody of which is of
classic purity and yet supremely expressive. Then a
few notes of the same strain repeated in canon form an
accompaniment upon which a man's voice ascends gradually, and this cry : ' Ideal Holiness, Justice, reveal thyself !'
Then the second part of the theme bursts forth in B major
in such a lyric rhapsody that one is carried to heights
unattainable except to genius. And to save our hearts
from being crushed by so violent a storm of expression,
we need all the gentleness of Christ's voice singing to
chords of ever waning *pianissimo*, ' Blessed are they that

hunger and thirst after righteousness, for in Heaven they shall be satisfied!'

The Fifth Beatitude: 'Blessed are the merciful, for they shall obtain mercy!' The text tells the oppression of the weak, and how their complaint cries for vengeance. 'Rise! mighty King, against injustice. Take our cause in Thy hand, and when in our turn we are victors, it shall be ours to oppress our former tyrants and to taste the triumphant joy of revenge!' This is sung by the full chorus. But Christ speaks, 'Vengeance is mine! Sons of Adam, forgive your brethren. Verily I say unto you: Blessed are the Merciful.' And the Angel of Pardon, in a beautiful strain, adjures men to forgive in order that they may be forgiven. And again the chorus sings, but now with how divine a gentleness! What calm! what serenity! and the hearer's soul is then soothed to rest.

The Sixth Beatitude: 'Blessed are the pure in heart, for they shall see God!' We must notice here the introduction of a new element in order to give variety to the work; a double chorus of women namely, whose burdens are admirably attuned, although one is throughout in the minor mode and the other in the major. This is another example of the composer's consummate dexterity. The Pagan women call vainly upon their ancient gods, the Jewish women equally in vain upon the God of Abraham, Isaac and Jacob, that He would reveal Himself to them as He did to their fathers; four Pharisees complacently relate their own virtues and deserts, and confidently, presumptuously, await the reward of their good deeds. The Angel of Death asks: 'Which of you can meet the King without trembling?' And, alternately with Christ's voice, the angel-choir comments upon the sixth Word of the Sermon, 'Blessed are the pure in heart, for they shall see God!' and the composer brings out that other Gospel thought: 'Verily I say unto you, unless ye become as

one of these little ones, ye shall in no wise enter into the
Kingdom of Heaven.' This chorus is indeed delightful,
full of evangelical feeling and grouped about a theme of
singular sweetness. Sweetness is indeed the note of this
sixth part, always excepting the Pharisee's quartet, which
is characterised by a vigour which recalls Handel, and
which is yet guiltless of a touch of archaism. Franck
wished this to be so, in order to throw the energetic,
almost brutal, seventh part into the higher relief.

The Seventh Beatitude: 'Blessed are the peace-makers,
for they shall be called the children of God!' Satan now
appears for the first time. Franck has portrayed him
terrible, untamed, colossal, the very Spirit of Evil; and
one is startled to find that the divine musician, who
excels in making angels sing, is equally able to render
the immeasurable pride, the eternal revolt, the fierce
hatred for all that is good and beautiful of this Prince of
Darkness, as he is here called. We find him summoning
his faithful, the wicked, the fratricides, the liars, the
enemies of peace; into them he breathes his own heinous
and rebellious soul, and all answer his call: tyrants,
priests of false gods, disturbers of order, despisers of
uprightness, master and followers of evil, they extol
hatred, revenge, warfare, assert the right of the strong,
and finally sing: 'Blessed are the powerful!' To all this
first part, which is not devoid of a wild majesty of its
own, the voice of Christ replies softly: 'Blessed are the
peace-makers, for they shall be called the children of
God!' Satan's head droops before this terrible voice,
but he does not yet acknowledge himself vanquished.
And the seventh part closes with the quintet of the peace-
makers, which is full of profound feeling, and celebrates
the universal brotherhood of nations drawn together in
love.

The Eighth Beatitude: 'Blessed are they which are

persecuted for righteousness' sake, for theirs is the Kingdom of Heaven!' We are now at the eighth and last stage of this wonderful road; we are upon the threshold of the finest portion of this sublime score. True that the Prologue is superb, and I have drawn attention to the merits of the fourth and sixth Beatitudes, but the eighth surpasses them all. The inspiration soars yet higher, the form comes nearer to perfection; Franck's soul develops into a very ecstasy of suffering! The joy of suffering which believes, of a suffering which hopes for justice in the Beyond, is glorified as never before in music.

Satan raises his head and hurls defiance at Christ:

> 'Christ, look backward thro' the years,
>   View the future, view the past;
> See the guiltless children's tears,
>   While their blood to earth is cast.
> See, how virtue is beset,
> See, with tears the earth is wet;
> All mankind does my behest.
> See the just in terror flee,
> Dost Thou dare to say to me,
> That thy faithful ones are blest?'

To Satan, who endeavours to prove the inefficacy of the work of Redemption, the chorus of the righteous answers:

> 'O Eternal Justice, for whose sake we endure,
>   Our souls are true to Thee;
> Thou alone art our reward,
>   It is sweet to die for Thee!'

And indeed this chorus seems to come from Heaven, so perfect is its purity. Twice does Satan try to tempt the just, who as often reply in tones more and more divine. It is as though one were initiated into the delight of martyrdom, wrapped in a mystic joy, penetrating, engrossing; one can never forget the emotion. And how exquisitely Franck has rendered Christ's Mother, who is also introduced in the eighth Beatitude: 'I am the Mother of the Saviour and all earthly sorrows pale before mine!' How touching is this musical phrase! Then, after the words, 'I give my Son to be sacrificed for humanity,' the orchestration is so light, so limpid, that it is as though a kindly dew were shed upon regenerate earth by the merits of the sacrifices made by the Mother of God. Above the instruments Satan's voice is heard threatening still, but confident no longer, and it is no longer the same proud being who now inquires: 'Is this that daughter of Eve who shall crush my head beneath her heel?' And the voice of Christ is lifted up: 'Blessed are they that are persecuted for righteousness' sake, their reward is in Heaven!' At length Satan acknowledges himself defeated, and the admirable Finale begins. The Christ-*motiv* which, in the words of a contemporary musicographer, has run through the score like a golden thread, develops and reveals itself in its full beauty as it soars. 'Come, ye blessed of my Father, come unto me. Come! my Cross has opened a way to eternal glory,' and, with a burst of Hosannas from angels and redeemed, to a slow majestic measure, the masterpiece is brought to a fitting close.

Now that I have run through the score of *Les Béatitudes*, I am only too conscious how inadequate is my treatment. Let any who think that they discern a certain exaggeration in my admiration open the score themselves and study it; or better still, let them hear it given more than once, and I am confident that they cannot fail to pronounce it a masterpiece.

True that the production is no easy task; it needs a numerous and enterprising chorus, a very complete orchestra, a host of soloists. But there can be no doubt about the result since the experience of M. Colonne, who gave *Les Béatitudes* in its entirety and met with complete success. There is therefore no longer any need to fear that the work should be too long, too monotonous for performance at one concert. At the Châtelet the performance was a very good one, and given three times in succession; the work attracted a numerous audience, so that we may hope that M. Colonne will ere long revive it.

I have praised Franck's unusual dexterity, but I have perhaps not sufficiently dwelt upon the abundance of his musical ideas. And it is especially by this quality of abundance that the great masters distinguish themselves. A faultless technique is not so rare as freshness, loftiness, fulness of melodious ideas. And this quality César Franck displays upon every page of *Les Béatitudes.*

I cannot have done with this score without quoting the opinions of some French musicians and critics. Arthur Coquard writes: ' The musical treatment is quite equal to the grandeur of the idea, and never did the master's idea soar so high. Where do we find accents more fraught with emotion and power, an idiom more modern, more clear, and, together with an astonishing and daring unity of scheme, a more abundant variety of ideas? We have come across composers whose methods had nothing in common with Franck's, who yet made *Les Béatitudes* a subject of unremitting study, a kind of musical Gospel. Of how many contemporary works can one say as much?' Ernest Chausson calls *Les Béatitudes* 'powerful, a work of genius.' M. Hugues Imbert writes: '*Les Béatitudes* is Franck's masterpiece . . . a fine Oratorio, massive in structure, which will tower above many works which at first met with more rapid, therefore more evanescent, success. This Oratorio alone would suffice as evidence of the composer's greatness.' We owe this last appreciation to M. Ch. Darcoms. It appeared in the *Figaro* after the Franck festival at the Concerts Pasdeloup : ' *Les Béatitudes*,

a series of majestic compositions, which occupy a unique
position in modern music.'

I come now to the second class of those into which I
have divided the works of César Franck—chamber-music
namely. It was in chamber-music that his earliest
inspiration found its expression, and he was not yet
twenty when already he had completed his four trios;
and if one compares them with the chamber-music then
(1840) in vogue in France, one marvels at the precocity
of a young musician who, as a first experiment in original
composition, produced works such as those which are
remarkable alike in melody and rhythm, and display a
firmness of touch altogether exceptional. The influence
of Beethoven is distinctly discernible, and indeed to what
other Master could Franck have looked for such sound
teaching in pure music? Still originality is by no means
lacking, and already there is distinct promise of what the
composer will achieve in the severe style of instrumental
music when he has come to his full strength. In this
connection let me refer especially to the trio in F♯ minor,
where there is an evident striving after achieving unity by
means of a *Leit-motiv* as yet timidly handled. The work
already reveals that musician to whom, some forty years
later, M. Gevaert, the learned and respected director of
the Brussels Conservatoire, could say, and say without
exaggeration, after the performance of the Quintet : 'You
have transformed chamber-music; you have opened a
new way!'

The Quintet, written if I mistake not in 1879, had a
great success among artists. Let me quote M. Ernest
Chausson, who has written so ably on the subject : 'It is
of the Quintet,' he says, 'that I wish to speak, but I am
at a loss for words in which adequately to express myself
on the subject of a work so powerful, so glowing in
expression, so divine. Nearly forty years elapse between

G

the composition of the Trios and the Quintet; the workmanship is entirely different, so is the system of harmony. We are plunged into a very torrent of tangled and delightful harmonies. The composer does not hesitate to employ all the keys, major and minor, and all progressions. But below all this luxuriance there is a scheme both finely conceived and logical. The work is ornate, yet there is no blurring of outline. The impression of unity is complete, and the leading *motiv* of the Andante is one of the most touching, one of the most penetrating ever written. It is impossible to resist the charm of the flowing harmony and of the melody, now spirited, now tender, and the emotion roused by so fine a work of art makes one for the moment lose sight of the artist's skill.'

M. Ernest Chausson has a special leaning towards the Andante, and in this he shows his discernment, although the entire work is deserving of unalloyed admiration. I so enjoy transcribing the words of others who share my devotion for Franck, that I cannot resist the temptation to quote M. Georges Peruvin, who wrote as follows of the very work which we are now considering :—' It is a perfect masterpiece, which will live among the monuments of modern music. I cannot recall any other work in which the inspiration is sustained at so high a level, or in which the balance between the three parts is so admirably maintained. They are drawn into amazing oneness by means of a phrase repeated in both Andante and Finale, after a long-drawn development in the opening Allegro— a phrase which hovers over the whole work like an overmastering idea, and by its very form suggests aspiration towards the Infinite.'

Next in order of time to the Quintet comes a Sonata written some years later. This work is by no means inferior to its predecessor, but it is totally different. It is for piano and violin, and having been completed in

September 1886, was first performed at the Salle Pleyel in Paris, on the 5th of March 1887. The work was interpretated by Mme. Bowes-Pene, a pianist of much talent, whose health just now deprives us of her presence on the concert-platform, and the incomparable violinist to whom the work is dedicated—Eugène Ysaye. It met with great success, for already the public were beginning to give the Master a hearing. The sublimity of thought, the purity of form, the wealth and freshness of the harmonies which place this Sonata in the first rank, met with due appreciation. The first movement offers no very startling developments, but does not fail to produce the desired impression of profound calm. Of the two *motive* upon which it is built up, the first is that which links together the four portions of the work. The second movement, the Andante, is very passionate, very human ; the Fantasia, which here replaces the Andante of classical tradition, alternating as it does between a wail and a poetic dreamfulness, is in violent contrast to the merry *Finale*, treated in continuous canon with consummate skill. The theme, which is of the simplest construction, is first rendered by the piano, while the violin plays the part of echo, but soon the *rôles* are reversed ; then the theme passes into the intermediary parts, going and coming, always interesting, each time presented in a new guise. And amid these variations, persistent as a peal of bells, the principal *motive* of the other movements are repeated, the most pathetic, that of the Fantasia, reappearing twice. Once more there is a return of the canon, the phrases hasten, close up into half-bars, and at the height of this admirable rhythmic progression the Sonata closes.

Up to this time César Franck had always availed himself of the piano in his chamber-music, but in his last achievement in that direction he selected the highest form —the string-quartet.

It is only the great artists who attain higher and higher. From the early Sonatas to the immortal latter-day Quartets, from *Rienzi* to *Parsifal*, Beethoven and Wagner progressed towards the Divine Unattainable. We have observed the distance which divides the work of Franck's twentieth year from his Quintet, his Sonata, but still greater than these is the Quartet for two violins, tenor and violoncello. It is indeed the Master's swan-song, rich in invention, dazzling in form, and fraught with a feeling so intense that I know several who cannot hear it without tears. And yet, after giving us this masterpiece, Franck was once more inspired, and from his very heart came his three last organ-pieces, which seem to be the last prayer of the righteous man before his entrance into glory.

But let me revert to the Quartet and briefly analyse its beauties. The construction of the first part recalls the first movement of the Symphony, but it is still more massive. The Poco Lento is a kind of introduction built up upon a sonorous phrase declaimed by the first violin, *fortissimo* in the triumphant key of D major; this the violoncello takes up, but *piano*. First period of the Allegro, the Poco Lento, serves as centre, reappearing in fugal form, the admirable writing serving but to intensify the thought. Return of the Allegro in the key of G minor, second period and conclusion on the Poco Lento repeated a third time in the original key. The second part is a winged and airy Scherzo, a fantastic dance of immaterial beings. Especially remarkable is the persistent recurrence of F♯ minor, for although the passages of the musical discourse may tend more or less away from the original key, yet they are invariably borne back again. Spite of this there is no suspicion of monotony. The trio is full of charm and poetry. Then the Scherzo is resumed, closing with a reminiscence of the trio. The Larghetto is one of

Franck's sublimest achievements. It sprang from the
over-flowing heart of the Master as though of set purpose,
by its length, to give the lie to such as pretend that the
leading characteristics of contemporary French music is
brevity of idea and flippancy of *motiv*. Now ensues a
second theme, wailing, agonising, torn from human pain
and again the first theme is repeated entire. A passionate
cry, and again the haunting burden recurs, but only its
first bars ; soon it expands, rises to the point of passion,
and dies away in ecstasy. Once more the second *motiv*
is repeated, but now in broken fragments, the tones
sinking to *pianissimo*. And now for the Finale—the
Allegro Molto! The four bows attack the vigorous
theme in unison : the beginning of the Larghetto—again
the theme of the Allegro Molto—snatches of the Scherzo
—the theme of the Allegro Molto for the third time—
that of the Poco Lento—and at last the Finale bursts
forth ! It is as though the musician, haunted by memories,
had laid them one by one by wilful repetition. Still
when, after an astounding exposition, after a caressing
snatch of melody, after developments displaying a
marvellous facility of invention, the first notes of the
Poco Lento serving for counterpoint to the second *motiv*
of the Finale, the artist is once more haunted by the Poco
Lento, and this time more persistently than ever, the
divers *motive* of the work intermingle until, triumphant
and sonorous, the Larghetto brings to a close the
greatest string Quartet in existence after Beethoven's
later ones.

Spite of the fact that pieces for piano solo do not
properly belong to chamber-music at all, I cannot refrain
from mentioning two among Franck's works : 'Prélude,
Chorale, Fugue,' and 'Prélude, Aria, Finale,' for in them
he has succeeded in giving quite new treatment of a style
of composition in which Bach excelled, in a manner

entirely novel. In the first-mentioned 'Prélude, Chorale, Fugue,' of proportions so unusual in piano music, the Chorale specially deserves note, as does the Fugue, in which the writer's modernity and chromatic range are pushed to their extremest limit.

Before bringing this division of my article to a close, let me quote the words of M. Alfred Ernst, the distinguished musicographer, the skilled translator of the Wagner dramas. It is ten years since, in the *Revue Wagnérienne*, he wrote as follows :—' I wish to return thanks to the Master for having given chamber-music in France new life by means of works of great sublimity and beauty, among others by the famous Quintet, whose fame is already European, and by a wonderful Sonata recently completed by M. Franck setting forth great musical ideas—which are not infrequently philosophical also and full of religious devotion—by means of dialogues between a small number of instruments, which are thus enabled to render from the fulness of their individual resource, all that is in them of intimate poetry. The musician, free from all stage-trammels, is thus able to devote himself entirely to expressing his thoughts, his pain, his dreams.'

It is curious that Franck, who was so essentially a musician, one for whom music was a language requiring no interpreter but itself, and governed by its own laws, should have strayed into the descriptive style. True, that his lapses in the direction of the symphonic-poem, properly so called, were few in number, and that even in them it is upon the musical side that the greater stress is laid. Save in the case of *Le Chasseur Maudit* suggested by Bürger's ballad, and in which music is certainly subordinate to the plot, whose action is unfolded by the orchestra, Franck's two other symphonic-poems, *Les Djinns* and *Les Éolides*, could well afford to dispense with a text commentary, and so depend solely upon the music. In *Les Éolides* especially, full of delicious subtleties, the title merely serves to indicate the general colour, the leading sentiment of the piece. In *Les Djinns* César Franck has most happily linked piano and orchestra, and, without giving the piano too important a place for its powers, has by judicious blending produced a charming sonority. But to *Le Chasseur Maudit, Les Djinns,* and *Les Éolides,* I infinitely prefer the *Variations Symphoniques,* which are likewise for piano and orchestra, and which, together with a Symphony of which I shall presently speak, are the finest of the master's orchestral compositions. And in the *Variations Symphoniques,* spite of the fact that the pianist has a more important part to play than in *Les Djinns,* we must not fail to notice that never for a moment is the opportunity for display afforded the pianist, which to my mind so disfigures works composed for solo and orchestra. The scheme of the *Variations Symphoniques* is full of charming fancy : the quartet plays a rhythmic accompaniment, a melody is suggested by the piano—a snatch of melody and rhythm together ; the second melody is sketched in lightly ; the first one is elaborated ; but now interrupted by the rhythmic beat, it gives place to the second *motiv,* which is subject to superb changes—now a gentle melancholy, now a great depth of expression. There is a short but extremely poetical episode in which fragments of the first melody are discernible, given upon the lowest notes of the string quartet, beneath a light piano accompaniment, and then ensues the Allegro, of delicate rhythm, picturesque light and shade, built up upon the first melody in the same key of F♯. Twice does the piano thrill with a phrase of passionate tenderness while the basses recall the second *motiv,* and a work of extraordinary resource of invention and incomparable workmanship is brought to a conclusion in canon form, sonorous, powerful, triumphant.

One autumn evening in 1888 I went to pay the master a visit at the beginning of vacation-time. 'Have you been working?' I inquired. 'Yes,' was Franck's reply, 'and I think that you will be pleased with the result.' He had just completed the Symphony in D, and he kindly played it through to me upon the piano. I shall never forget the impression produced on me by that first hearing. Notwithstanding the great oratorios, the organ-pieces, the chamber-music, it is the work I prefer of all that the master composed.

I will do my best to analyse it as clearly as it is possible to do when one is denied the expedient ,of transcribing the different themes in musical notation.

The Symphony is divided into three parts : Intro-duction (*Lento* and *Allegro non troppo*): Allegretto: Finale (*Allegro non troppo*). But we shall see that in the Allegretto, which here replaces the usual Adagio, the Scherzo is, so to say, enshrined, and so co-exists with it : if one considers them separately, they, with the other two parts, make up the four of classical tradition.

The orchestra is very complete, and César Franck enlists the services of the English horn, the bass clarinet, and harp.

The Introduction suggests the first theme of the *Allegro non troppo*, and no sooner has this theme been displayed by the strings to a rhythmic accompaniment of chords from the remainder of the orchestra, than the Introduction is repeated a minor-third lower, that is in F minor. A brief transition leads to another theme of most penetrating charm which I will term the Hope-*motiv*. Soon it is repeated a major-third lower. This phrase is full of un-earthly tenderness, pure as the seraph choirs that sing in the master's oratorios. And now ensues the theme which

binds the part of the Symphony in one. It is declaimed
by the whole orchestra like a mighty *Credo*. An ascending progression in major-thirds vibrates in the bass,
and inspires the leading quartet with enthusiasm : soon
the sound diminishes, and one by one the instruments
become silent. Then a horn plays the four first bars of
the Faith-*motiv*, and it seems like a great mark of interro-
gation upon the threshold of the mystery underlying all
things. Amid the wonders of an ever-varied instrumentation there is continual development; it is as though the
themes were inexhaustible mines whence the composer
derives treasures of melody and rhythm. So ingenious
are the transformations of the original ideas that they
seem ever new, and yet so closely is the texture woven
that one can hardly discern the points at which they
begin or end. And yet a careful analysis reveals the
plan of the work beneath this musical abundance, and the
plan is a classical one. The Introduction reappears in
a new form. The Faith-*motiv* is chanted in D major, and
once more inspiration soars. This first part closes upon a
triple repetition in canon of the first bar of the Introduction, leading up to the final chord of D major by a
plagal cadence.

The Allegretto is composed in a form entirely new.
Sixteen bars of *pizzicati* on the strings and chords upon
the harp outline a kind of vague silhouette of the leading
phrase, and when the horn recites this phrase, first alone,
and then with a melody upon the tenors for counterpoint, the *pizzicati* and harp-chords act as accompaniment.
There is a sweet melancholy about this phrase which
reminds one of a shepherd's song in the evening twilight.
And how kindly the ray when the first violins chant the
Faith-*motiv* in another form, while the second violins and
the tenors beat the measure! Now the English horn
repeats a snatch of the principal phrase, while a clarinet

responds. Next a second theme in triplets on the violin's lowest register; it is actually the theme of the Scherzo, if we regard each beat of a moderate movement as a bar in a rapid one; nor does this Scherzo lack its trio, which, with another *motiv*, completes the charming *genre*-picture. And again the melancholy phrase recurs, blended now with the Scherzo in one of those combinations of two apparently unlike passages in which Franck's great talent delights itself.

The strings, followed by the whole orchestra, burst with the joyous key of D major, and now, borne up by violon-cellos and bassoons, there ensues a theme of overflowing joy, which I will call the Joy-*motiv*. The violins take it up eagerly, and in their turn the clarinets, the flutes, the hautboys claim it also; it soars on high. Modulating in ascending major-thirds, it gives place to a second theme, Triumph-*motiv*, which is also joyous, for the whole Finale is joyous, although it is according to Franck's wont, a synthesis of the whole Symphony, so that into it all the themes are gathered. Before the principal phrase of the Allegretto, allotted to the English horn with the same accompaniment of *pizzicati* and harp-chords, besides a counterpoint in triplets upon the first violins, recalling, but solely in its rhythm, the theme of the Scherzo, a *motiv* (Grief-*motiv*) which seems sentimentally akin to the first theme of the *Allegro non troppo* wail, first in the bass, then higher, and seems preparing for the triplets to which I have drawn attention, the Joy-*motiv* is further elaborated: fragments peep out here and there, now in canon, now accompanied by strains of the string quartet. The time increases until the whole orchestra bursts into the Triumph-*motiv*. Four times it is repeated, modulating by ascending major-thirds, only once again to die away. Snatches of the Sorrow-*motiv* alternate with reminis-cences of the principal phrase of the Allegretto. The

Joy-*motiv* struggles vainly for the mastery. Again the
entire orchestra wails in the melancholy phrase of the
Allegretto, while the first violins contribute a counterpoint in minims. And now the Faith-*motiv* recurs,
soaring from the bass to the highest notes of the violins,
growing ever more piano after lingering among the wood.
Now begins the Finale, which seems as a blossoming of joy
through the triumph of faith. Listen to the violoncellos
and double basses sustaining a rhythm reminding one of
a peal of bells! In their turn wood instruments and
trombones contribute *piano* passages. The harps tell
their pearls, and the *motiv* of the Introduction reappears,
but now in the major key, soon to be followed by the
Faith-*motiv*. Thus grouped, the *motive* progress in
ascending semitones, accompanied by the ceaseless bells;
the tone increases until, like an apotheosis, the Joy-*motiv*
triumphantly asserts itself, and brings an admirable work
to an admirable conclusion.

I have been compelled, in order to achieve some degree
of clearness, to affix some sort of literary title to the
principal *motive* of the work, but these are of course
purely arbitrary, for in composing it the master had no
literary aim.

To the class of symphonic-poems belongs also Franck's
'Psyche,' a symphonic-poem with choruses in three parts,
which was performed at the Colonne Concerts in 1890;
but although this composition includes several passages
of a high order of merit, such as 'Psyche's Dream' and
'The Love-scene in the Garden of Eros,' still it seems as
though the master, a Christian mystic, were out of his
element in dealing with Pagan beauty, and 'Psyche' is
not worthy to be compared with the other orchestral
works which we have been admiring together.

The sacred music composed by Franck comprises on

the one hand motets, a Psalm, a Mass; on the other, organ-pieces. The first-named are of indubitable merit and full of intense devotional feeling, but the organ-pieces are yet more worthy of admiration. There are twelve of them, of which the last three are the Chorales to which I have already referred, and since Bach no one has written so admirably for this sublime instrument. The organ-pieces are really symphonies, sublimely conceived, magnificently wrought. César Franck was himself a remarkable organist, full of love for his instrument and careful to avoid degrading it, as do, alas! too many of his fellows, to the poor part of entertainer of the swarming crowd that fills the churches. At Ste. Clotilde, where he was organist for thirty-two years, crowds of music-lovers would assemble Sunday by Sunday to hear his admirable improvisations, and had any one noted them down Art had been the richer by a series of compositions as finely constructed as those which he so long thought over, so carefully wrote down.

.   .   .   .   .   .

I shall not dwell long upon the subject of Franck's dramatic contributions. They comprise but two works, *Hulda* and *Ghisèle*, neither of which operas was ever given in the composer's lifetime. Since his death they have both been produced at Monte Carlo, but I had not the pleasure of hearing them. Still, to judge from a mere reading of the score, it is evident that Franck, who was an innovator in all other branches of his art, did not feel called upon to follow the dramatic movement so proudly evolved in our day. Certainly the artist's hand is discernible on every page of the score, but neither can one credit Franck with having been a great dramatic composer.

There are many other works of Franck's scattered here and there—songs, choruses, etc.—which deserve at least mention ; but in order not to exceed the limits set me for this brief article, I have abstained from noticing any save his principal works.

.   .   .   .

To sum up : César Franck was a great Master, and his work will live. I am aware that there are critics who deny this last. I am also aware that we are still too close to him in time to deliver final judgment. But when one cannot deny that a musician has a spontaneous, abundant, passionate, profound gift of melody and a wealth of resource in harmony—and there is no one but admits that Franck's system of harmony was all his own, and that he contributed an incredible number of new harmonies to the musical world—nor solidity of construction, nor that skill in development that makes development beautiful, it is difficult to grudge him the title of genius !

Let me conclude by quoting M. Arthur Coquard, who says—' Franck's place in the history of music is beside Bach.'

Vincent d'Indy

HUGUES IMBERT

En ce siècle où les Dieux sont tous éteints, j'estime que l'artiste est un prêtre, et doit, pour rester tel dévouer tout son cœur à l'art, seul Dieu réel, comme un Consul Romain une dépouille opime. . . .
L'Art, A. Vincent d'Indy, *Paul Bourget.*

AMONGST the figures of the young French school Vincent d'Indy is one of the most arresting. Fascinated by the new formulæ of musical art, he had the courage from an early age to proclaim at the top of his voice the character of his preferences, and to break with the past. He has fearlessly climbed the slopes of the sacred mountain, and his path has always been a straight one. From his first work, *La Chanson des Aventuriers de la Mer*, to *Fervaal*, the last, not a single thing that is imperfectly realised has come from his hand. At once a poet and a musician, he has lived alone for Art. Like Berlioz, Vincent d'Indy, though born in Paris in 1857, on the 27th March, has natural connection with the southern provinces of France, for his family came from Verdieux (Ardèche), where they still hold property. From the beauty of the country which surrounded him, from the mountains of Vercors,

110

from the plain of the Rhone, from the fair forests of beech and pine he has sucked his profound love of Nature. Like Berlioz, he will be found to have had very marked tendencies towards symphonic art; and when, in 1867, he had before his eyes the treatise on the orchestra by the Master of the Côte St. André, it was a revelation to him : the gods of the musical Olympus—Gluck, Spontini, Beethoven, Weber—appeared before him in all the grandeur of their masterliness and pomp. Nature and Berlioz were the two first teachers of Vincent d'Indy, and they were teachers of no mean power. Is not the whole problem of his destiny contained in these two constructing forces? 'It is a hypothesis of contemporary literary philosophy,' said Paul Bourget, 'that the mind grows like a plant, absorbing in unconscious and yet profound travail all the nourishing matter of the *milieu* in which it is placed.' You have only to visit the hills and mountains of Vercors, the picturesque peaks and slopes of the Cevennes; you have only to call to memory the theories, the preferences, the hatreds, the enthusiasms of Berlioz, and you will get a vision of the physical and moral *milieu* in which Vincent d'Indy lived; the quality of his soul will be unmasked to you. Later, when a thunderbolt bursts in the musical heavens and Richard Wagner appears, he is fascinated, overwhelmed by the power of this genius. He seeks to imitate him (certain of his works show traces of this); soon he perceives that he is on the wrong tack. He falls back upon himself, retains only the outlines of the Bayreuth master, and, spurred on by a musician like César Franck, he writes beautiful works in which, in spite of some Wagnerian reminiscences, a marked personality displays itself. Take for example the *Chant de la Cloche*, the *Trilogie de Wallenstein*, and *Fervaal*.

'His delicate and firm features,' says M. Edouard Schuré of him, 'betray an original character, a very accentuated individuality, a will concentrated in itself. He does not let himself go until he is dealing with music, and then we may note that under a severe, almost hieratical exterior lie hidden deep wells of energy, of dreamy imagination, and of thought.'

It was his mother, Mme. Théodore d'Indy, a woman with a genuine passion for art, who guided the first steps in his career. He began to study the piano at the age of nine, and at fourteen he was absolute master of the instrument; he lived in close colloquy with the classics, Bach, Haydn, Mozart, Beethoven. From 1862 till 1865 Diémer teaches him a deeper knowledge of the mechanism of the keyboard; after this Lavignac teaches him the technique of harmony, and the first principles of composition. At the same time he follows the lectures of Marmontel. In 1867 one of his uncles, M. Wilfrid d'Indy, a passionate lover of music, introduced to his notice the *Treatise on Orchestration* by Hector Berlioz, which was destined to disclose a new horizon to him. Then in 1868 or 1869 comes his intimacy with a very gifted musician, M. Henri Duparc: they work together at the scores of Wagner, for which they both have a great enthusiasm. Nor are the beautiful works of John Sebastian Bach treated with less reverence, for these are also performed in their little club, especially the 'Passion according to Saint Matthew.'

In 1870 d'Indy dons the soldier's helmet and flies off to the defence of his country—a grievous page of history, in which the brightness of many minds is dimmed, but in which also we read of great acts of heroic devotion. For the composer, it meant a grave loss in the death of his grandmother, Mme. Théodore d'Indy, a little while after the armistice had been declared.

At this period César Franck became his master, and under his direction we find the young musician again studying harmony, composition, counterpoint, and fugue. In 1873 he was enlisted in the organ-class at the Conservatoire; in 1874 he gained a *secundus*, and in 1875 a *primus accessit.* While yet a member of this class he did his preliminary parade of arms as titular organist of the church of Saint-Leu Taverny, near Ermont, which, thanks to the liberality of Napoleon III., possessed a very fine instrument by Cavaillé-Coll. On reading the marvellous ' German Requiem ' of Johannes Brahms, he at once entertained the highest opinion of the great German symphonist, and his one wish was to see the author of such a masterpiece. His expedition to Germany in search of Brahms was a true Odyssey. He at last succeeded in picking him up at Tutzing, a rakish little village situated on the river opposite the royal castle of Berg, where King Louis of Bavaria met with his tragic death.

What Berlioz did when, after maternal excommunication, he took a post as chorist at the Théâtre des Nouveautés, to minister to the first necessities of life, Vincent d'Indy did also when, in the year 1875, on leaving the Conservatoire, he entered the Société des Concerts du Châtelet as second kettle-drummer and choirmaster, with the intention of familiarising himself with the use of the orchestra and forming a connection with the majority of the players, and perhaps also with a view of putting to the test a well-defined determination to follow up a musical career. In this year, 1875, his first work was performed in Paris under the direction of Pasdeloup, at the ' Concerts Populaires.' This was the overture to *Piccolomini,* second part of the *Trilogie de Wallenstein,* after Schiller's tragedy, which was destined to be one of his fine creations, of which we shall make mention in due season. Then came the years of production : in 1876, at the ' Concerts Populaires,' was heard the overture to Shakespeare's *Antony and Cleopatra*; on the 24th March 1878, a setting of Uhland's *Forêt enchantée*. In the same year the quartet (Op. 7), for piano and strings, was played both at the Société Nationale de Musique and at the Trompette. We will pass rapidly over *Attendez-moi sous l'orme*, a one-act operetta, after a story by M. Robert de Bonnières, which was performed in 1881 at the Opéra-Comique, and come to the *Poème des Montagnes*, a suite for piano (Op. 15), which dates from the same time, and is included under the same category as those works directly inspired by nature.

His first marked success was the *Chant de la Cloche*, a dramatic legend in a prologue and seven tableaux, which gained the first prize at the competitions opened by the town of Paris in 1886. Here is the personal impression of one of the jury: '*Le Chant de la Cloche*, by Vincent d'Indy, is not perhaps a masterpiece, but it is legitimate to hope that a composer who starts like this may reach to the summit of perfection. The whole picture of *l'Incendie*, certain parts of *la Vision*, the Latin chants, and the apotheotic chorus of the last tableau are the work of a master. The author springs from the musicians which he has most studied—Berlioz, Wagner, Franck. He is a little too fond of polyphony, of complex writing. As soon as he introduces into his compositions a little more air, a little more of what the old Italians called *bel canto*, as soon as he shall shake himself free from foreign influences, I think we shall find ourselves confronted with a man of whom our country will be very proud. Up till now I see no one with us, or indeed amongst other nations, who has greater strength. The competitions of the Town of Paris had not until now produced work of this quality.' Composed between 1879 and 1883, this beautiful composition was drawn from the drama of Schiller by Vincent d'Indy. The poem as well as the music is the work of the composer, who followed the example of Berlioz and Wagner. *Le Chant de la Cloche* was performed at the expense of the Town of Paris, at the Eden, on the 25th February 1886; it has been heard at numerous concerts in France and abroad with growing success. Though impregnated with the Wagnerian school, Vincent d'Indy has known how to use *Leit-motive*, or leading themes, without imitating the Bayreuth master in servile fashion. He has preserved his originality, and tableaux such as *le Baptême, l'Amour, la Fête, la Vision, l'Incendie, la Mort, le Triomphe*, have furnished him with opportunities to show his mastery in a variety of instrumental combinations, and in the infinite wealth of musical colour.

Sauge-Fleurie, a legend for orchestra after Robert de Bonnières, was composed in October 1884. This poetic fairy-story was calculated to fascinate the musician, who in his childhood had manifested an exclusive passion for the popular or fantastic stories of Hauff, Andersen, and others. It disclosed a vast horizon to his dreamy muse who doted on symbols. The young fairy Sauge-Fleurie wanders along the edge of a blue-watered lake overgrown with jonquils. The son of the king, in pursuit of a stag through the forest, sees the fairy and stops, struck with wonder at the sight. For Sauge-Fleurie the love of man means death; but she prefers to give up her immortality for the joy of possessing, even for an instant only, the heart of so fair a prince. Here is a charming love-scene, in which Sauge-Fleurie gives life to her lover, who swiftly makes off to the hunt:

> 'Amour et mort sont toujours à l'affût.
> Ne croyez pas que celle que je pleure
> Fut epargnée : elle sécha sur l'heure
> Comme une fleure de Sauge qu'elle fut.'

From this finely chiselled work, the product of a poet-

musician in whom the science of the old masters is allied
with the richness of modern harmony, comes a charm
that is no less sure because it is delicate.

Vincent d'Indy played a leading *rôle* in the adminis-
tration of the Société Nationale de Musique. In 1885
he took over the management in consequence of the
changes made in that year regarding the admission to
the programmes of works by old and foreign composers
—by which means it became possible to perform whole
acts of Gluck, numerous cantatas of J. S. Bach, or Handel,
and chamber-music of Schumann, Brahms, Borodine,
Grieg, Glazounoff. . . . After the resignation of the old
committee César Franck was nominated President in
place of Bussine ; but he only exercised honorary powers,
being burdened with more business than he could get
through. The actual work fell upon the two secretaries,
Vincent d'Indy and E. Chausson. Since the death of
César Franck the Société Nationale de Musique has
become a republic without a President, administered by
the two secretaries.

.   .   .   .

In October 1886 was finished the Symphony in G (Op.
25) for orchestra and piano on a French mountain song.
It was heard at the Concerts Lamoureux in March 1887,
with Mme. Bordes-Pêne at the piano. Vincent d'Indy
has availed himself of the resources of the keyboard with
much skill. The symphony is divided into three parts,
which are no more than variations of a theme submitted to
an infinite number of transformations. The English horn,
from the opening of the first part, gives the pastoral *motiv*,
which is developed by the other instruments in turn. In
the second part the piano assumes greater importance,
and gives the reply to the orchestra, in which the most
conflicting rhythms, the most imaginative combinations,
may be distinguished. The calls of the horn, an alto solo

full of tenderness, suggest very effectively the scenes of woodland life. And as an apotheosis we have a Kermesse, in which the rhythms are full of swing and humorous fancy.

On the 3rd May 1887 took place that unique performance of *Lohengrin* at the Eden. It was Vincent d'Indy whom Charles Lamoureux gathered to his side to direct the choral studies and the *musique de scène*. The memory of that masterly performance of Wagner's work, which has never been surpassed at the opera, is still green.

Wallenstein, a symphonic trilogy, one of the most characteristic works of the musician, was written between 1873 and 1881, to serve as a preface and musical commentary to the three dramatic poems of Schiller, *Le Camp*, *Les Piccolomini* (Max and Thécla), *La Mort de Wallenstein*. The first complete performance took place at the Concerts-Lamoureux in 1888. The distinguishing feature of the symphonic music of Vincent d'Indy is that it paints with forcible truth, marvellous vividness and astonishing vigour, the various episodes in the drama of Schiller. For instance, in the first part (*Le Camp*), after the slow valse, comes the savage dance with its determined rhythm, the sermon of the Capucin father given to the bassoon, the theme of Wallenstein energetically illustrated by the trombones, and then the final tumult, in which we hear a few notes of Wallenstein's theme thrown out by the trumpets amid the *fortissimi* of the orchestra. In all this you will recognise the mastery of the musician who has approached very nearly to a musical translation of a scene crowded with movement. You will find not only the painting of events and acts, but the painting of the moral sentiments which animate the persons in the drama.

Is there anything more exquisitely tender than the love

episode between Max and Thécla (second part)? With
what felicity do the two themes of the lovers unite and
embrace each other; yet with what inevitability are the
ideal transports of the happy pair stifled by the inter-
vention of Fate, whose fell design has been suggested in
the brief introduction by the horns! The third and last
episode is the death of Wallenstein. Very dramatic is the
opening, in which strange chords, that recall the splendid
sonority of the organ, characterise the influence of the
stars on human destiny. These chords are the poetical
rendering of this beautiful saying of Wallenstein in the
Piccolomini (Act II. Scene 6) :—

'Yet the mysterious force which labours in the bowels
of nature—the ladder of spirits that stretches from this
world of dust up to the world of stars with a thousand
ramifications, this ladder on which the heavenly powers
mount and dismount ever restless—the circles within
circles that grow narrower and narrower as they approach
the sun their centre,—all this can be witnessed alone by
the eyes of the heaven-born joyous descendants of Zeus
—those eyes from which the veil of blindness has fallen.'

After several episodes, an ascending progression of the
basses brings back the complete statement of Wallenstein's theme in B major, which ends in a very widely
constructed movement, in which the *starry* chords of the
opening are reproduced, covered over with the wind
instruments, while the quatuor winds its way rapidly in
and out of them, and the trombones thunder out the fate-
fraught song. Soon calm is restored, and the sound dies
away gradually in a long *pianissimo* of the stringed
instruments.

What a number of interesting compositions might be
quoted from the period between 1886 and the production
of *Fervaal*! We may note briefly the *Suite* in D for
trumpet, two flutes, and strings (June 1886), the *Nocturne*

in G flat minor (November 1886), *Promenade* for piano (August 1897), *Sérénade et Valse* for small orchestra (August 1887), *Trio* for piano, clarinet, and violoncello (October 1887), *Schumanniana*, two piano pieces (October 1887), *Fantasia* for orchestra and principal hautboy *On popular French airs* (September 1888), *Sur la Mer*, chorus for female voices (October 1888), *Tableaux de Voyage*, thirteen piano pieces (October 1889), *Karadec, musique de scène* for a drama, by André Alexandre (1890), *Quartet*, for two violins, viola, and violoncello (August— December 1890), *Tableaux de Voyage*, suite for orchestra in six parts (1891), then a *Cantata*, chorus and orchestra (Op. 37), for the inauguration of the statue of Emile Augier at Valence (Drôme), June 1893.

Since this period Vincent d'Indy has completed other works, amongst the chief of which the *Variations symphoniques* were performed at Brussels at the Ysaye Concerts in January 1897. It is worth noticing how many representatives of our young French School have received a kindly welcome in Belgium and in Holland; their works have been more often performed, and consequently are better known in these countries than they are in France. One of the chief promoters of the widening of their fame has been the eminent violinist Ysaye. At his quartet meetings, at the grand concerts directed by him in Brussels, he has never ceased to champion the cause of the young. The *Variations symphoniques* were enthusiastically received in Brussels: this little symphonic poem is a translation into music of the descent into hell of Istar, the Assyrian Eurydice, in search of her husband. The treatment is free and the orchestral minutiæ are perfectly charming, especially the *Allegretto* corresponding to the episode in which Istar is robbed of her jewels, and the fascinating embroidery of the flute on the violin at the moment when the last veil falls from her.

This new work will take its place beside *Wallenstein* ; at Brussels it formed a kind of preface to *Fervaal*, that fine lyrical drama at which Vincent d'Indy has laboured without interruption during five years with the assiduity and the faith of the artist who is never satisfied with his work.

Fervaal, a musical play in three acts and a prologue, was given for the first time on the stage of the Théâtre Royal de la Monnaie in Brussels, on the 12th of March 1897. Like Massenet's *Hérodiade*, like Reyer's *Sigurd* and *Salammbô*, and other operas, the dramatic work of Vincent d'Indy will have glowed under the bravery of foreign footlights before being accepted and played in its native country. In *Fervaal* the composer has not been false to his original incentives : Nature, Berlioz, and Wagner. The last chiefly seems to have inspired him by his great conceptions and fine style, as well as by his poetical and musical force. But this is no case of plagiarism ; we have rather to observe a clever parallel instance. Certainly there is matter for much lament in the reckless way in which certain young composers gifted with the power of imitation play fast and loose with the style, the rhythm, and the colour which are exclusively Wagner's ; we have already more than once expressed our opinion on this subject. Vincent d'Indy furnishes us with no case in point, for, in spite of his deep belief in Wagner's works, and notwithstanding the thorough study of them to which he devoted himself, there are numerous examples of his having preserved his own personality. We have only to remind ourselves of the best portions of *La Cloche* and of *Wallenstein* to be assured of this. In *Fervaal*, we repeat, that whatever comparisons may be instituted between his method and that of the Bayreuth master, and however genuine they may be, he has fully realised his own independent self.

The persons in the drama move in the territory of the Cevennes, where the composer's family lived, and where he himself resides during part of the year; the *milieu* then is familiar to him, and the action is unfolded in times not prehistoric, but sufficiently remote to permit the introduction of legendary matter. Moreover, the country being, little known lends itself to an imaginative story. Descended of a divine race, Fervaal is destined to save his people who adhere to the religion of the Druids, but, like Parsifal, he must remain pure. After an attack in ambuscade by Saracens, he is received in company with the old Druid Arfagard, by the fair Guilhen, daughter of an Emir who conquered the country. The bewitching Saracen maiden conceives a passion for the young hero, and he is destined not to leave the enchanted spot where she detains him until he has succumbed to love. Led by Arfagard, who reminds him of his duty, he returns to his own people in the mountain, is elected chief, and holy war is declared against the enemies of the old Cravann. But Fervaal's sin brings in its wake the defeat of his people. In the last act Fervaal wanders among the mountains in the midst of snow and corpses : a scene at once gloomy and grandiose ! Arfagard prepares to offer him up as an expiatory victim, when in the distance the despairing voice of Guilhen is heard. She calls her lover. Fervaal strikes Arfagard, and throws himself into the arms of Guilhen, who is frozen and on the point of death. The cruel cold of the mountain has destroyed the frail southern plant. She dies, and Fervaal, seized with a holy exaltation, mounts one ridge after another, carrying the body of Guilhen, and singing the triumph of the new God Jesus.

The musical quality of the score is very remarkable ; we have from it an impression of a constant straining after the attainment of perfection. Though he borrows from Richard Wagner a little of the richness of colour on his orchestral palette, the eminent composer has in his new work given us the quintessence of the qualities revealed in *La Cloche* and in the *Trilogie de Wallenstein.* The music, which is intensely dramatic, is incorporate with the poem ; the *Leit-motive* are developed with striking felicity ; and there are many passages no less daring than successful. What splendid examples might be quoted : the very beautiful prelude, the love idyll of the prologue and the first act, the imposing narrative passages of Arfagard, in which the Druidical themes are displayed ; the apparitions in the second act, which contains a very fine development of the theme of Cravann, the call of the shepherd in the myxolydian mode, the brilliant colour of the regathering of the tribes, and, lastly, the whole of the third act, in which one might say that the author has taken a leap 'as if to land him in the Infinite.'

        .   .   .   .

M. Etienne Destranges, the author of an interesting study of *Fervaal,* had written to the composer to reproach him for having given his consent to the fragmentary performance of this work at the Concerts de l'Opéra in Paris before it was produced in Brussels. The following is the splendid reply of Vincent d'Indy :—

'If I have given a fragment of the work into the hands of the Opera it is because . . . how am I to explain it? . . . because I have no personal feeling of coquetry about the execution of my work before the public. I think the principal and the true *rôle* of the artist is to *create the work*, and once this is done, *completely done*, whether that work be a *painting*, a *sculpture*, or an *engraving*,—from the moment, in a word, that the work exists, the artist is entitled to free himself from all interest in what shall happen after. If the work is good and noble it will live in its entirety, in spite of the mutilations and outrages to which these purveyors of art may have submitted it ;

if it is bad, no meticulous care in execution, no rich clothing will rescue it from the oblivion which is its destiny.'

Might one not believe that one was reading one of those enlightened pages of Gustave Flaubert in which he exposed so unflinchingly his theories on art?

Beneath a somewhat severe exterior Vincent d'Indy conceals a quality of intense sentiment and of deep sensibility. In public he shows a strong reserve, in private a wide affability. Of tall build, with long hair swept back in the manner of the revolutionary artist or philosopher, his forehead a little narrow, but widening near the temples, his eyes very deep set under arched brows, his face long, his features fine and sharply defined, a small mouth and moustache—such are the separate details that go to make up a very characteristic whole. The general bearing suggests infinite control : the face is one which, once seen, is never forgotten ; it reflects a great will-power, a marked individuality, deeply rooted convictions. At the bottom of all the man is a modest person who seems always afraid of boring the public with his personality. But in spite of his reserve this personality has emerged in a strong form and has won the keen admiration of the musical world. Realising that the favours of fortune should turn to instruments of high intellectual activity in the hands of those who possess them, he is one of that distinguished class of people, too rare with us, alas ! who, hating the commonplace, cultivate the ideal and the religion of Beauty.

The Conception of
Love in Wagner

CLAUDE PHILLIPS

LOVE is the spirit that informs and colours the whole of
Wagner's life-work—love from the deep pit of the lowest
lusts to the radiant heights of the most sublime self-
sacrifice—love so universal, so infinitely various in its
manifestations, that with him it is almost the equivalent
of life itself. It is wholly inadequate to say that of the
great succession of Wagnerian music-dramas—leaving
out of the question the purely historical *Rienzi* and the
youthful efforts which preceded it—the dominating motive
is love. This would not suffice to establish any distinction
of kind between the Wagnerian theatre and the great
stage-plays of the modern world, with the Renaissance
at its base. The vast, tangled Elizabethan drama,
culminating in Shakespeare, is like life itself—a field in
which the fairest and also the most baleful flowers of love
spring up, as they do in life, side by side with the
stronger, coarser plants. Love gives to it its charm, its
passion, its lurid intensity, its horror, but does not so
wholly envelop it as to dwarf and extinguish all other
influences. In the pseudo-classic tragedy of Louis XIV.,

the heroic Corneille might roughly be taken to represent for the seventeenth century the great aspirations of Æschylus, the sublime and the more faultless Sophocles. All the same, Racine, the poet of passion and sentiment— of passion loving to dwell upon its own sweet anguish, of sentiment loving to lay bare its most secret fibres— corresponds much more closely to his prototype Euripides. He is, nevertheless, essentially of his own time, in which even love was reduced to a system, in which amorous ardour smouldered under a crust of conventional decency, and when it at last leapt forth was compelled to follow in the channels already hollowed out for it. Euripides represents to the scholar and the critic of literature a far lower stage of excellence than that supreme altitude attained by Æschylus and Sophocles when they took, as their central theme, the national mythology and legendary history—

> ' Presenting Thebes' or Pelops' line,
> Or the Tale of Troy divine.'

For them, we may infer, the mere love of two human beings, unattended by world-moving portents, uncrushed by the iron hand of Destiny, would have been deemed too trivial a motive to be presented in the vast Athenian theatre before audiences of some thirty thousand spectators, by beings already in the fixity of their tremendous tragic masks, in the intonations of their voices, in their increased altitude, imagined by the poet as something more than merely mortal. And it must be taken that this was, with the necessary qualifications, the view of Greek tragedy in general. It was reserved to Euripides, the dangerous innovator whom many hold to have permanently lowered the tone of the Greek stage, to put forth the passion of love — in its aberrations rather than its normal manifestations—as the principal subject of tragedy. And he did so by creating his heroines,

Alcestis, Medea, Phædra, Iphigenia, Helena, Electra, so exceptional in love, in woe, in vengeance, that their destinies are almost beyond the capacity of the mere mortal to conceive by comparison with his own. One stands forth, the very type for all time of sublime conjugal devotion ; another, of vengeance so exalted in its horror as to be above and beyond punishment ; yet another of love-torment armed with a sting so intolerable that as a release from it death seems sweet and easy. It is in the development of this element of vastness and heroic breadth in passion that a point of contact is afforded between the later Greek stage of the great tragic period and that of Wagner. With Shakespeare and his contemporaries the human note with its supreme pathos dominates, thrilling through the whole of the Elizabethan drama, and lighting that vital flame which maintains it in perpetual youth. Shakespeare's magic can awake in our breast an interest more passionate and more enduring for mere men and women seen in their most human aspects than for the mighty, stricken races of the dim past, for the heroes or the gods who loom vast and terrible in the tragedies of antiquity. And so, too, we wear Goethe's heroines next our heart. We may tremble in contemplation of Medea and Electra and Phædra ; we may gaze up in awe at the sublime figures of Antigone and Alcestis ; the august calm of Goethe's own ' Iphigenia in Tauris ' may lift us high above the realities of life ; but our tears are for Gretchen, for Charlotte, for Mignon, for Klärchen. Only in that great musical comedy on Shakespearian lines, *Die Meistersinger*, has Wagner emerged from his favourite atmosphere of rainbow-hued mist and luminous shadow, from his favourite system of heroically exaggerating human proportions, into the bright sunlight of happy day, to show us human beings— *Menschen wie alle*—palpitating with life, and moved

by love, yet only as one factor among many others in
life.

Wagner's essential conception of love is something
vaster and less human — not necessarily greater — than
this. With him—let it be said once more, at the risk
of monotonous repetition—it is the vital principle of
the world, the fire at its core, without which it would
freeze and cease to be. What is it that Wellgunde, in
Das Rheingold, says, exchanging the careless chatter of
the creature something lower than mortal for a prophetic
solemnity :

> ' Denn was nur lebt will lieben,
> Meiden will keiner die Minne ' ?

But the definition of love must here be widened so as to
include much more than the love of man for woman. It
must include paternal love—the love of Wotan for Brünnhilde, and for that hapless race of the Wälsungen, which,
cherishing, he so cruelly tries. It must include brotherly
love—that complicated web of ties which binds Siegmund
to Sieglinde, the brother to the *bräutliche Schwester.*
It must include that curious combination of vehement
passion with the maternal instinct which is to be found
in the relation of Brünnhilde to the boy-hero Siegfried.
It must include that friendship which, in its aspiration
after self-sacrifice, is the highest type of love—the friendship of Wolfram for Tannhäuser, of King Mark for
Tristan, the brotherly love which binds together, or should
bind, the Knights of the Holy Grail. It must include
something higher and greater than all this—the love of
suffering man for all his suffering brethren, the love of
Parsifal for humanity, whose bleeding wounds he divines
in that poisoned one of the stricken Amfortas. We may
get at Wagner's conception of love in yet another way—
that is, by looking at the beings whom he condemns to
live loveless, and perceiving how altogether abnormal,

how entirely outside the world he deems them. Take the gnome-king, black Alberich, whom love eludes, scorched though he is with the fires of the lower lusts. *Erzwäng' ich nicht Liebe, Doch listig erzwäng' ich mir Lust.* Cursing the love that he has vainly grasped at, renouncing its joys, he fashions from the pure gold of the Rhine the avenging ring, he scourges his brother-gnomes into a submission beneath which groan hate and fruitless rebellion, he vainly reigns over arid rock and useless treasure until superior craft and violence cast him down again. Then look at the greater, the more fatal figure of Hagen, half-man, half-demon, the offspring of loveless lust and violence, born of a mortal mother who has been compelled by the ravisher Alberich. His blood will not mix in the draught of 'Blut-Brüderschaft' with the generous blood of Siegfried and Gunther; it will not flow freely and nobly as theirs; cold and stubborn and sluggish it moves; no generous human emotion tinges his pale cheeks. Accursed in his birth, he groans forth to Alberich in the awful night-scene of *Götterdämmerung* on the Rhine shore: *Frühalt, fahl und bleich, Hass' ich die Frohen, Freue mich nie!* In Klingsor, the Oriental magician, the baleful heathen influence ever hovering on the border of Christ's country, lust and ambition have stifled love and life. Dark, mysterious sins, which the poet but touches upon lightly as he passes on, have stained and dragged him down, until, frenzied like the Attis of Catullus, he reduces them by hideous violence to the silence of death. Impotent now to harm, yet still unpurified, he burns to obtain possession of the Holy Grail, that he may rule over its Brotherhood, not as the spiritual pontiff, but as the temporal sovereign, the tyrant. These are the loveless, and Wagner holds them accursed in the very fact that they lack the vivifying spark of love which is life.

Let us glance rapidly at some of the great music-dramas in their order, and see how it stands with the characters called into being by the Promethean fire of Wagner's genius. In *Der Fliegende Holländer* is to be found the first germ of that self-sacrificing love, of that absolute subordination of the whole being to another, which in *Parsifal* reaches its fullest, its most sublime development. Senta is, however, a creation infinitely lower down in the scale than Parsifal. She is of the tribe of the *illuminées*, hypnotised by the vision of anguish suffered through the centuries that has fixed itself in her mind. She is impelled less by love or reason than by some dominant force outside herself to save the Holländer from that eternal life which is eternal death, though she must, in the effort, sacrifice father, lover, and all that makes life dear.

Tannhäuser is, perhaps, the most pathetic figure to be found among all the characters of Wagner. Noble aspirations, the dreams of the knightly poet possess him, his eyes are turned imploringly to heaven, his hands are clasped in prayer, but his feet are glued to earth. The lusts of the body hold him fast in their vulture's claws, and holding cruelly rend. His physical nature is enslaved by the subtle delights of the Venusberg, by the rhythmical harmony in the dance of the Graces, by the treacherously alluring pictures which they present to the eye, preparing the beholder for the higher voluptuousness of Venus herself. Yet he yearns for the pure air of the Wartburg, for the nightingale's song, for the innocence of the saintly virgin Elizabeth, and the holier delights of a clean life. Not for him, alas! is such a code as that which the spotless Wolfram embodies in his Rhapsody addressed to the court of the Landgraf. For the platonic lover, for the anchorite by nature, such a profession of love is easy enough, but not for Tannhäuser, in whose

I

veins still lurks the sweet poison of the Venusberg, in whose ears, even while he struggles, echo its most intoxicating harmonies. The struggle is not over until he sinks lifeless at the dead feet of the holy woman who has faded out of life even that she may intercede for him in heaven. Then over the pair, united at last in death, is poured the purifying sweetness of the young pilgrims' song, as they hold aloft in solemn gladness the miraculously blossoming wands which symbolise the Divine pardon. We may shudder and weep with Elizabeth, but let us not, like the angry knights, Tannhäuser's brothers, strive to pierce again the thrice-wounded heart, or relentlessly, like the Sovereign Pontiff in St. Peter's Church, cast down the agonised sinner who, with bleeding feet, has crawled to the foot of the throne. Tannhäuser is a man, in all his weakness, in all his aspiration, in all the passion of his appeal.

The loves of Elsa and Lohengrin are as unequal as those of Faust and Margarethe. In both cases with the woman it is all love, all life that is at stake; with the man it is a mere episode of bliss imperfect, of which from the very beginning the end is foreshadowed. Lohengrin, valiant as Sir Launcelot and pure as Sir Galahad, is loftily compassionate, tender and forgiving, rather than passionately loving.

Elsa is not the heroine steadfast and valiant enough to battle against fate, or to resist the corrosive venom of Ortrud's promptings. She is all woman, with her charm of the white lily bent by storm-winds, woman in her clinging affection, but also in her inconsistency, in her ungovernable curiosity. Her love, like her being, is weak and negative. While Senta's vision is of self-sacrifice and redemption, Elsa's is but of salvation for herself, of the dazzling lover, heaven-sent to crush her enemies and vindicate her innocence. Ortrud, the baleful sorceress, queen-like even in her malignity, is one of Wagner's most effective stage figures, but also one of his most conventional. She is of the family of the Frédégondes and Brunehauts of Merovingian times, and stands in still closer kinship to the vengeful Kriemhild of the *Nibelungenlied.* Perhaps under her insatiate lust for power lies a spark of half-contemptuous love for the miserable Telramund, whom her dark counsels have brought so low—a little of that feeling which animates Lady Macbeth, the virile, the steadfast in evil, when she is brought face to face with the terrors of her half-distraught lord.

The great figures of Tristan and Isolde tower as lovers high above those of any other pair created by Wagner, save only Siegfried and Brünnhilde. Here is frenzied passion at a height hardly ever before reached in stage-drama—vast in its dimensions as the passions of antiquity, yet wholly modern in its exasperation, its incapacity for self-restraint, its impatience of all curb from without. Not a few have seen in the strange communings of the lovers in the night-scene of the garden a high philosophic love disdaining the mere delights of common mortals. Indeed, in some notable performances of the mighty music-drama, divergence of view between the chief performers on this cardinal point has produced strange results ; the passionate ardour of the Isolde contrasting with the pensive calm of the Tristan in a fashion which a little too much called up a certain Biblical scene which the painters of the Renaissance have made all too familiar to us. But no, the music of Wagner is here to give the lie to such an interpretation, with its waves of burning lava pouring one over the other perpetually ; with its hate, its scorn, its fatefulness colouring even love with the hues of death, with its large spaces of silence and pause, more voluptuous than passion itself. When the sym-

bolical love-philter has broken down the last barriers—on
the woman's side those of royal dignity offended, and
blood of kin crying out for vengeance, on the man's that
strongest one of honour—well might the one or the other
of this ill-fated pair cry out with Phèdre:

'Ce n'est plus une ardeur dans mes veines cachée,
C'est Vénus tout entière à sa proie attachée!'

The love of Tristan and Isolde is sublime in its
measureless egoism. For it the mere earthly satis-
factions of passion are too limited, too incomplete.
It would blot out all that is not itself, burst the walls
of the world, quench the very sun as Isolde puts out
the torch, and remain alone with measureless, eternal
night, in which, and not in the deceitful light of day, for
them is truth. The vision thus conjured up is one of
vastness and horror that might have been evoked by
Victor Hugo himself. Delight has in it hardly a place,
though we remember the dissolution in a frenzy of
expectant love of Tristan, the love-death, too, of Isolde.
Rather are we brought to think of Francesca and Paolo
as they appeared to Dante and Virgil, whirled together
in eternal torment through the spaces of night and time.

How to deal with the guilt-stained, the infinitely
pathetic Wälsungen pair—Wotan's children, Siegmund
the brother, and Sieglinde the 'bridal sister'? Not again
had consciously incestuous love formed the chief subject
of stage-tragedy since the Elizabethan dramatist Ford
produced his famous play, from the very name of which
modern squeamishness shrinks. The stain and guilt of
the two hapless, storm-tossed beings, united by destiny
in one ephemeral moment of happiness, is redeemed by
the tragic pathos of their ending. If we may not say,
as does Wotan, seeking to stem the flood of Fricka's
righteous wrath, *Was so schlimmes schuf das Paar?*
we may at least pity and forgive. All sin is washed

away from the love which is that of brother and lover at once in that scene of *Die Walküre*, in which to Siegmund, while he supports Sieglinde unconscious in his arms, appears the warrior maid Brünnhilde, claiming him for Wotan and the joys of immortality. With what scorn, when he hears that Sieglinde, the mournful bride, will not there greet her brother, does Siegmund repudiate the tinsel joys of Walhalla, and devote himself to hell itself rather than face an eternal parting! Brünnhilde, fateful and impassive as Destiny, has delivered the message of the gods ; but the woe, the infinite devotion of the mortal lover move her to disobey the command forced from the unwilling Wotan by his angry consort. Her eyes, which hardly yet have known tears, are dimmed, her heart for the first time beats in unison with that of a man, though in pity, not in love. Not yet deprived of her divinity by the Father of the Gods, she is for all that half woman already in her compassion.

There is about the union of Siegfried and Brünnhilde the same element of the colossal, the superhuman, that strikes us with awe in the contemplation of Tristan and Isolde's fortunes. But here the parallel ends. Until black Alberich and his sinister child, the pale, cold-blooded Hagen, begin to weave their dark spells round the hero and the goddess transformed into woman, the radiant, all-piercing light of day envelops their loves, and even in the white heat of their passion there is perfect purity. Siegfried, the boy-hero, has in the sombre cave of Mime the dwarf yearned for love ; his whole heart is filled with unsatisfied aspirations after mother, father, kindred, after something, too, that is beyond these things, and, as yet, undefined. It is the note of the bird, his monitor at the cave of the dragon Fafner, that sets ablaze the latent fire in his heart, filling his whole being with expectant longing, even before he has beheld woman.

With Brünnhilde the awakening to mortal life and mortal passion is only the achievement of that destiny which was foreshadowed when divine pity led her to save the offspring of the Wälsung in the womb of the doomed Sieglinde. With the prophetic soul of her mother Erda, who bore her to Wotan, she foreshadows, even in the moment of her wildest ecstasy, the end. Yet, while she entreats Siegfried to forbear, her love blazes forth in such beams of dazzling light, of devouring heat, that we fear to see the audacious mortal reduced to ashes under our very eyes. Before the curse of the Ring has darkened her brightness to deepest shadow, her love is as unselfish as that of Isolde is in its unquenchable yearning purely egoistic. Brünnhilde has—it has been said already—the protecting instinct of the mother joined to the love-passion in its highest and noblest phase. She will enrich her youthful hero with every gift of might and wisdom with which she herself is endowed, making of him a very Achilles in war, making of herself a mere woman, *Des Wissens bar, doch des Wunsches voll; an Liebe reich, doch ledig der Kraft.* More than mortal is the heroism of her renouncement; when sending him forth, she thus entreats and admonishes : '*Willst du mir Minne schenken, gedenke deiner nur, gedenke deiner Thaten.*'

Yet shall nothing be allowed to stand between her and the treasure that is hers as a woman, escaped from the distant, mist-enwrapped realms of the gods, sunk to a lower level than theirs, yet with one inestimable gift to replace all that she has lost — Siegfried's love. To Waltraute's solemn appeal to save the gods, ere they pass from their august twilight to annihilation, by giving back the ring—Siegfried's ring—to the Rhine-maidens, she but answers : *Die Liebe liesse ich nie, mir nehmen sie nie die Liebe, stürzt auch in Trümmern Walhall's strahlende Pracht.* And the key to Wagner's own inter-

pretation of the whole great Trilogy is in the infinitely
consoling words of her solemn leave-taking over the
corpse of the slain hero:

'Verging wie Hauch der Götter Geschlecht, lass' ohne
Walter die Welt ich zurück; meines heiligsten Wissen's
Hort weis' ich der Welt nun zu. Nicht Gut, nicht Gold,
noch göttliche Pracht; nicht Haus, nicht Hof, noch
herrischer Prunk ; nicht trüber Verträge trügender Bund,
noch heuchelnder Sitte hartes Gesetz : *selig in Lust und
Leid lässt die Liebe nur sein !*'

It was left to Wagner in old age to show in *Parsifal* a
love even higher than this—the all-embracing love of
man for his brethren, the merging of his whole individuality in theirs. This religion of humanity, which some
have of late thought fit to mock at as the mere catch-
word of the modern schools, is perhaps the keynote of
the finest art, of the finest literature of the time—the all-
penetrating influence which will serve to distinguish the
nineteenth century in its creative aspects from preceding
ages which in so many other aspects overshadow it.
Parsifal is like St. Francis of Assisi : the man became
almost divine in his infinite pity, in his infinite desire to
console and save. Looking on, a blind, foolish youth, at
the anguish of mind and body that the sinful being
Amfortas must endure, as he drags down with him, as
he stains with the soil of his sin, the whole Brotherhood
of the Grail, he is pierced to the heart; yet, in his
unreasoning pity, he remains merely amazed and helpless. It is only when the sorceress Kundry, compelled
by the will of her master Klingsor, seeks to infuse into
his veins, with the first kiss of woman, the maddening
poison of physical lust, that the scales fall from his eyes
and, staggering, he awakes and sees. His infinite purity
is unreceptive of sin, and the allurements of the flesh
which vanquish a Tannhäuser or an Amfortas are power-

less to touch him. The poison which would corrupt and slay others works as an elixir within him, to transform by its vivifying power the boy groping in the dark into the Christian hero passionately aspiring to heal the wounds of mankind. The love of woman may well, to the man who is now the lover, the champion of all his brethren, who will henceforth stand supreme as the guardian of the Holy Vessel symbolising the Godhead itself, seem a small and trivial thing, which, in his life, can have no place. When Wagner had given in *Parsifal* this last and greatest conception of his, he could not have returned to the favourite themes of his splendid maturity, even to paint the supreme passion of Tristan and Isolde, or the more radiant and Godlike love that bound Brünnhilde, in the annihilation of a world, to Siegfried. He might, had he been longer spared to the century, have given to it a 'Buddha'—nay, even a 'Christ'; he could not again have descended to the lower level.

Tristan and Isolde

GABRIEL D'ANNUNZIO

GIORGIO AURISPA had not forgotten a single episode of
his first religious pilgrimage towards the Ideal Theatre;
he could recall every instant of his extraordinary emotion
in that hour when he had first seen on the fair hillside, at
the further extremity of a long leafy avenue, the building
dedicated to the supreme festival of Art; he could re-
construct the amphitheatre in its solemn vastness, girdled
by columns and arches, the mystery of the Mystical Gulf.
In the shadow and the silence of the enclosure, in the
shadow and ecstatic silence of every soul present, a sigh
rose up from the invisible orchestra, a moan floated on
the air, a gentle voice gave utterance to the first plaintive
cry of yearning in solitude, the first vague agony in the
foreboding of future suffering. And that sigh, and that
moan, and that voice, changing from an indefined suffering
to the intensity of an impetuous cry, rose up telling of
the pride of a dream, of the terror of a superhuman
aspiration, of the fierce and implacable will to possess.
With a devouring force, like flames bursting forth from
some unsuspected abyss, the yearning grew and spread,

and blazed upwards ever higher and higher, fed by the purest essence of a double life. All things were enveloped in the intoxication of the harmonious flame ; the whole of the sovereign world vibrated madly in the boundless rapture, and gave forth their most occult joys and sorrows, rising heavenwards in a final consummation. But suddenly the forces of resistance, the anger of strife, quivered and shrieked in that wild upward rush, and the great vital current flung itself suddenly against some invisible obstacle, fell earthwards, smothered in its fall, and did not rise again. In the shadow and the silence of the enclosure, in the shadow and the hushed silence of every soul present, over the Mystical Gulf a sigh breathed, a moan died away, a faint voice spoke of the sadness of eternal solitude, of the yearning towards the eternal night, towards a return to divine oblivion.

And behold, another voice, a living human voice modulated by human lips, young and lusty, tinged with melancholy and irony and menace, sang a song of the sea from the masthead of the vessel that bore to King Mark his fair Irish bride. He sang : 'Westward the eye roams, eastward the vessel glides. Freshly blow the breezes towards our native shores. O, daughter of Ireland, why dost thou delay ! Must my sails be swelled by thy sighs? Blow, blow, oh wind ! Woe, woe, oh maiden of Ireland, my wild love ! ' It was the warning, the prophetic augury of the sentinel, gay and threatening, tender and mocking, indefinable. And the orchestra remained silent. 'Blow, blow, oh wind ! Woe, woe, oh maiden of Ireland, my wild love.' The voice floated over the tranquil sea, over the silence, and within her curtains Isolde lay motionless on her couch, plunged in the dark dream of her destiny.

Thus the drama opened. The breath of tragedy by which the prelude had already been stirred, swept and reswept the orchestra. Suddenly the power of destruction displayed itself in the woman endowed with magic gifts against the man of her choice, doomed by her to death. Her anger broke out with all the fury of the blind elements ; she invoked all the terrible forces of earth and heaven against the man whom she could never possess. ' Awake at my appeal, oh intrepid will ! Arise from thy hiding-place within my heart. Oh, wanton breezes, pay heed to my commands. Shake the slumbering sea from her lethargy ; draw forth from the depths implacable greed ; show her the prey that I offer. Let her shatter the ship and engulf the wreck ! And to you, oh winds, I give as a reward all that breathes and palpitates within her.' The forebodings of Brangaene respond to the warning of the sentinel. ' Alas, alas ! what ruin I foresee, oh Isolde ! ' And the gentle, faithful woman hastened to appease the wild fury. ' Oh, tell me the cause of thy sorrow, tell me thy secret, Isolde ! ' And Isolde : ' My heart will burst—draw back the curtains, wide, wide.'

Tristan appeared, standing motionless, with folded arms, his gaze fixed on the distant horizon. From the masthead the sailor began his song afresh, on the rising wave of the orchestra. ' Woe, ah woe ! ' . . . And while the eyes of Isolde, burning with a hidden flame, were fixed on the hero, from out of the Mystical Gulf there rose the death-motive, the mighty and terrible symbol of love and of death, which contains within it all the essence of the tragic romance. And Isolde, with her own lips, pronounced his doom, ' Chosen by me, lost to me ! ' Her passion seemed to have infused into her a homicidal desire, to have roused deep down in the very roots of her being an instinct hostile to life, a craving for dissolution, for annihilation. She grew more and more exasperated, seeking within herself, around herself, some flashing power which would strike and destroy, without leaving any trace. Her hatred grew even more intense at the

sight of the hero standing calm and motionless, conscious
of the hatred that was being concentrated upon his head,
and recognising the futility of resistance. Her lips
curled with bitter sarcasm. 'What thinkest thou of the
knave?' she inquired of Brangaene, with a strained laugh.
She would have made of a hero a dependant, asserting
her own supremacy. 'Tell him that I command my
servant to approach his sovereign, I, Isolde.' Thus she
defied him to the supreme struggle; thus she flung down
the challenge of force against force. A solemn hush
accompanied the steps of the hero towards the threshold
of the tent, when the irrevocable hour had struck, when
the potion already filled the goblet, and destiny had
drawn its thread closely round the two lives. Isolde leaned
against her couch as pale as if all the blood in her veins
had been consumed by fever, and waited in silence; in
silence Tristan appeared on the threshold; both stood
erect, drawn up to their full height, but the orchestra
betrayed the unspeakable tumult of their hearts.

In that instant was heard once more the wild ascending
scale. It seemed as though once again the Mystical
Gulf flamed upwards like a furnace, with sonorous flames
leaping ever higher and higher. 'Sole truce to eternal
sorrow, oblivion's kindly draught. I drink without fear!'
And Tristan lifted the goblet to his lips. 'For me the
half; I drink to thee!' shrieked Isolde, snatching the cup
from his hands. Had both drunk their death? Must
they both die? An instant of sovereign agony. The
death-philter was no other than a love-potion which
penetrated them with an unquenchable flame. And
motionless, they gazed at one another, seeking in each
other's eyes for a sign of the approach of death, to
which both believed themselves condemned. But a new
life, incomparably more intense than any they had lived
before, flowed through all their veins, throbbed in their

temples and their pulses, swelled their hearts in one
vast wave. 'Tristan!' 'Isolde!' They called one
another face to face; they were alone; no one remained
near them; the past was blotted out, the future was a
mist which could only be pierced by the lightning shafts
of this unforeseen intoxication. They were alive; they
called one another with living voices; they yearned one
towards the other with a fatality against which, henceforth, no power could prevail. 'Tristan!' 'Isolde!'

And the love-motive burst forth, rising and swelling
it; panted and sobbed, shrieked and sang on the deep
tempest of palpitating harmony. Now plaintive, now
joyful, it soared irresistibly towards the heights of
undreamt-of ecstasy, towards the summits of supreme
voluptuousness. 'Freed from the world, I now possess
thee, thou who alone dost reign in my heart, oh, highest
rapture of love!'

'Hail, hail to King Mark! All hail!' shouted the
crew amid the blare of trumpets, saluting the king, who
was rowing out from the shore to meet his fair bride.
'Hail to Cornwall!'

It was the uproar of vulgar life, the clamour of profane
joy, the dazzling splendour of day. The Chosen One,
the Lost One, lifted his eyes, in which floated the dark
clouds of dreamland, and questioned, 'Who is approaching?' 'The King.' 'What King?' And Isolde, pale
and trembling beneath her royal mantle, asked, 'Where
am I? Am I alive? Must I still live?' Sweet and
terrible rose up the love-charm motive, enveloping, em-
bracing them in its passionate ascent. The trumpets
resounded, 'Hail to King Mark! Hail to Cornwall!
All hail to the King!'

But in the second prelude all the sobbing of an over-
mastering joy, all the yearning of frustrated desire, all
the tremors of uncontrollable expectation alternated

one with the other, blended, mingled together. The
impatience of the woman's soul communicated its
vibrations to the night, to all things breathing and
watching through the pure summer night. On all things
the intoxicated soul urged the prayer that they should
remain vigilant beneath the stars, in order that they
might assist at the festival of her love, at the nuptial
feast of her joy. Over the ruffled surface of the ocean of
harmony floated the death melody, now clearly, now
darkly. The waves of the Mystical Gulf, like the
breathing of some superhuman breast, heaved and
swelled, sank back in order to rise again, to sink once
more, to fade gently away.

'Dost hear? To me it seems the clamour has already
died away in the distance.' Isolde only heard the sounds
which her wishes created. The horns of the nocturnal
huntsmen still re-echoed clearly through the forest. 'It
is the deceitful rustling of the foliage that the wind stirs
in its pranks. . . . No horns can give forth so sweet a
sound. It is the murmur of the stream bubbling and
rippling in the silent night.' She could hear nothing
save the insidious sounds which excited in her soul the
longing which contrived the old, yet ever new witchcraft.
All the murmuring voices, all the insinuating allurements
enveloped the breathless watcher, full of suggestions of
the coming intoxication, while Brangaene warned and
entreated in vain in all the terror of foreboding. 'Oh, let
the protecting torch yet burn! May its light show thee
thy peril!' But nothing could illuminate the blindness
of desire. 'Were the torch my very life, I would extinguish it without fear. Without fear I extinguish it
now.' With a gesture of supreme disdain, proud and
intrepid, Isolde flung the torch to the ground, offered her
own life and that of her Chosen One to the fatal night,
and entered with him into the eternal shadows.

Then the most intoxicating poem of human passion swept triumphantly upwards to the supreme heights of spasmodic ecstasy. It was the first frenzied embrace, a mingling of bliss and anguish in which the souls, thirsting for communion, encountered the impenetrable barrier of the human form. It was the first regretful moment for the time in which love was non-existent, for the empty and useless past. It was hatred towards the unfriendly light, towards the perfidious day which intensified every sorrow, which encouraged deceitful appearances, which favoured pride and hindered tenderness. It was the hymn of the friendly night, the benign darkness, the divine mystery from which sprang the marvels of internal perception, within which bloomed ideal blossoms on stately stems. 'Since the sun has hidden himself in our breasts, the stars of joy lighten us with their smiles.'

And in the orchestra all the raptures found expression, all the joys sang, all the sorrows wept to which the human voice has ever given utterance. Up from the symphonic depths the melodies emerged and developed, interrupting one another, replacing one another, mingling, dissolving, melting away, disappearing in order to reappear. A note of unsatisfied yearning growing ever more haunting and acute swept over the instruments, indicative of the vain and ceaseless effort to attain to the unattainable. In the transports of the chromatic progression could be discovered the mad pursuit of an aim that evaded all capture, though hovering near at hand. In the variations of tone, of rhythm, of measure, in the succession of suspensions there was a seeking without intermission, a limitless lust, a ceaseless torment of desire, ever frustrated and never quenched. A motive, symbolising the eternal yearning, eternally embittered of fallacious possession, recurred again and again with cruel persistency; it swelled and dominated, now illuminating the crest of the harmonic wave, now darkening it with a tragic gloom.

The irresistible power of the love-potion acted upon the soul and the flesh of the two lovers, already consecrated to Death. Nothing could extinguish or modify their fatal ardour ; nothing save Death itself. Both had attempted in vain every caress, had summoned in vain all their energies, to unite themselves in one supreme embrace, to possess each other utterly, to become a single being. Their voluptuous sighs were changed into sobs of anguish. An inviolable barrier interposed between them, separated them, kept them estranged and solitary. The barrier lay in their corporal substance, in their living persons. And in both a secret repulsion sprang up, a craving towards destruction, towards annihilation, a longing both to kill and to die. In their very caresses they realised the impossibility of transcending the material limits of the human senses. Lip joined to lip felt checked in the embrace. 'Who would ever succumb to death,' asked Tristan, 'save for that which separates us, which with-holds Tristan from eternally loving Isolde, from living for her alone through all ages?' Already they were entering the infinite shadows. The outer material world was fading away. 'Thus,' exclaimed Tristan, 'thus may we die, unwilling to live save through love, inseparable, ever united, without end, without awakening, without fear, nameless, in the arms of love.' The words were heard distinctly above the *pianissimo* of the orchestra. A fresh ecstasy enwrapped the two lovers and lifted them to the threshold of the marvellous realm of night. Already they enjoyed a foretaste of the transports of dissolution, they felt themselves freed from the weight of matter, already they felt their very substance etherealised and floating on the waves of eternal bliss. 'Without end, without awakening, without fear, without a name.'

'Take heed! Take heed! See, the night fades before the day!' warned the invisible Brangaene from her turret. 'Take heed!' And the shiver of the morning frost passed over the park, awakening the flowers. The cold light dawned slowly, and concealed the stars which twinkled unceasingly. 'Take heed!'

In vain the faithful servant gave the warning. They did not listen; they would not, could not, rouse themselves. Beneath the threat of daylight they buried themselves ever more deeply in those shadows through which no shaft of light could penetrate. 'May the night envelop us to all eternity!' And a whirlwind of harmony enveloped them, wrapt them round in its emphatic ascensions, transported them to the remote shores that they yearned after, there, where no anxiety restrained the impulse of the human soul, beyond all languor, beyond all suffering, beyond all loneliness, in the infinite serenity of their supreme dream.

'Save thyself, Tristan!' It was the cry of Kurwenal, following on that of Brangaene. It was the unforeseen and brutal attack interrupting the ecstatic embrace, and while the orchestra maintained the love theme, the hunt-motive burst out with a metallic crash. The king and the courtiers appeared. With his flowing mantle Tristan concealed Isolde reclining on the bank of flowers, sheltered her from the light and from curious eyes, affirming his authority by the gesture, establishing his undoubted right. 'The dreary day—for the last time!' For the last time, in the calm and firm attitude of a hero he accepted the contrast with external forces; convinced that in the future nothing could alter or arrest the course of his fate. While the over-mastering grief of King Mark found vent in a slow and mournful lament, he remained silent, absorbed in his secret thoughts. And at last he replied to the queries of the King: 'I cannot reveal this

K

mystery to you. You can never learn that which you seek to know.'

The love-charm motive enveloped the reply in the obscurity of mystery, in the gravity of an irreparable event. 'Wilt thou follow Tristan, O Isolde?' he asked the queen, simply, in the hearing of all. 'In the land where Tristan hopes to go the sun never shines. It is the land of shadows, the land of night, whence my mother sent me when, conceived by her in death, I passed from death into light.' . . . And Isolde, 'There where Tristan finds his home, there Isolde will follow him. She is ready to follow, gentle and faithful, by the road that he will show her.'

And towards that land the dying hero preceded her, wounded by the traitor Melot.

From out of the third prelude there rose a vision of a remote shore, of desolate and arid rocks, in whose hidden cavities the sea moaned ceaselessly, as though in inconsolable grief. A cloud of legends and of mystical poetry enveloped the storm outline of the rock, which appeared as if in an uncertain dawn, or in a deepening twilight. And the sound of the shepherd's pipes reawakened confused memories of his past life, of things lost in the nights of time.

'The old lament! What does it say?' sighed Tristan. 'Where am I?'

The shepherd modulated on his slim pipe the imperishable melody that had been transmitted to him by his forefathers through all time, and he remained untroubled in his supreme unconsciousness.

And Tristan, to whose soul the simple notes had revealed the whole truth, murmured, 'I did not dwell where I awoke. But where have I wandered? That I cannot tell thee. There I beheld neither sun, nor landscape, nor people; but that which I saw I cannot reveal.

I was there, where I have ever been, whither I shall
return for ever: in the vast realms of universal night.
One single solitary gift is vouchsafed to us there: divine,
eternal, never-ending oblivion!' A delirious fever agitated
him; the love-potion still worked evil in his innermost
fibres. 'Ah, that which I suffer thou canst not suffer!
This unquenchable yearning that devours me, these implacable flames that consume me. . . . Ah, would that I
could tell thee, would that thou couldst understand!'
And the unconscious shepherd piped his melody again
and again. It was always the same tune, the same notes ;
they told of the life that was no more, they spoke of
things lost far away.

'Old and mournful melody,' said Tristan, 'with thy
pathetic notes thou didst penetrate to me on the evening
breeze in the far distant time when the child heard of
the death of his father. In the grey dawn, even more
mournful, thou didst seek me when the son learnt the
fate of his mother. When my father begot me and died,
when my mother gave me life in death, the ancient
melody struck upon their sad and languid ears. One
day it questioned me, and behold, it questions me still.
For what destiny was I born? For what destiny? The
ancient melody repeats it again and again: To yearn
and to die! To die of yearning! . . . Ah! No! No!
That is not thy meaning. . . . To yearn, to yearn, to
yearn even until death, but not to die of yearning!'
Even more ruthlessly, more actively, the love-potion
gnawed his very vitals. His whole being writhed in
unendurable spasms. The orchestra crackled like a
funeral pyre. At intervals the pain overwhelmed him
with all the force of a thunderbolt, adding fresh fuel to
the flames. Sudden spasms shook him; horrible groans
escaped him; suppressed sobs burst from his lips. 'The
potion! The potion! The terrible potion. With what

madness I feel it mounting from the heart to the brain! Henceforward there is no hope for me ; no gentle death can release me from the torture of my desire. Nowhere, alas, nowhere can I find peace. The night flings me back upon the day, and the eye of the sun gloats on my ceaseless misery. Ah! how the blazing sun scorches and consumes me! And nowhere a refreshing shade from this withering heat. What balm could afford relief to my ghastly tortures ?' He bore in his veins and in his very marrow the desire of all men, of the whole human species, built up from generation to generation, aggravated by the sins of all the fathers and all the sons, by the passions of all, by the anguish of all. Within his blood the germs of all the concupiscences of the flesh flourished anew, there mingled every form of impurity, together with the most subtle and acute poisons which, from time immemorial, the sinuous purple lips of woman have infused into her eager male victims. He was the inheritor of eternal evil. ' This terrible love-potion, which has given me over to torment, I, I myself composed it. With the ardour of my father, with the transports of my mother, with all the tears of love shed in days gone by, with laughter and with sobs, with passion and with wounds, I, I myself mingled the poison of the potion. And I quaffed it in a long draught of delight. . . . Cursed be the potion! Cursed be he who composed it!' And he fell back on the couch, exhausted, lifeless, only to live on in the spirit world, to feel once more his burning wounds, to see once more in the hallucination of his brain the sovereign image in the act of crossing the seas. ' She comes, she comes, gently lulled on great waves of inebriat- ing blossoms, floating towards the shore. With her smile she pours out upon me a divine consolation ; she brings me the supreme refreshment.' . . . Thus he evoked, thus he *saw* with eyes which were for ever shut to the

light of day, the Enchantress, the wonder-worker, the
healer of wounds. 'She comes! She comes! Dost
thou not see her, Kurwenal, not yet see her?' And the
tumultuous waves of the Mystical Gulf swept up once
more from their depths in a confused medley all the
previous melodies, mingling them, developing them, en-
gulfing them as in a whirlpool, flinging them once again
on the surface, crushing them to fragments; the melodies
that had expressed the terrors of the decisive conflict on
the deck of the ship, those in which had been heard the
gurgle of the beverage poured out into the golden goblet,
and the tingling of the arteries invaded by the liquid
fire; those which told of the mysterious breathing of the
summer night, tempting to endless passion; all the
melodies, with all the images, with all the memories.
And over that vast shipwreck the death-motive, high,
overmastering, implacable, drifted at intervals, repeating
the awful sentence : 'To yearn, to yearn, to yearn even
unto death, but not to die of yearning.'

'The ship is casting anchor! Isolde, Isolde is here!
She springs to land!' shouted Kurwenal from the roof of
the turret. And in the delirium of his joy, Tristan tore
the bandages from his wounds, incited his own blood to
flow in torrents, to inundate the earth, to incarnadine the
world. At the approach of Isolde and of Death, he
seemed to hear the light. 'Do I not hear the light?'
A great interior glow suffused his being; from all the
atoms of his substance rays of sunlight sprang, and
spread themselves in harmonious and luminous waves
over the universe. The light was music—the music
light.

And at this moment the Mystical Gulf, in very truth,
seemed to throw out rays of light. The harmonious
notes of the orchestra seemed to repeat those distant
planetary sounds which in past ages vigilant watchers

fancied they could discern in the silence of the night.
Little by little the long vibrations of terror, the long sobs
of agony, the moans of vain longing, the outbursts of
ever-frustrated desire, and all the varied emotions of
human misery were allayed and died away. Tristan had
crossed the threshold of the 'marvellous realms,' and had
entered at length upon the eternal night. And Isolde,
prostrate on the lifeless remains, felt at length that the
burden that oppressed her was fading slowly away. The
death-melody, which had become ever more clear and
more solemn, consecrated their marriage in death. Then,
like ethereal threads, the slender notes wove round the
living woman diaphanous veils of purity. Thus there
began a species of joyous ascension of jewelled steps on
the wings of a hymn. 'See how sweetly he smiles. Do
you not see? His smile is radiant as the stars. Can
you not see? Can you not hear? Do I alone hear this
new melody, infinitely tender and consoling, which rises
up from the depths of his being, enveloping me, penetrating me, enrapturing me?' The Irish enchantress, the
awe-inspiring maker of potions, the hereditary arbiter of
secret terrestrial powers, she who from the deck of the
ship had invoked the storm and the whirlwind, she who
had chosen as the object of her love the strongest and
the noblest of heroes in order to poison and to destroy
him, she who had closed the path of glory and of victory
to a 'conqueror of the world,' she the poisoner, the
murderess, was transfigured by the power of death into
a being of light and of joy, cleansed from all impure
stain, free from all degrading bond, breathing and living
in union with the soul of the universe.

'Maybe these sounds which murmur ever more clearly
in my ear are the soft breezes of the air. Shall I breathe
them, drink them, fling myself into them, drown myself
gently in the vapours, in the perfumes?' Everything

seemed to dissolve within her, to melt away, to return to its original essence, to the numberless elements of the ocean from which forms spring up, into which forms disappear, in order to renew themselves, to be born again. In the Mystical Gulf the transformations and the transfigurations, from note to note, from harmony to harmony, followed in an endless succession. It seemed as though everything was being decomposed, everything was giving out its secret essences, everything was being metamorphosed into immaterial symbols. Colours which have never been discovered in the petals of the most exquisite of earthly flowers, perfumes of almost imperceptible delicacy floated in the air. Visions of hidden paradises flashed past, germs of future worlds sprang into life. And the wild intoxication rose even higher and higher ; the great Choir drowned the solitary human voice. Transfigured, Isolde entered triumphantly into the marvellous realms. ' To lose oneself in the infinite throbbing of the world's soul, to plunge into it, to fade away, without consciousness! Highest bliss!'

Rembrandt and

Richard Wagner

HUGUES IMBERT

LIGHT AND SHADE IN ART

LIGHT and shade, harmony and dissonance! Do not these four terms, which determine the limitations of the visual and auditory faculties, also include painting and music, the visible and the invisible world, the world of forms and that of substance? What an infinite number of luminous vibrations exist between a midday sky and a starlit night, through all the shades of daybreak and of dawn, of sunset and of twilight! Can we not trace a multitude of sonorous vibrations in the murmurs of a crackling forest in which are predominant the majesty of perfect harmony and the shrill hissing of a storm at sea, when all the superposed notes tear and annihilate each other in a furious and weird affray? Painting, which reflects the visible world by the aid of colour, and music, which expresses the invisible world of sentiments, exist between the two extremes of light and shade, harmony and dissonance, both corresponding to those two conditions of the soul known as joy and sadness.

Our senses do not enable us to detect anything in common between painting and music, which appear as irreducible to one another as light would be to sound. But our souls tell us that they correspond to each other, just as the external world communes with the internal world, by means of thoughts and sentiments. It is worthy of notice that music, whether symphonic or vocal, evokes images at its highest pitch of intensity, just as perfect painting can engender a rhythmical and melodious vibration of the soul, similar to musical waves. A temperament, ever so commonplace, could not listen to a symphony of Beethoven, to a fragment of Berlioz or Wagner, without perceiving a vision of landscapes or human dramas. No one, however devoid of sensitive feeling, could gaze upon one of Correggio's nymphs, or upon a Madonna of Memling, or a prophet of Michael Angelo, without feeling certain vibrations of the innermost self, mysteriously impelled by human or heavenly harmonies. There is thus a 'chiaroscuro' and colours in music just as there are harmonies and tones in painting. The two arts meet at that depth of the soul where sentiment and form are born of a common idea, where the vibration of sentiment creates visible form, and where the beauty of the form awakens the musical vibration.

The originality of painter and musician are shown in the way in which they oppose light to shade, harmony to dissonance. In this, Rembrandt and Wagner can be considered brothers, not because they are identical in every detail, but because their temperaments are so much alike. They show the same contempt for hackneyed methods, the same yearnings for new ones, the same delight in rare and intense sensations. But the strongest link between them is that wonderful gift they both possess of awakening in us the sense of external life,

of stirring the inner man by effects that are both delicate
and violent, of bringing, as it were, the soul into light,
by a clash between light and shade.

In this rapid study of the two great masters, we
purpose submitting some examples of the secret but
striking correlations between their sensitiveness and their
systems. We shall then endeavour to show the differences
that exist between them.

.   .   .   .

It has often been said that a great genius is not
produced all of a piece, that he is the result, the echo
of all the efforts and the aspirations of many preceding
generations. Rembrandt undoubtedly can be traced from
Lastman and Pinas, while Wagner owes his origin to
Gluck and Weber. But have they not vastly extended
the modes of their masters and predecessors? They
have engraved upon steel the timid lines of the past and
interpreted in a strong and majestic language the first
stammerings of the muse.

Do they not seem to have broken off with past traditions,
to have snapped the chain of art? Have they not introduced into this art, apart from new plastic beauty,
sublime moral beauty, the poetry of the supernatural
and that intense passion? They are the inventors of a
sublime æstheticism, the creators of an ascensional movement. How has this understanding come about between
two men so separated by time and distance? This is
a mystery that can only be explained by the instinct
which they both possessed of a new poetry. They have
made their art immaterial : in their creations we find
nothing but the human soul. They both revered Psyche ;
and for them she unfolded her wings.

.   .   .   .

Admire Rembrandt's masterpieces in the principal
museums of Europe, read the beautiful books that have

been written about this great genius, in which his pictures, his drawings, and his sketches are faithfully reproduced.[1] The originals and the reproductions, especially those consecrated by Van Ryn to the translation of Divine subjects, to the principal stories of the Bible and the New Testament, seem to create the same weird impression as do those musical pages with which Wagner resuscitated the olden legends. In both their works mystery hovers, the pathos and the magic of the 'chiaroscuro,' of light and shade, are felt.

When Rembrandt attacks scenes that have often been painted by his predecessors or by his contemporaries, when he is dealing with the various episodes of the life of Christ, the Crucifixion, the descent from the Cross, the Entombment, the Ascension, what sublime lights he imparts to his visions that go back to the early periods of Christianity! He certainly ignores tradition, conventional laws; but all the scenes depicted by him have the hall-mark of genius, of genius made of light and shade, of that genius that bears you away to dreamland.

In that wonderful etching in which he makes Jesus say to Lazarus, 'Rise and walk,' he masses the shades behind Christ and projects the stronger light upon Lazarus rising from his coffin and upon the bystanders, who shrink back in fear and amazement, and the whole constitutes a formidable *crescendo* in the intense light that illumines the drama. Mary alone comes forward, arms outstretched, for she has recognised Lazarus. This is indeed the miraculous scene, the extraordinary deed of a resurrection surrounded by all the majesty of emotion which it deserves.

Christ has only to raise His left hand, and a sudden light is produced, giving a supernatural character to the

---

[1] The most important of these works is entitled *Rembrandt, His Life and Works, and His Times*, by Mr. Emile Michel, Membre de l'Institut.

episode. Clad in a long toga, standing barefooted upon the flagstones, He towers over the whole scene by His greatness and His powerful will.

Do we not find identical effects of light and shade, so dear to Rembrandt, produced in the Temple scene of *Parsifal*, that majestic and seraphic page of the drama that was so justly christened *The Canticle of Canticles of Divine love?* While the orchestra plays the characteristic march, to which are soon added the *sounds of the horns and the chimes of the bells*, the whole panorama of the different places that Parsifal and Gurnemanz have passed through on their way to Mount Tabrat is unfolded in one progressing scene. Then we see the interior of the Temple with its huge cupola, whence fall the sounds of the bells, and whence soon will descend *an intense, an almost supernatural light.*

From the depths of the sacred building, the slow procession of the knights of the Holy Grail proceeds, singing the chorus on the same motive as that of the orchestral march. *Gradually light is thrown on the stage.* The knights gather round the Communion tables, followed by their equerries and the lay brothers, the former carrying King Amfortas, still suffering from his wound, the latter bearing the tabernacle which contains the Grail. The emotion increases, as the voices of the knights in the midst of all this pomp are heard in gradations, together with those of the youths in the centre, and of the children *at the top of the cupola. It is indeed the unfolding of a mystery with alternatives of dazzling light and dark tenebræ,* just as noticeable in the scenery as in the music. Then comes the terrible episode in which Amfortas describes his sufferings, refuses to celebrate the Divine mystery, and finally consents to do so, remembering the promise of redemption. This pathetic scene, the anguish and sorrow of which baffle description, puts an

effectual stop to the prayers of the knights, the invocations
of the boys, and the ineffable canticle of the children,
'Uncover the Grail.'   And then the act of consecration
begins, *in the darkness of the twilight that invades the
temple*, the supper-theme being delineated by the orchestra
and the children's voices, who sing while Amfortas
prays :—

> Take this bread, it is my body,
> Take this wine, it is my blood,
> Which my love has given thee.

Can we not liken the long tremolo of the basses to an
effect of darkness, of shade, which throws out in bold
relief the theme of Redemption?

As Amfortas slowly raises the Grail cup and the scales
above the kneeling knights, *the darkness is replaced by a
dazzling light which falls upon the sacred cup*, and is
refracted by it into a thousand brilliant corruscating rays.
The supper-theme is interpreted again by the orchestra,
with all its wealth of sound.   Little by little these
musical splendours die away ; the knights rise, the feast
begins, with the songs of the knights alternating with
those of the children and youths ; the knights then
solemnly leave the Temple after the feast, while the
tabernacle of the Grail is being removed.   Once more
the orchestra, having unfolded the theme of *faith*, takes
up the motive of the first march.   Here occurs that short
and very curious episode, during which Gurnemanz
remains alone with Parsifal, upbraids him for his stupid
silence, and throws the artless one out of the Temple.
But, in the cupola, a heavenly voice is heard, supported
by the chorus of youths and children, singing *Blessed are
those who have Faith.*

We have intentionally italicised the principal passages
referring to the effects of great light and darkness, which
are determined by the *crescendo* or *pianissimo* of the

orchestra, so as the better to mark the similarity between the work of Rembrandt and that of Wagner. The stratagems of harmony, composition, vocal and orchestral instrumentation, concentrate the whole light upon one principal point, the scene of the Grail! The beautiful sonorous effects, mysterious and veiled, such as the master of Bayreuth conceived them, and executed them, coming from under the stage where all the orchestra is placed, are truly capable of making the illusion more complete, and causing a more intense emotion. These sounds, these effects of light and shade, are doubtless analogies between the mysterious and vibrating ray that is produced by the ecstatic and bloodless face of the Christ of Rembrandt in the *Pilgrims of Emmaus*, which we admire in the Louvre Museum! Has not the enigmatic physiognomy of Kundry a family look of the Magdalen of *Christ and the Magdalen* in the Brunswick Museum, where in this marvellous scenery of Good Friday the sinner kneels, humble and contrite, to wash the feet of Parsifal and, like a new Magdalen, stoops to wipe them with her long tresses?

We venture to quote some extracts from the interesting work of Mr. Emile de Saint-Auban,[1] who was also struck by the great affinities that exist between the geniuses of Rembrandt and Wagner. In the Good Friday scene, when Parsifal appears clad in armour by the side of Gurnemanz and Kundry, Mr. de Saint-Auban draws the following parallel:—

'It is not the magic roar that we hear this time; the melodious forerunner does not come from the infernal regions; it is the harmonious image of the providential hero Parsifal who must be near. . . . But is it not a ghost? The chords that precede his arrival have a sound from beyond the grave; they are phantom chords. So

---

[1] *A Pilgrimage to Bayreuth*, pp. 202, 333, 334.

can I fancy the *Leit-motiv* of that Christ of Rembrandt,
who, after His resurrection, appeared to the people of
Emmaus in His deathlike splendour as a transfigured
corpse!'

And, in his conclusion, Mr. de Saint-Auban lays special
stress upon the similarity that can be noticed between
the genius of Rembrandt and that of Wagner:—

'The meditative study of a Wagnerian score evokes
the recollection of a Rembrandt canvas. We stand before it; it is in powerful darkness; an incipient design is
perceptible; then, again, comes darkness. The puzzled
eye awaits a further development. Soon the clouds
become animated, and spread their latent light. A
richer light is kindled, dilates, expands, envelops its
surroundings, penetrates them, searches them in their
innermost crevices, glides upon the cornices, accentuates
the angles, reveals all that is visible, and makes one
anticipate the rest. From the black darkness men,
groups, houses, furniture, glasses, potteries, familiar
realities sally forth, each one playing a part; and far
back in a corner you perceive a winding staircase
leading up to a garret, down to a cellar, receding walls,
rooms that grow bigger, and new expanses full of breath
and life.'

Rembrandt was not directly inspired by the sacred
books, but by the legendary interpretation of them,
which from century to century had become acclimatised
among the people.

Before composing *Parsifal*, Wagner had, of course,
thought of a life of Christ; but the legend obtained the
upper hand, and it was the legend that guided his steps.

Both painter and composer rejuvenate tradition, and
infuse into it a new life.

The consecrated themes are rendered without any rule
or local veracity, but their spirit is so personal, so weird,

that the subjects become impregnated with it, while it imparts to them an exalted and admirable expression.

The most exalted among these works of art almost always symbolise the feeling of sorrow in the Passion drama.

Rembrandt and Wagner have expressed with sublime intensity that poetic contemplation, that intimate comprehension of the sensation of pain, to which our nature has doomed us the moment we stand upon the threshold of life.[1]

Wagner's *Parsifal*, and the *Good Samaritan* of Rembrandt, are *dramas* of Pity and of Faith.

.　　.　　.　　.　　.　　.　　.

The sword, buried to the hilt in the oak-tree of Hunding's hut, and suddenly shining with a brilliant flash, the quick irruption of light which flows into the dwelling the moment the door is thrown open by the strength of a vernal breeze, with the luminous effects of the orchestra underlying the whole, are these not pictures worthy of Rembrandt's brush?

The orchestration of the principal passages presents the most striking analogies between the methods of Wagner and of Rembrandt; both possess the same art of bringing into full light the *theme* or principal motive, the one which produces the culminating point of sensation, of the idea which the author has propounded, and which he wishes the audience to conceive.

Study the orchestration of the 'Nornes' scene in *Götterdämmerung*, the evocations of Alberich in the same

---

[1] 'Forse in qual forma, in quale
    Stato che sia dentro covile o cuna,
    È funesto a chi nascea il di natale !'
                    Leopardi (*Canto notturno*).
    Whether we were born in high or low degree,
    In a cavern or a mansion,
    The day of our birth must bring sorrow to us all.

work! Consider the part played by the strings and the
bass clarinet in the colouring of these pictures! Recall
the storms in *Die Walküre*, the scene of the Nibelheim
in *Das Rheingold*, and in *Siegfried* the scene of Wotan
and that between Alberich and Mime before the Dragon's
cave (last act)—are they not so many dark pages, intensely black and mysterious, in strong contrast with the
preceding or the following scenes, that are illumined by
the brilliant orchestral colour and the feverish inspiration
of the melody? Let us admire the second act of *Tristan
und Isolde*, which is like a starlit, mysterious night, coming
between the dazzling light of the first act and the sorrow-
ful splendour of the third. Are not these contrasts of
the Rembrandt school?

In the third act of *Tristan und Isolde*, the crowning
event, the arrival of the ship so long hoped for, is introduced by the unmixed brilliancy of beautiful sounds.

What a stage effect is produced, in a purely musical
sense we mean, by the sudden irruption of this flash of
light in the midst of the dark shades, where inexpressible
sufferings were relentlessly, pitilessly meted out!

What object had Wagner at heart? It was to develop
on the stage the inner motives of the action, to inculcate
into the drama its utmost value ; the musical elements,
like all the other elements which he borrowed from the
different branches of art, are only used to accentuate
the action better. He imparts life to his heroes, and the
leit-motive in the orchestra are most powerful agents in
the enlightenment of their souls. He envelops them
in a light of great intensity, and increased strength is
borrowed from the darkness of the whole theatre at
Bayreuth. Are not these the ideas, so dear to Rembrandt,
which lend such animation to the different characters of
the drama, that one gets an insight into their inner
lives?

L

The great intensity of the drama is present in the works of both masters.

Whether Rembrandt takes his subjects from legends, from the Scriptures, or from everyday life, he always invests them with supreme power by the aid of light and shade.

Whether Wagner is representing the heroes of the Edda, a spotless character like Parsifal, or the deeds of the Master Singers, he will always impart to them almost supernatural force by means of the *forte*, light, and the *pianissimo*, shade.

These two great geniuses always put their will into effect ; all of their sublime conceptions were completely and perfectly carried out.

.   .   .   .

Rembrandt and Wagner belong to that species of impulsive minds who entirely create their own æstheticism, borrow little or nothing from their predecessors, develop mysteriously, and leave no heirs. Rembrandt's pallet was so powerful, so foreign to all rules, that his most famous pupils sank their own individuality in his method. Will not the same happen to Richard Wagner's pupils ? He had no pupils properly so called ; but those of the young school who were hypnotised by his genius and his methods had much difficulty in becoming known. They copied the system, but really had no creative genius.

Mr. Emile Michel, in his study on Rembrandt, shows clearly the danger of working under such masters.

'Logic alone cannot explain genius, especially Rembrandt's genius, which was perhaps the most original ever known. We lose ourselves in trying to follow him, and it would be rash to take him as a model. We do not think that his pupils had in him a very safe guide, or that his influence had a healthy effect upon their education. His powerful temperament compelled him

to tower over them, and notwithstanding all the pre-
cautions he took to isolate them and safeguard their
independence, they nearly all lost their own individuality
through the mere strength of his ascendency. They
were protected against the influence that they might
exercise on one another, but they were defenceless
against their master. The best among them, in their
best works, succeed in being like him, and the highest
honour that they have attained is that they are sometimes mistaken for him. But, as a rule, they only
imitate his external methods, his quaintness, his modes
of composition. They borrow his subjects, his costumes,
his system of effects; they copy him, they counterfeit
him ; but his original and individual pride only accentuates the docility of their submissiveness.'

Are not these words applicable to Wagner and to his
disciples? Fanaticised, they imitated him more than
any other master had ever been imitated, and many
amongst them who were mere copyists took exactly
what should have been avoided.

.   .   .   .

Now, having endeavoured to show the bonds that exist
between the great Dutch painter and the great German
symphonist and dramatist, we must state the points that
separate them and distinguish the one from the other.
A complete identification of them would mean the
complete suppression of their originality. We may
understand them better if we throw the light of the one
upon the other, but it would be equally unjust to painter
and musician if we were to confuse their two geniuses.

Eugène Fromentui, the remarkable painter and admirable writer, has defined, in his book, *Maîtres d'Autrefois*,
the *chiaroscuro*, or light and shade, of Rembrandt, as only
a professional and an artist could define it. We cannot
do better than quote him :—

'The *chiaroscuro* is undoubtedly the incipient and necessary form of his impressions and of his ideas. Others besides him have used it; but none used it so continuously or so ingeniously. It is pre-eminently the mysterious form, the most hidden, the most elliptical, the richest in hints and in surprises, that can be found in the picturesque language of the poets. It is light, vaporous, veiled, discreet; it lends its charms to hidden things, it excites curiosity, invests moral beauty with greater attraction, and gives more grace to the speculations of conscience. It is composed of sentiment, emotion, uncertainty, the indefinite and the infinite, dreams and idealism. And that is why the *chiaroscuro* is, as it should be, the poetic and natural atmosphere in which Rembrandt's genius ever dwelt.'

This definition clearly shows that Rembrandt is, above all, the past-master of light and shade. His genius resides entirely in his etchings. His art is satisfied with black and white, which he bathes in a yellow mist in his oil paintings. Wagner, the magician of sound, also makes use of these spectral oppositions of daylight and darkness; he, too, is a great illuminator of darkness, but he is also a painter of extraordinary power, who requires the free run of the whole gamut of colours, because he alternately inhabits all the regions of nature, and deals with the whole scale of human passions.

The harmonic and orchestral colouring of Richard Wagner resembles most the light and shade of Rembrandt, in one of his early works, *Der fliegende Holländer*, which, by the way, is founded upon a Dutch legend. This drama, the frame-work of which is composed of Norway and the North Sea, contains nothing but lightning and darkness, white upon black. The heroic and tender figure of Senta stands out luminously on the dark surf of the ocean which carries the accursed sailor.

In *Tannhäuser* the sensual and pagan tendencies of Wagner burst forth in all their strength. In order to find analogies for the ballet of Venusberg alone, in the masterpieces of painters, we should have to combine Rubens, the painter of shuddering nudes, with Titian, who bathes his Fauns, his Bacchants, and his courtesans in the sumptuous light of Venice and of the Italian Tyrol. The brilliant sonorousness of *Lohengrin* recalls the style of Correggio; diaphanous bodies on warm backgrounds, dazzling whitenesses upon rich yellow canvases. Here the light itself acts as a shade and as a contrast or set-off to the light. Recall the prelude which unfolds itself like a cloth of gold upon an azure sky, and the introduction of the third act, in which the flourish of the trombones rebel against the sparkling trepidation of the trumpets!—*Siegfried* brings us to the freshness of the sunlit forest. Here we have innocent joy, light and warbling. On the awakening of Brünnhilde, torrents of light fall upon the whole creation. It is not only the Valkyrie who has been changed into a woman —it is the whole orchestra that seems to exclaim through all its chords and all its mouths : 'Hail, sun! hail, oh earth! hail, resplendent light!' In the farewell scene between Siegfried and Brünnhilde in the first act of *Götterdämmerung*, the musician's magic concentrates, as it were, the blinding strength of the rising sun upon the heroic couple as they leave the cavern. Here the effects produced are so intense that the art of painting can provide no analogies to it, as they can only be found in the greatest effects of nature itself. The instruments all sounding together are, at that moment, drowned by the noise of the brasses and the cymbals, just as the rising sun re-absorbs and embodies for a moment all the colours of the sky and the earth.

How can we describe the death and the transfiguration

of Isolde, who appears enveloped in pink gauze and
caressed by the vast embrace of a setting sun? It seems
then as if the sorrows, the ecstasy, the terrors of the
great tragedy of love were vaporised and had resolved
themselves in that ethereal pink as in an ocean of supreme
unconsciousness.

It would be easy to furnish many more examples;
but we have said enough to show how much more varied
and exclusive is the gamut of Wagner's colours. We do
not say so in order to deprecate the rare and original
genius of Rembrandt, but to make it more evident by
means of the contrast. This difference of the methods
employed corresponds to a different conception of life
and the human ideal.

Rembrandt is a dreamer who kindles life in the shadow,
who etherises light and spiritualises the body. By means
of his light and shade, composed of black and white, he
gives us the sensation of the supernatural and the world
beyond. He transports us to a mysterious region, that
of the soul separated from nature, plunged in its own
element and face to face with itself. He holds up a
mirror to that soul in which it can fathom unknown
depths. In a word, Rembrandt is a transcendent
Spiritualist, as far as a painter can be. On the other
hand, the pantheistic genius of Wagner takes delight in
the whole universe. He resorts to the kingdoms of
nature, and analyses all the layers of the human soul.
He is as much at home on the mystic heights whence
comes Lohengrin, and to which Parsifal repairs, as he is
in the abysses of diabolical wickedness and animalism
from which Alberich and Ortrud have sprung. But one
feels with him that it is the same breath that goes through
the whole of his creation, that hell, heaven, and earth
are joined together by infinite and necessary gradations,
and that this great whole is but one real living creature.

The most sublime harmonies in *Parsifal* are still drenched by the tears of Christ. Wagner humanises divinity, his heaven is only the crowning of earth. These are the reasons why his orchestration corresponds so marvellously with the definition which Schopenhauer gave of music : ' It roars, it sings, it cries, like " The Soul of the world." '

Wagner in London in 1855

A. J. JAEGER

OF the publishing of Wagner letters there seems to be no end. What a voluminous correspondent the master was; and how few of his communications to friends and acquaintances there are that do not provide most excellent reading, besides shedding fresh light on the life and work of this truly extraordinary man of genius! A very large number of his epistles have already been published; and yet hardly a year passes in which some periodical or other does not add to the rich store of Wagneriana by bringing to light still further instalments. There must be plenty more to come, though not all Wagner's correspondents took the precaution to preserve his letters.[1]

[1] For instance, I happen to know of a certain German composer, not altogether unknown to fame, whose sisters proudly showed a lady friend of mine a long row of jars filled with home-made jam. Their pride was in the quantity and quality of their jam, and not in the fact that all these same jars were covered with what, on inspection, proved to be *original letters of Wagner*, addressed to the said composer! The dear ladies told my friend that they had used 'lots' of the 'Meister's' epistles in place of parchment paper, because their brother had no further use for them. This was some years ago.

168

In some recent numbers of our excellent contemporary, the *Allgemeine Musik Zeitung*, there have appeared several long and highly entertaining letters addressed by Wagner to one Herr Otto Wesendonck. They possess exceptional interest for English readers, since they were written in London in 1855, when Wagner conducted a series of the Philharmonic Society's concerts. It will be remembered that he was at the time engaged on the scoring of his *Die Walküre*, the first act having been finished on April 3—'with great trouble,' according to a letter dated April 5. He wrote from 22 Portland Terrace, Regent's Park. This house, situated on the north side of the park, near the canal, still stands. He calls it an 'expensive lodging,' which, however, seems to have possessed one advantage to a great lover of animals like him, in that it was quite close to the Zoological Gardens. These he seems to have frequently visited, for he writes in the same letter : 'We shall have fine weather. I shall often go and see the wild beasts,' etc. Perhaps it was in the dear old Zoo, then, that Wagner made some of the preliminary studies for the 'menagerie' he was at that time introducing into *Der Ring der Nibelungen*, though I cannot trace that it ever possessed a 'fearful wildfowl' like Fafner the Worm. That Wagner's tenure of the conductorship was by no means an unequivocal success is, of course, well known ; and that he was terribly chagrined at the lack of appreciation and the open hostility of a great portion of the London press is also no secret. His own interpretation of the motives and actions of the critics of the period may be wrong in some details ; but that it was not altogether incorrect, those who have studied the musical history of London of the year 1855 can hardly deny.

The letters are, as usual, full of complaints and groans about his lack of success, the bother of having to earn money, threats to give up Art, and even to do something desperate to 'end all.' That an abnormally sensitive genius like Wagner should vent his spleen as he does in these letters is not surprising. Proudly conscious as he was of his own transcendent genius and the greatness of the message it was at once his ecstasy and his agony to have to deliver to an unappreciative world, he must have suffered almost the anguish of Amfortas on seeing the English completely given up to that hysterical Mendelssohn worship which made the appreciation of other men of genius, such as Wagner himself, Schumann and Brahms, all but impossible, or at any rate greatly retarded it. Wagner's sweeping remarks about the English and their 'sheep-like' characteristics can only raise a smile, and no Englishman is likely to propose retaliating with a boycott of the poor disappointed master's music.

The first letter is dated March 1855, without giving the day :—

'DEAR FRIEND,—What I have to communicate shall be told you to-day, so that I may let you know at the same time how grateful I am for your many kindnesses. I should be delighted if I could write to you in a better temper, because I know that I could only gladden your sympathetic heart with news about my well-being. But even to obtain this good object, I will not tell any lies, and I will, therefore, confess at once that if you still cherish any hopes for my earthly welfare, I can give but little encouragement to such hopes. London is a very large and very rich city, and the English are exceedingly clever, prudent, and intelligent; but I, unhappy man, have nothing in common with them. For a time they will take me for something different from what I am, and we shall thus get on together without any great annoyance; and, as I am by no means inclined nor conceited enough suddenly to dispel their illusion, I can only wish that that time may soon pass. Once more : I have no business to be here. If you ask where I ought to be, I reply : wherever I would meet the fewest people. But here, on the contrary, I am being advised to call upon this one and

that one, *e.g.* Davison (*Times*), Chorley (*Athenæum*), etc. I
am told that they are . . ., but influential, and that, moreover,
it would be a pity to allow my abilities and talents to be
altogether wasted here. I do not know what *you* think of this.
I am always of opinion that I have no business here with all
my talents; and besides, I should certainly not require the
recommendation of those gentlemen. If I wished to become
duly appointed (*wohlbestellter*) conductor of the " Philharmonic "
for a number of years, I could no doubt easily attain this
object, for people see that I am a good conductor. But that
would be about the *sole* delight to be expected ; besides that
there is nothing. To entertain even the faintest hope of
creating any special interest—more particularly on the part of
the Court—in my operas, or in a good German theatre is quite
chimerical, . . . and certainly nobody here would have the
very least sympathy with anything out of the common. One
can see that from the character of the people. Real art is
something utterly strange (*wildfremdes*) to them, and it is impossible to affect them, except through their pockets (*Aus- und
Einkommen*). For instance, to see with what imperturbability
these people listened while, thirty seconds after the finish of
the *Eroica*, a tedious duet was sung to them, was truly a new
experience for me. Everybody assured me that no one took
the least offence thereat ; and the duet was applauded quite
as loudly as the symphony. Well, this by the way.

I had placed all my hopes in the satisfaction to be derived from
my intercourse with the orchestra—which is very devoted to me
—and in the prospect of fine performances. I was particularly
anxious to be given *two* rehearsals for the next concert, because
I hoped on that occasion to give the orchestra a thorough
" drilling." But after yesterday's first rehearsal, I had to abandon
even that hope, for I came to the conclusion that for my
purpose even *two* rehearsals would be too few. I had to pass
over a good many important things, and I see that I cannot
possibly go over them at the final rehearsal. So, after all, I
shall have to be content with only a *very* comparatively good
performance of the Ninth Symphony. As regards my music to
Lohengrin, I felt this time especially, with deep sorrow, how
sad it is for me to have to come before the public always with

such very meagre extracts from this work. I appeared quite absurd (*abgeschmackt*) to myself, because I know how little people can learn about me and my works from this poor little "sample card," with which I'm travelling about like a *commis voyageur*. And thus I spend my best years, with my artistic activity completely hindered as regards my coming before the public. I would very much prefer to renounce every attempt at such activity, for my martyrdom during the same, *I alone* can feel! Under these circumstances only one satisfaction would therefore remain—to have done something for my worldly prospects. I should be very glad if I could do it. But how, if not by stealing? We will see how "fat"[1] my prospects will become through my London concert fee. Although my lodging is expensive I do not contemplate any real extravagance, and I hope therefore to save something. But that is about all *this* time, and *every* time!

'Parliament recently passed a Bill according to which no copyright can be obtained of works which have already appeared abroad, but only of those which were written in England, or for England, and first published here. Accordingly the "Evening Star" and "Lohengrin's Rebuke to Elsa," published in an elegant translation by Ewer, greeted me upon my arrival here; and I am assured that a further complete selection of my lyric pieces may be shortly expected. Anybody has the right to reprint them at pleasure, so I very much regret the postage which I paid a short time ago, when I asked for these things to be sent to me to England. Dearest friend! cease trying to make me "independent." I shall always remain a good-for-nothing (*Lump*), especially in the Englishman's sense. I can only wish that nobody were dependent on me, for whoever clings to me is not likely to get on.[2] It can't be helped! Perhaps I may soon give up Art altogether, then everything will be right. Art alone upholds me for the time being, but with delusions which may have dangerous consequences for me. At times it makes me reckless, and you know that recklessness does good to nobody, least of all to him who gives way to it.

---

[1] Wagner uses the word 'fett.'

[2] 'Und muss somit nur wünschen, es hinge auch Niemand von mir ab; denn wer an mir hängt,' etc. ; a play on the word 'hängen.'

But of this I am certain—only a little more is required to decide me to stop completely this source of all irrationality (*Unvernunft*) in my existence. Reason enough I should have —the agonies which even my Art causes me enormously outweigh the rare moments of ecstasy which it holds for me. Little is required, ay, only one single thing, and I give up this game—then it will appear probable, though in a different manner from what some people would imagine.

' I visited Herr Benecke in the city. The day after to-morrow he will send his carriage for me, to drive me to his house in the suburbs. You have certainly recommended me very well. He and his people really belong to the *Times* set, also in musical matters. His wife is a relation of Mendelssohn,[1] for whose antagonist people will insist on taking me, though they assured me that they had never heard his " Hebrides " overture so well done as under my direction. The Beneckes are well known here as a very Art (?) loving and rich family ; we shall see ! At any rate, I thank you for your kind solicitude.

' Up to the present my dearest London acquaintance is the first violinist here, Sainton, a native of Toulouse, fiery, goodnatured, and amiable. He alone is the cause of my coming to London. He has for many years lived with a German, Lüders, on terms of the most intimate friendship. Lüders had read my books (*Kunstschriften*), and through them had become so prejudiced in my favour that he communicated their contents as well as he could to Sainton, and both concluded from them that I *must* needs be an able fellow (*ein tüchtiger Mensch*). So when Sainton suggested me to the directors and was asked to explain how he came to know me, he lied that he had actually seen me conduct, because, so he said, the real reason for his preconceived opinion of me would not have been appreciated by those good people. After the first rehearsal, when Sainton, full of enthusiasm, embraced me, I could not help calling him a *téméraire*, who ought to be glad to have got off scot-free this time. Sainton is very congenial to me. Yesterday, after the rehearsal, when he noticed my great exhaustion and ill-temper, he would insist upon driving me home and waiting until I had changed ; after which he countermanded my lonely dinner and

---

[1] By marriage.

took me to his rooms, where I dined with him and Lüders quite cosily (*gemüthlich*) *en garçon*, until my temper improved. Such a man, in London amongst the English, is a real oasis in the desert. Anything more objectionable than the real, genuine, English type I cannot conceive. The prevailing type is that of the sheep; and the Englishman's practical sense is as sure as is the instinct of a sheep for finding his fodder in the meadow. The Englishman is sure to find his fodder, but the whole beautiful meadow and the blue sky above it do not exist for his perceptive organs. How unhappy every one living in their midst must feel who, on the contrary, perceives only the meadow and the sky, but alas! hardly the fodder.[1]

'I have also taken a great fancy to a young musician— Klindworth—whom Liszt recommended to me; if the fellow had a tenor voice I should kidnap him for certain, for, apart from that, he meets every requirement for my Siegfried, especially as regards physique. By the way, I have now a beautiful Erard grand in the house; I had to get a carpenter to make a writing-stand[2] specially for me, as I could not procure such a thing anywhere. So I have for some days past been fitted up for work, though able to do but little. The interruption was too great, and too violent, so that at first my composition[3] appeared utterly strange to me. Let us hope that I may soon find myself again—or shall I give it up altogether?

'But, heavens! what stuff I am writing; see if you can make head or tail of it. Sainton fills your cigar cases for me regularly with excellent weeds.

'I am longing for beautiful spring weather; before we get that, my cold is not likely to disappear. I should love to make a few excursions, but I dare say I shall have to deny myself everything, so as not greatly to increase my expenses or disturb my arrangements, made with a view to the greatest possible

---

[1] Wagner uses the word *Schafgarbe* (yarrow) here for the sake of the play on 'Schaf' (sheep). I am not aware that sheep eat yarrow, but quite ready to believe that Wagner knew all about it. Anyhow, a punster would ignore such a trifle.

[2] Wagner means a *high* desk, at which he could write while *standing*.

[3] Die Walküre.

economy; for without a fearful lot of money it is quite impossible to get on in this place. You hardly seem to realise this.

'Yesterday I received a letter from my good wife; my best greetings to her, and let her know whatever there may be sensible in this letter, because I must to-day refer her to you as regards news from me. Tell her to rest assured that she is a thousand times better off in Zürich than I am in London, and that I am looking forward with pleasure to my return.

'My kindest regards to Auntie Wesendonck and Auntie Myrrha. Tell them that everything is all right, splendid, first-rate—but they will take that for granted. Remember me also to the esteemed Sunday guests, and tell Baumgärtner [1] it is said that even in London "gute Wy" [2] can be had. Accept a thousand thanks for your true and heartfelt (*innige*) friendship. If you ever think of giving me up, let me know in good time; in that case I shall remain in London! Farewell, and keep in your heart your   R. WAGNER.'

II

'*April* 5, 1855.

'DEAR "UNCLE,"—Continue like this, and you will soon be promoted to "father"! I was on the point of writing to pour out everything to you, from the creation of the world to the development of English music, when your last letter arrived, which necessitates my beginning at once somewhat more promptly and precisely. Well, then: What the joke in *Punch* [3] means I do not know; I can only assure you that I have not raised any money by means of a promissory note. After the

---

[1] Wilhelm Baumgärtner, composer of songs, vocal quartets, etc., Musikdirektor at St. Gall, died at Zürich March 1867, aged 47.

[2] I cannot guess what 'Wy' may be; perhaps some Zürich or Swiss reader can enlighten me?

[3] This is the joke in *Punch* (March 31, 1855, page 127). No wonder Wagner couldn't see it :—

A WAG ON WAGNER.

We do not know what Herr Wagner's new musical theory may consist of, but we should say that 'the Music of the Future' must be composed principally of 'Promissory Notes,' made payable at two, three, or six months after date.

second concert Mr. Anderson inquired of Sainton whether he knew how they were to arrange about my fee, to which Sainton replied: "How should I know? *Faites ce que vous voulez!*" Thereupon Mr. Anderson sent me a cheque for fifty pounds, my fee for the first two concerts, which I cashed, and with which I mean to manage for a long time to come. What *Punch* means should therefore worry you as little as it affects me. I may add that nobody here had mentioned the matter to me; nor had I read it. Perhaps I may learn what the point was; in that case I shall let you know.

'Now, then, let us leave English business matters for English music, by which latter also—as you learn from *Punch*—only business is meant. You, too, appear to cherish some hope that I may yet be able to do some English music, that is, business here. My letter about the second concert seems to have been the cause of it. However unpractical I may be, and however little of the man of the world there may be about me in your opinion, I really must this time counsel my enthusiastic friends to be more sober and moderate, and ask them not to expect anything from me in English music. It may be true that latterly my music has pleased the public; I receive proof of this even now. Good! but that ends the matter. The people are as pleased with the dullest stuff as with my music; and quite as much as my own performances, they applaud, on the following day, performances of the most atrocious kind. So I have indeed succeeded in raising myself to the height of the most miserable London music-making (*Musikmacherei*), and I stand on a level with other local heroes. That is something like!

'Now the thing would be for me to do exactly what the others do, so as to derive some advantage from their appreciation; in fact, I ought to be able to do it better than they, if I meant to expect anything from it. But here, dearest friend, we arrive at the point where I am of no use at all. In the end, and under strong guidance and inspiriting instruction, I should even have to reconcile myself to being a ne'er-do-well amongst ne'er-do-wells (*mit Lumpen ein Lump zu sein*). Oh! what does not a man learn when he has an aim, an object in view, which he must absolutely and of necessity reach! But the difficulty is this, that with the best will in the world I cannot find any aim which I could attain thereby. My aims, dearest Uncle, are else-where, and as remote as Heaven itself from all one can attain here! I thought you knew that. But enough of this! I am here, and shall hold out until the eighth concert. Surely you expect nothing further from me? You ask for newspapers. Very well, but what are they to contain? Something with which you can throw dust in people's eyes with regard to my successes here? Only the *Illustrated* [*London*] *News* and the *Daily News* would answer for that purpose. These are supplied by the paid secretary of the Philharmonic with appreciative articles about the Society's concerts, and consequently also about my perform-ances. Several critics find the tone of Messrs. D. and C.[1] too impertinent, and therefore write lukewarm reports in which they give me credit for one thing or another that is good, but, on the other hand, do not deny other qualities that are bad. The ability to judge me, yea even to listen without prejudice to what I perform, I must deny to every one of them. The two I have named know best what they want; they are paid to prevent me from succeeding, and thus they earn their daily bread, which is not so cheap in London as many an American fancies. Every one who lives here is so thoroughly convinced of the rascality, impertinence, corruptness, and blackguardism of the London press that—in all sincerity—I do not like to soil my hands even by touching such papers. Whoever really does know some-thing, and really *has* an independent opinion, does not mix with this crew. Thus I have been assured that a certain careful veering round on the part of the critic of the *Morning Post* after the second concert was anticipated, because *The Times*, etc., had pounced upon me so unmercifully. This necessitated caution on the part of the former, because not one of them cares to entirely dissociate himself from his colleagues, as occa-sions may ultimately arise when they have to be of service to one another.

'The Editor of *The Times* alone seems to have considered D.'s invective too strong and coarse, for which reason he is said not to have inserted D.'s account of the second concert. Now it is possible that this unexpected incident may react encouragingly upon the other papers, and that an advance in my favour may

---

[1] Davison and Chorley.

M

again be observed. It may be that in this manner, and with the continued favourable disposition of the real public, everything may turn in my favour after all, to which end this and that manœuvre of the Philharmonic—which is fighting for its very existence—might contribute a great deal. Therefore you may be quite right when you say: "It can't be helped; it is the way of the world, and you will ultimately be appreciated!" Is it possible? But I? What purpose have *I* in view? To conduct symphonies which—to be sincere—I made it my business to do in Zürich only in exceptional cases and to please *you* and *yours*? And what else? The "Tannhäuser March" and one of my overtures? And then? Thank you!

'You see that my mood is none of the sweetest; it is not because I expected anything here in which I am now disappointed, but because others continue to expect something from a wholly fruitless conflict between my real being (*Wesen*) and another being utterly strange to me. I, for my part, have already found the necessary repose to look at the matter with equanimity and irony, and to wait until the thing comes to an end. We shall have fine weather; I shall often go and see the wild beasts, and in the end I shall return home with a few pence saved. What more can one want?

'Oh! what a quantity of lovely music they make here. I was recently at a concert of the New Philharmonic Society. We had overtures, symphonies, concertos, choruses, airs, etc., one after the other; it was a real joy. Dr. Wylde conducted everything, slap-bang (*Klitsch-klatsch*) until the whole was got through, which was rather late. *Publicus* applauded as usual, and the next day this concert was described in all the papers as the most beautiful of the whole season. Directly after the second concert which I conducted, this "New Philharmonic" concert was praised by the critics most favourably disposed towards me in exactly the same terms as mine. Perhaps you would like me to send you these papers?

'But the real delight of the English is the oratorio; in that, music becomes to them the interpreter of their religion—*passez-moi le mot!* For four hours they will sit in Exeter Hall and listen to one fugue after another with the sure conviction that they are doing a good work, for which by and by, in Heaven, they shall hear nothing else but the most lovely Italian operatic airs. Mendelssohn has beautifully grasped this ardent longing of the English public. He has composed and conducted oratorios for them, whereby he has become the real saviour of the English musical world. Mendelssohn is to the English exactly what the Jehovah of the Jews is to the latter. So now Jehovah's wrath strikes unbelieving me, for you know that amongst other great qualities a vast deal of vindictiveness is attributed to the God of the Jews. Davison is the High Priest of this divine wrath. What does Auntie [1] say to my writing an oratorio for Exeter Hall?

'Now I must tell you something about the Beneckes. That will be no small matter, for they are a very large family. They live in Campervall (*sic!*) eight miles from my house, and regularly every Sunday evening they gather to the number of about a quarter of a hundred heads. He is a very nice fellow, bourgeois from head to foot, well meaning and musical. *She* is a relation of Mendelssohn, clever, reserved and—not bad. Daughter, sons, brothers-in-law, sisters-in-law, cousins, male and female, sit down to tea directly after dinner—quite different from your home—and let two or three other relations sing or play to them—of course only Mendelssohn. I have passed through this experience twice already; next Sunday I am unfortunately otherwise engaged. The "quarter hundred" are as yet, perhaps, hardly clear in their own minds what to think of me; probably this will come in course of time. I fancy that Benecke's goodwill may show itself in a little quiet influencing of the press (*gemüthliche Bearbeitung der Presse*). If this should result in the production of a really thoughtful article, I will send it to you. At present the only thing of interest I could send you is the programme book of the second concert with the translation of the *Lohengrin* extracts and the explanatory remarks anent the Ninth Symphony. But such things, unless printed in newspapers, cannot be sent *sous bande* in this country, and if enclosed in a letter it might cost you too much at this time, when you are about to start building. You see how passionately I am given to saving.

[1] Mrs. Wesendonck.

'Now what else can I have to tell you? I really cannot
remember anything interesting. I have accepted your long
letter with deep thanks as the heartfelt outpourings of a friend,
and have made everything in it my own, excepting the consolation, for which I have no longer a proper organ. If I need
encouragement to live happily in my mission as artist (*um
meiner inneren Aufgabe als Künstler froh zu leben*), assurances
of friendship such as yours will contribute not a little to that
end; of that you may rest assured. Give my thanks also to
Auntie, and tell her that I shall stick to my post, but that my
work[1] is progressing slowly. I have almost completely forgotten my composition, and have often to think for a long time
how I intended this or that in it; here in London I have completely lost my inner consciousness of it. The day before
yesterday I completed the First Act with great trouble, and
already I am satisfied with the hope of finishing at least the
Second Act here. But the Third Act I must keep for Seelisberg,[2]
where, however, I shall not unfortunately be able to begin *Jung
Siegfried*. I shall be happy if there I find my work once more
and regain courage for *Jung Siegfried*. Believe me, I ought not
to have come to London! But that is the result *quand on n'a
pas l'esprit de son âge*, as you gave me to understand. Well,
everything will turn out all right, and I shall bring 1000 francs
with me. So after all the whole affair has its reward: how
many risk the scaffold for much less!

'My greetings to my old lady; she has learnt to-day all about
my lodging. Greet Myrrha also, and remain true to me, even
if I cannot send you any nice newspaper articles soon. Wish
that I could say "Auf baldiges Wiedersehen!"—Your R.W.'

III

'A thousand hearty thanks for your kind letter; it has given
me great and true joy and has done me good, through and
through! I send you these lines immediately after the receipt
of yours so as not to let any London air blow between its
effect upon me and my reply to you. Believe me, my yearning

---

[1] The scoring of *Die Walküre*.
[2] A lovely spot on the Lake of Lucerne.

for home is great. I have neither rest nor happiness, and if you can imagine a tiger in its cage for ever turning round and round, with the one single thought of how to manage to get through the bars, you have a picture of my daily unrest before you. But be assured that I do not blame you for having advised me to start on this London expedition. I can think of no one who would not have advised me thus. Indeed *I* ought to have known myself better; *I* was guilty of an inconsistency for which I must now quite rightly suffer. Were I only a musician, everything would have been quite in order; but unfortunately I am something more besides, and this is the reason why it is so difficult to find a place for me in the world and why there must needs be a thousand misunderstandings. It is a great nuisance; but this much is certain: I am not in the world to earn money, but to create, and the world should see to it, that I can do this *undisturbed*. But, as you know, the world cannot be compelled; it does exactly whatsoever it pleases, just as I would like to do myself. So here we are, the world and I, two obstinate heads, one against the other. Of course the thinner skull is likely to be broken; hence probably my frequent nervous headaches! You, dearest friend, have placed yourself between us with the best of intentions, no doubt, for the purpose of weakening the blows: take care lest you receive a share! But the cause of my present deep dejection lies really more in myself than in the unexpected in my London experiences. These experiences only confirm what I have long known, and as I have lately always been anxious to have to do with a few choice spirits only, claiming nothing from the general public except, perhaps, the respect due to the higher rank (*dem Höheren*), I might console myself with the thought that I have at least become very dear individually to many. The really repugnant and deeply humiliating thing to me is, to a large extent, the character of my work here, since I am compelled to play the *rôle* of concert-conductor and put up with the most inartistic views and customs without having even the satisfaction of knowing that my objections are understood. Well, I have committed a folly, and however hard it may be for me, I have decided to hold out, to please my wife, who otherwise would be greatly troubled.

'But this latest experience will decide me never again to risk an inner conflict of this kind, and completely to shun this unsatisfying music-making, so that I may concentrate all my powers on my creative work. My sojourn in London has been very detrimental to my work. It has put me back almost a whole year, as my spirit (*Geist*) is now so exhausted that for the rest of the year I must be satisfied if it proves equal to *Die Walküre*. I must needs reserve *Jung Siegfried* for next year. This resignation alone gives me a little peace.

'To my great inward satisfaction I find, after your dear letter of to-day, there is no need for explanations as regards all my London affairs; you understand all, and feel with me! Believe me, I hold this to be gain! The sharpness of every pain is soon blunted when one meets with sympathy. Verily, this is perhaps the only source of the truest and happiest love. Let us, therefore, only think of a happy meeting!

'I learned, with heartfelt joy, that your dear wife is quite well again. Give her my best thanks for the Bass-theme. I am not to make a fugue on it, am I? and get another purse! Heavens! Those who know my stock of purses must verily believe that with reference to your dear wife I have become a stock-jobber.[1] I do not get a real chance of wearing them out, and there are reasons for it. But, perhaps, an occasion may yet arise when I can stuff them all full to bursting. From New York I have just received a preliminary inquiry, whether I feel inclined to accept a special invitation from several societies to go there—perhaps in two months—personally to continue the propaganda of my compositions, which has already been begun with great success by others. So you see that the second edition of London is already in preparation. Indeed, if necessary, I need not unpack in Zürich, but continue at once to America. Or shall I wait till you are settled in your country seat? I see you call it "Hochwyl"; but I don't care, I shall call it "Wesenheim," and shall always call it so. Now we will see which name will prevail! To-day give my greetings to the

---

[1] 'Wer meinen Vorrath an Börsen kennt, müsste wahrlich glauben, ich sei in Beziehung auf Ihre liebe Frau Börsenspekulant geworden!' A quite untranslatable play on the word *Börse*, which means both purse and Exchange.

Hotel Baur, and all that therein is ; in doing so, do not forget wife and child. "Gott befohlen !" "Auf Wiedersehen !" This day five weeks I start ; may I find peace and refreshment in your midst ! A thousand thanks for all your friendship. Your R.W.'

The above is the last of the letters addressed to Wesendonck from London. Our contemporary, the *Allgemeine Musik Zeitung*, published many others, dating from the years 1853 to 1870, and written from Palanza (Lago Maggiore), Zürich, Mornex (Lake of Geneva), Venice, Lucerne, Paris (with particulars of the *Tannhäuser* rehearsals and the composition of the new *Venusberg* music, which it appears was finished at 2.30 A.M. one night in January 1860), Bieberich (re *Die Meistersinger*), showing his special fondness for the character of Pogner,[1] Munich and Triebschen. That all of them are full of interest goes without saying ; but the never-ending groans respecting his terrible financial difficulties and worries, and the letters of thanks for assistance promptly and frequently rendered by his friend, cannot but prove somewhat depressing.

Otto Wesendonck died in Berlin in November 1896, aged 82. His wife, Mathilde, survives him. He was a rich, cultured, art-loving merchant, and had made Wagner's acquaintance at Zürich in 1852. It was he who placed the little villa in Enge, a suburb of Zürich, at Wagner's disposal, in which the master sketched *Tristan* and wrote the Second (Forest) Act of *Siegfried*, and I believe it was there also, one lovely spring morning, that he conceived the unspeakably beautiful 'Charfreitags-zauber' in *Parsifal*. That the great master was happy under Wesendonck's roof, this lovely, sunshiny music amply proves. Frau Wesendonck is the poet of the 'Fünf Gedichte,' composed by Wagner, 'Der Engel,' 'Stehe Still,' 'Im

---

[1] In which he fancies he 'has erected a monument to a friend' (meaning Wesendonck, no doubt).

Treibhaus,' 'Schmerzen,' and 'Träume.' The orchestral
arrangement of the last-named famous song was played
for the first time outside her rooms early one December
morning in 1858, by a small band of eighteen, conducted
by the composer. It was her birthday, and this beautiful
Morgenmusik the master's delicate and thoughtful birthday present to his friend and poet, just as the delicious
'Siegfried Idyll' was composed for and performed on
Frau Cosima Wagner's birthday in 1870. The 'Album
Sonata' in E flat was also written for the same lady. It
bore originally the inscription: 'Sonate für Mathilde
Wesendonck,' and the motto: 'Wisst ihr, wie das wird.'[1]

Many other particulars of Wesendonck's friendly intercourse with the master was given by Mrs. Wesendonck in
No. 7 of last year's (1896) *Allgemeine Musik Zeitung,* to
which I must refer those who, like myself, consider every
little detail of a great man's life and work of the utmost
interest.

One more extract from a letter dated 1852, before I
conclude. Wagner writes from Palanza:

'How is Donna Mathilda's study of Thorough Bass progressing? I hope she will have finished her first fugue by the
time I return. I will then teach her how to compose operas à
la Wagner, so that she may, at least, make some use of her
knowledge. Afterwards you will have to sing in them; we must
get your part translated into English, because you only sing in
English.'

Query: What English songs can Wesendonck have
sung in 1852? *and to Richard Wagner!*

---

[1] A quotation from *Götterdämmerung.* Wagner little suspected the answer
to his query, viz. that his P.F. Sonata would ere long become an orchestral
piece !

Purcell's 'King Arthur'

J. A. FULLER MAITLAND

MOST people, even among musicians, have so little idea
of what is implied in the work of editing the music of a
past day for performance in the present, that I may
perhaps be excused for giving a more or less detailed
account of the various processes by which one of Purcell's most famous compositions was prepared for the
Birmingham Festival of 1897.

As with a good many other things, the work was a
good deal easier to undertake than to carry through. In
suggesting the choice of *King Arthur* to the committee, I
was partly guided by the patriotic nature of Dryden's
play, which seemed particularly suitable for a year of
loyal rejoicing, and partly also by the fact that a certain
amount of editorial skill had been bestowed upon the
work by Professor Edward Taylor, who edited it for the
Musical Antiquarian Society in 1843. Thus it seemed
that one would at least be guided to the most important
sources from which a complete edition might be made.
It is curious that no vocal score of a work so well known
by name, and one containing so many numbers familiar

to all English musicians, should have been accessible. So far as I am aware, there was only one edition made between 1843 and the year of the Festival ; it was prepared by a conscientious and thoroughly competent musical antiquary, but for some reason or other the copies were withdrawn from circulation soon after its appearance. The same bad luck seems to have pursued this music from the beginning, and it is probable that no work of equal celebrity has had a more chequered career. It was, perhaps, not much to be wondered at that the composer's own score of the incidental music and Dryden's play should have been lost soon after its first production, and Mr. W. H. Cummings is probably right in surmising that some careless manager is to be blamed for the loss, and that in the disappearance of the MS. is to be found the reason of the comparative paucity of the extracts included in the posthumous collection of airs called 'Orpheus Britannicus,' as well as for the incorrect version in which some of them appear there. The pieces that were accessible to 'Madam Purcell' after her husband's death seem to have come to light gradually, as the second part of the collection, issued four years later, contains no addition to the extracts, and in the second edition of the whole, in 1712, five more numbers, including three of the longest and most important in the work, made their first appearance in print. The overture in D minor (placed in my edition before the fourth act), and the *entr'actes*, or 'act-tunes,' as they were called, together with other pieces, to the number of thirteen in all, were included in the 'Ayres for the Theatre,' another posthumous publication, containing the instrumental portions of many compositions by Purcell, written as incidental music to plays. Besides these two printed collections, of the vocal and instrumental portions respectively, a good many MSS., dating from various periods in the eighteenth century, exist, all of which have this peculiarity—that they agree in omitting the interludes which find a place in 'Ayres for the Theatre.' Very few of these MSS. present exactly the same sequence of numbers, and each has its own peculiarities of reading in matters of detail; if it were not that Dryden's play has been preserved in absolutely authoritative form, we should be completely at a loss to decide upon the right arrangement of the various sections.

The first systematic attempt to put the *King Arthur* music in order seems to have been made by Arne, in view of the revival of the play in 1770 at Drury Lane. He preserved all the music of Purcell that was then to be found, adding music of his own for certain numbers for which no music was forthcoming. Five later revivals are mentioned by Professor Taylor, the second of which, in 1803, included Charles Kemble and Mrs. Siddons in the principal parts of Arthur and Emmeline. The part of the 'airy spirit,' Philidel, was taken, during Hawes's direction of the Royal English Opera House, by Mrs. Keeley, in all probability the only member of the theatrical profession now living who has appeared in Dryden's play. The same part fell to the share of Miss Priscilla Horton (afterwards Mrs. German Reed) in 1842, when Mrs. Nisbett played Emmeline, the princess whose sight is restored after a number of thrilling adventures. The scene in which the cure is performed is now the only one of those evidently intended for musical setting for which no music exists. There were various other *lacunæ* in the piece, but now all but one of the four missing numbers occur in this section. There should be two solos for Philidel, 'We must work, we must haste,' and 'Thus I infuse the sovereign dews,' as well as a song, ' O sight, the mother of desires,' for an 'airy spirit.' The other absent number is a solo for a siren, with chorus, ' O

pass not on, but stay,' which should immediately precede
the duet, 'Two daughters of this aged stream are we.'
The opening of the fourth act, in which this last duet
occurs, seems to have been lost, as there is none of the
'act-tunes' which bears evidence of having introduced it,
and I have, therefore, inserted the overture in D minor at
this point, choosing the more effective overture in D
major, found in many of the best MSS., for the opening of
the whole, as it is set for comparatively full orchestra.

From the absence of all trace of music for the scene of
Emmeline's restoration, I am inclined to believe either
that it was never composed, or that it was cancelled at
first, perhaps because the introduction of music at a point
of such dramatic importance was felt to be a little out of
place. I am not very sanguine as to any prospect of its
ever turning up, though I should not be surprised to find
the siren's song in some hidden treasury of eighteenth-
century MSS.

Every conscientious editor of old music will agree that
the object which it is first of all necessary to keep in view,
is to restore the composition to the shape in which it
originally left the author's hand, unless there is something
to show that he himself undertook or sanctioned alterations or corrections, in which event these carry the
utmost weight. For this reason, as in literature, the first
printed edition of the work, if issued during the author's
lifetime, or even soon after his death, is of greater weight
than his autograph, if there is reason to assume that the
former had the benefit of his corrections for the press.
Here there is neither autograph nor a complete first
edition to claim the supreme authority, and of the two
printed sources, the 'Ayres for the Theatre' are evidently
more complete and accurate than the songs in 'Orpheus
Britannicus.' With regard to these instrumental numbers,
it has been assumed by Mr. Cummings, in his life of

Purcell, that the act-tunes, etc., are incomplete, since they consist of four string parts only, and it is argued that as Purcell had other orchestral resources open to him he must have introduced wind instruments into some or all of them. But I do not think we need come to so disheartening a conclusion, for it must be remembered that the idea of the orchestra as a composite body was a creation of a very much later date than Purcell. Even in the time of Bach and Handel, the continuous use of a whole body of wind instruments together with the strings was not thought of as indispensable. Our sense of orchestral colouring in the present day has been so refined by acquaintance with the gradually increasing elaboration from Mozart and Haydn, through Beethoven to Wagner, that it is hard for us to realise the simple manner in which instruments, other than strings, were formerly employed. Almost until the time of Mozart the custom prevailed of using single instruments or pairs of instruments in the manner of an obbligato accompaniment throughout a whole number or section. As often as not, the employment of two flutes, for example, in the accompaniment of a song, rendered the presence of all the stringed instruments (except the bass) superfluous; other numbers would be accompanied by strings alone, and in many other ways it is clear that our forefathers' perceptions of tone-colour were comparatively elementary. If an instrument were introduced at all, it was expected to have a good deal to do in its own special sections, and then to be silent for many numbers together. We may compare the old composers' way of treating the various parts of the orchestra in successive numbers to a number of drawings in monochrome, now a picture in brown, now one in green, now one in black and white, while the modern orchestra finds its familiar analogy in a picture made up of a multitude of colours. In the parts of *King*

Arthur, which do not occur in the printed 'Ayres,' there are several instances in which instruments are used in this individualised way, without any trace of accompaniment for the upper strings.

The duet for sopranos, 'Shepherd, shepherd,' is accompanied by flutes, oboes, and basses, while the song for Honour near the end has trumpet and bass alone. In parts of the fine 'passacaglia,' the oboes and violins carry on a dialogue, and in other numbers the two violins are used as obbligati without any support from any other strings, except the basses. I do not, therefore, think that the *entr'actes* were played by more instruments than the strings alone, and my opinion is confirmed by the internal evidence, for there is hardly one of the whole set which have any incompleteness in the harmonies, and very few in which it is necessary to fill up the harmonies of the figured bass. Such filling-up as I have undertaken in these portions of the work, have been mainly with a view to variety of effect, and is not due to any such imperfection in the existing parts as would lend support to the theory that other instruments have once been employed.

As a rule, in editing a work of this kind, it is necessary to prepare a text as the groundwork of collation, that is, on which all varieties of reading in the various MSS. may be noted. In the present case, the Musical Antiquarian Society's edition was ready to hand, and its wide margins allow plenty of space for annotation. The task of identifying the MSS., cited by Professor Taylor, was by no means easy, for he was not careful to give signs by which each might be recognised. But, although I cannot be certain with regard to the six manuscripts he mentions, I am fairly sure that I have seen all of them, excepting only one formerly in the collection of Dr. Corfe, of Salisbury, dating from about 1720. As I have collated

eight MSS. unmentioned by Taylor, none of which contain
the fine song for Honour, I infer that it exists in Corfe's
MS., which hitherto I have been unable to trace. As it
bears strong traces of being a genuine specimen of
Purcell's work, I have included it, this being the only
case in which I have taken anything upon the sole
authority of Taylor. He speaks of a score in his own
collection, 'nearly contemporary with the time of
Purcell'; I take this to be the earliest MS. extant,
namely, the text of Act I. only, which afterwards passed
into the possession of Sir F. A. Gore Ouseley, and is
now in the library of St. Michael's College, Tenbury.
Another of the earliest scores existing is also at Tenbury;
it is in the handwriting of Travers, who indicated the
fact, and the limits of his knowledge of the Greek
language, in the inscription, ' Travers εγραπσε ' (*sic*).
The score in Croft's handwriting, in the Fitzwilliam
Museum at Cambridge, is of high authority, and some
early fragments at Christ Church, Oxford, are among the
more important sources. The Royal library at Buckingham Palace contains a score, portions of which are early,
the remainder having been filled in in the latter half of the
eighteenth century. The completion of this score was
effected by copying either a MS. formerly in the possession of a Mr. Windsor of Bath, or a MS. from which Mr.
Windsor's was also copied : the two scores (Windsor's is
now in the British Museum) are so closely allied in readings
of doubtful passages, that a connection between them is
easily inferred. Two other MSS. of the eighteenth century
are in the British Museum, and another of later date than
these is in the Royal College of Music. Three late MS.
scores are in the possession of Mr. W. H. Cummings, who
kindly lent them to me to work upon, and at Gresham
College there are a score and parts.

It was necessary in the first place to note every devia-

tion from Taylor's edition in the margin of my copy, and
this involved the most minute examination of all the
MSS. I have referred to.   As I have already said, no one
of these is of such paramount authority as would belong
to the composer's autograph, since of only one, and that
an incomplete MS., can it be asserted that it is even
'nearly contemporary' with Purcell. So far as it goes, this
oldest MS. has the utmost weight, of course.   It is when
one comes to the later copies that the chief difficulties
arise in choosing the reading which seems most likely to
be the right one.   In editing a classic of literature, the
readings of the various authorities are weighed, with due
regard to their antiquity as well as to their number, and
the reading which has the greatest amount of support is
chosen.   But in music it is not always possible to do
this.   The weight of MS. authority may oblige one to
put a certain note in the violin part which, perhaps,
follows the soprano vocal part in unison through some
particular passage ; but if we examine the various MSS.
in respect of the soprano part at the same point, a note
would have to be chosen which would contradict the note
already fixed upon for the violin part.   Therefore, at
every turn one's choice is conditioned by a thousand
considerations, and it is sometimes impossible to do more
than make a compromise between various conflicting
evidences.   Here, as a matter of course, the closer acquaintance one has with the other works of the composer
in question, the more likely one is to be able to decide
rightly on what are called questions of internal, as
opposed to documentary, evidence.   There is a whole
class of differences and variations arising from the lack of
systematic and scientific knowledge of Purcell's style and
manner of workmanship, or perhaps I should rather say
from a lack of reverence for his characteristic habits of
expressing himself.   In regard to certain uses of 'false

relations'— a sharp or flat in one part clashing, more or
less simultaneously, with a natural in another—Purcell
was far bolder than the later men, and the transcribers of
the later scores did not scruple to adopt various expe-
dients for smoothing away these passages, which, to their
ears, no doubt seemed very ugly. In such cases, the rule
of textual criticism, that 'the more difficult reading is to
be preferred to the more obvious,' is to be steadfastly
kept in view, for, after all, what we want to get at is what
Purcell wrote, not what various good people in the
eighteenth century thought he ought to have written.

The text once determined upon, the next point was to
decide upon the manner in which the harmonies, indicated
as usual by figures above the bass part, should be filled
up, and whether additional accompaniments should or
should not be introduced. By 'additional accompaniments,' I should explain, are generally meant real parts
written for instruments not occurring in the score, such as
the wind parts inserted by Mozart in the score of the
Messiah ; and by 'filled-up harmonies' musicians understand the use of a keyed instrument to play the chords
shown by that kind of shorthand which is known as
thorough-bass. While admitting that Handel's music, in
the present day, would sound very bare without the
enrichments of the later writers to which we have been
accustomed from childhood, it seemed to me desirable on
this occasion to let Purcell 'speak for himself,' to use the
time-honoured phrase of the programme analyst. Undoubtedly in the orchestras of Purcell's time a harpsichord
would have been employed for the harmonies, and they
would have been played, whether by the composer himself or another, from the single bass line, above which the
usual figures would be placed to denote the chords required. I therefore took advantage of the fact that
Mr. Dolmetsch's new harpsichord is perfectly audible in

N

every part of the Queen's Hall and of Covent Garden
Theatre, and wrote out the harmonies for this instrument,
reinforcing it with a second harpsichord in the choruses
and other louder portions. In one or two places the
second harpsichord echoes or answers the first, but as a
rule it has the same part to play. Thus, with one exception, to be mentioned shortly, nothing has been added
from conjecture in the way of adding to the orchestral
disposition of the work. Perhaps I had better enumerate
those passages in which I was compelled to exercise my
discretion, and to make a choice between two evenly
balanced sets of readings.

In the first place, the 'act-tunes' in 'Ayres for the
Theatre' had to be apportioned to their proper places, for
their sequence in the part-books is clearly wrong, since
an instrumental version of 'Come if you dare' (Act II.)
comes near the end of the set of act-tunes, and one of
'Fairest Isle'—a song occurring in the last act of the
play—stands fourth in the series of interludes. This
obvious blunder in arrangement showed pretty clearly
how little value was to be attached to the rest of the
sequence, but the play itself contained, in its stage directions, indications as to dances, etc., which enabled me to
fix a certain number of the incidental numbers in their
places, and with some few exceptions I adopted Taylor's
arrangement of the *entr'actes*. By a curious oversight, he
omitted the 'trumpet tune,' which I have placed at the
beginning of Act V. In regard to this, I have made my
only addition to the score, but it amounts to nothing
worse than letting a trumpet play in unison with the first
violins, for although it is called 'trumpet tune' in 'Ayres
for the Theatre,' no trumpet part is given there. In that
publication, as I have already said, the overture in D
minor comes first, which I have put as an introduction to
Act IV., preferring the overture in D major to open the

work with. This only occurs in the MS. authorities. The
'Sacrifice scene' stands exactly as it is in the best MSS.,
and in the 'Battle scene' the little interlude on p. 24 of
my edition of the vocal score is placed between the two
verses of 'Come if you dare,' for two very good reasons :
in the first place it is put there in the fragmentary score
already mentioned as being at Tenbury, and in the second
some musical description of a battle is implied in the
stage directions as occurring between the challenge given
in 'Come if you dare' and the victorious announcement
'The fainting Saxons quit their ground.'

The arrangement of the words in the 'Spirit scene'
(p. 29, etc.) indicates not only that Philidel's good spirits
are inviting the warriors to follow them, but that Grimbald's spirits, employed by their enemies, are at the same
time tempting them to risk their lives in the treacherous
marshes. Beyond the rhythmical interchange of the word
'hither' there is no identification of either body of spirits
with one or other section of the chorus, but I have adopted
the hint given in one of the later MSS., that the tenors
and basses are supposed to represent Grimbald's attendant
sprites. I have suggested the contrast between the two
by means of alternate *piano* and *forte*. After Grimbald's
vain attempt to lure the soldiers away, there is a charming
movement for Philidel's spirits alone, 'Come, follow me,'
in which I have again followed a single MS. in the allot-
ment of the opening bars to a quintet of soloists. I have
also omitted the bass at the passage 'We brethren of air,'
as it is undoubtedly more effective if sung unaccompanied.
The words of the duet in the 'Sylvan scene,' pp. 52, 53,
had to be changed ; those given occur in one of the scores,
and are there ascribed to a Mr. Jones, whose claim to
poetical honours is indeed so slight that the absence of
further identification need hardly be regretted. Dryden's
original words at this point are not very wicked, as they

only represent a couple of cautious nymphs who require
definite contracts of marriage from their swains before
joining in the dance; still, having in remembrance the
action of a provincial choir which declined to sing Stanford's *Phaudrig Crohoore* because it contained the word
'thigh,' and guessing at the susceptibilities of the singers
and audience at the Birmingham Festival, I thought it
wiser to be on the safe side. The splendid 'Frost scene,'
the most celebrated part of the music, is entirely unaltered;
that is to say, I have adopted the reading of the best
MSS. in matters of detail. With regard to the history of
the device whereby the 'shivering' effect is given to the
voices, first to that of the 'Cold Genius' and then to the
chorus, I am indebted to Mr. R. A. Streatfeild for the
discovery that the indication of a tremolo by a wavy line
over the repeated notes (*see* pp. 58, 64) was not an invention of Purcell's, but that it occurs first in Lulli's *Isis*,
where a chorus of 'inhabitants of frozen countries' sing in
an exactly similar manner. After Purcell, it was copied by
Jeremiah Clark in an anthem, and finally used in Gossec's
Requiem to express the terror produced by the 'tuba
mirum spargens sonum.' Barring the insertion of the
overture, the fourth act, with its wonderful 'Passacaglia,'
is exactly as it stands in the best authorities. In the
dialogue between the three nymphs and the three shep-
herds at the end, I have allowed the second harpsichord
to accompany the higher voices, and the sonorous first
harpsichord to support the lower. The musical portion
of the fifth act consists of one long pageant in glorification
of England; and the fine song in which Æolus stills the
tumult of the seas before the island arises is fitly preceded
by the trumpet-tune already mentioned. No former
edition of the music has contained the song for Comus
and his three peasants, 'Your hay it is mow'd,' p. 106.
The book of the play indicates that it is a quartet or glee,

but the tune that stands in D'Urfey's *Pills to purge Melancholy* over these words is evidently intended as a solo with choral refrain. No chorus parts are given there, nor does the number appear in any of the older MSS. In the later supplementary part of the Buckingham Palace copy it appears with blank lines for string parts and choral accompaniments. The first part of the tune is not the same as D'Urfey's version, bearing a terribly close resemblance to 'Girls and boys come out to play.' The bass line is given, and is as good a bass to D'Urfey's tune as to the other : I have ventured to fill up the choral parts of the refrain for male chorus, and have altered a note in the third bar which in D'Urfey is clearly due to a misprint. The words are the first and fourth of Dryden's. In deference to clerical prejudices, I have omitted the others, one of which runs—

'We've cheated the parson, we'll cheat him again,
For why should a blockhead have one in ten?'

In the lovely song of Venus, 'Fairest Isle, all isles ex-celling,' I have fitted the string parts given in 'Ayres for the Theatre' into the accompaniment, so as to allow some relief from the harpsichord and bass.

The 'trumpet tune' on page 118 stands in 'Ayres for the Theatre' for strings alone ; the addition of oboes, trumpets, and drums appear in the Buckingham Palace MS., and bears strong internal evidence of being genuine. The next number, the soprano air, 'Saint George!' is given, as I have already said, on the sole authority of Professor Taylor; the bulk of the MSS. now existing either ignore this verse, or fit it to the music of No. 33, the final chorus. The final *chaconne* is a splendid example of Purcell's skill in varying a repeated bass, and a worthy pendant to the 'passacaglia' of the fourth act.

For a *résumé* of the action of Dryden's play, upon

which the music is little more than an excrescence, though
a very beautiful one, I must refer readers of *The Musician*
to my edition of the vocal score, published by Messrs.
Boosey and Co., to which the page-numbers given above
belong.

Alfonso Ferrabosco

the Younger

G. E. P. ARKWRIGHT

THE Ferrabosco family was remarkable for the number of musicians which it produced in different countries, and in several generations. No fewer than five of the name published compositions in Italy, Germany, and England in the sixteenth and early seventeenth centuries, and some half a dozen more are known to have held appointments as professional musicians. It is not surprising, therefore, that historians of music from Burney's time onwards should generally have failed in distinguishing between the different members of the family, especially as three of them were named Alfonso. An attempt to bring together into a brief biography such references to one of these as are scattered through the Public Records and elsewhere, may not be without interest.

The second Alfonso Ferrabosco, though probably of less importance as a composer than his father or grandfather, had nevertheless a very high reputation in his day, and as a performer on the lyre[1] was unsurpassed. He

---

[1] See the interesting letter from André Maugars, published in *The Musician*,

has also a special interest to the student of Jacobean literature as having provided the musical part of some of the sumptuous Masques produced at Court by Ben Jonson and Inigo Jones. He was 'born of Italian parents, at Greenwich,' says Anthony Wood, on the authority of Dr. Wilson ;[1] but Wood, curiously enough, omits to tell us that he was the son of the well-known Alfonso Ferrabosco, whose friendly contests with William Byrd, as reported by Morley and Henry Peacham, are familiar to all musical antiquaries. Of this elder Alfonso Ferrabosco it is not necessary to say much here. He was the son of Domenico Maria Ferabosco,[2] at one time Master of the Choristers at St. Petronio, Bologna. He arrived in England before 1562, where he seems to have devoted himself, with some success, to feathering his nest ; and returned to Italy in 1578, leaving his children behind him in the charge of Gomer van Awsterwyke, one of the Queen's musicians. He entered the service of the Duke of Savoy, and settled with his wife Susanna at Turin, where he died in 1588. He had previously sent for his children from England, but the Queen refused to let them go—it is not clear why. Probably she wished to show her indignation with Master Alfonso, to whom she had shown many favours, and who, after he had bound himself in writing never to leave her service for any in the world, was enticed away to Turin, presumably with the prospect of getting better pay. Or perhaps she regarded the children as hostages, in the hope of his eventually returning. The following letter,[3] in

page 215. It is curious to find the second Alfonso called the 'great' Ferrabosco. The Lyre here spoken of was presumably the same as the Lyra Viol.

[1] 'He [Dr. Wilson] did often use to say for the honour of his country of *Kent*, that Alfonso Farabosco was born of *Italian* parents at Greenwich.'— Wood. Fasti Oxon. 'John Wilson,' anno 1644.

[2] For these particulars I am indebted to the kindness of the Avv. Leonida Busi, who has made several interesting discoveries relating to the Ferrabosco family, which it is to be hoped he may be induced to publish.

[3] This letter has been published in an Italian translation in the *Rivista*

which most of these matters are to be found, is among the Hatfield Papers.

[*Historical MSS. Commission. Hatfield House. Part III.,*
p. 869.]

To the Right Hon. the Lord High Treasurer of England.

RIGHT HONORABLE: & MY VERY GOOD LORD: It hath pleased Mr. Vice chamberlain to move her Majesty concerning my suit of the surrender of my patent of £20 per ann. for a lease[1] in reversion according to your Lordships good liking : but since I did get your Lordships honorable hand, for the good liking of it, I understand that Alfonso Ferabosco is dead, & upon this occasion, I did most humbly beseech her Majesty, to augment the lease aforesaid, in consideration of my keeping of his children, & her majesty was partly offended therewith, but by the honorable persuasion of Mr. Vice Chamberlain her Majesty was pleased again, & said that she would speak unto your Lordship for it. Wherefore I beseech your Lordship to grant me your honourable & accustomed favour therein. Right Honorable, the cause of my suit, for the keeping of Alfonso's children is this, I have kept two children of his the space of 11 years, & about 5 years past Alfonso did send commission, unto one Lawrentio Dondieno to bring him his children, & also to pay me for their keeping, but then her Majesty commanded me by my Lord Admiral that now is, that I should not let them depart, by reason whereof I am still unpaid for the said childrens keeping. And now Alfonso being dead it is apparent that I shall be constrained to keep them still without any recompense, unless her Majesty of her accustomed clemency & goodness, take pity upon her poor servant, that hath performed her commandment, most humbly beseeching your honour likewise to consider of it. And I according to my

Musicale Italiana, Vol. IV., January 1897, with letters from the elder Alfonso. It is printed by kind permission of the Marquis of Salisbury.

[1] Mr. H. Davey has pointed out to me that in the Record Office there is a book of Particulars relating to Leases in Reversion of Elizabeth's time, from which it appears that Gomer van Osterwike had lands granted to him in reversion for twenty-one years for services done, though the services are not specified.

bounden duty shall daily pray unto God for your good L. long & happy life. Your most humble servant

GOMER VAN AWSTERWYKE.

[Endorsed.] The humble petition of Gomer van Awsterwyke musicŏn to the Queens most excellent Majesty. 8 May 1589. The Queens grant to be shewed forth.—W. BURGHLEY.

The younger Alfonso no doubt was one of these children. The year of his birth is not known (the Greenwich Parish Registers not going back to so early a date), but it may be placed somewhere about the year 1575, as it is evident from Awsterwyke's letter that he was still a child in 1589.

'From his childhood,' says Anthony Wood in his MS. Notes on Musicians [Bodl., Wood, 19 D. (4)], 'he was trained up to musick, & at mans estate he became an excellent composer for instrumental musick in the raigne of K. Jam. I. & K. Ch. I. He was most excellent at the Lyra Viol & was one of the first yt set lessons Lyra-way to the viol, in imitation of the old English Lute & Bandora. The most famous man in all ye world for Fantazias of 5 or 6 parts.'

The first allusion to him by name occurs on Nov. 27, 1604, when he was intrusted with £20 to be laid out in buying two viols with cases and a box of strings for Prince Henry [See Cunningham's *Accounts of the Revels at Court*, p. xxxvii.]. It is not known whether he was then actually in the Prince's service, but that he certainly was after the following Christmas is shown by this document. (*State Papers, Domestic. James I., Docquet.* 21 Feb., 1605.)

A pension of 1ˡⁱ by yeere for Alphonso Ferabosco, in regarde of his attendance upon the Prince & Instructing him in the arte of musik, from Chrmas last past, during his lyfe, payable at th' excheqʳ quarterly, wᵗout the proviso of not selling or cŏvayeng the same to any othʳ parson.

[Endorsed.] xxi Febr. 1604. Dockett.

The Patent, dated March 22, 1605, is printed in **Rymer's** Fœdera (see *The Musician*, Historical Notes, p. 159);[1] it shows that Alfonso was at the time one of the Extraordinary Grooms of the Privy Chamber.

About the same time, Ferrabosco first appears as a writer of Masque music. On Twelfth-night, 1604-5, Ben Jonson's Masque of Blackness was produced at Court, for which Ferrabosco seems to have written some of the music. His name does not, indeed, appear in the printed Description of the Masque, but a song from it is included in his book of 'Ayres' of 1609. From this time for some years he seems to have been regularly associated with Jonson and Inigo Jones in the production of Masques. He wrote for the ' Hymenæi,' performed at the marriage of Lord Essex and Lady Frances Howard, on the Eleventh and Twelfth Nights from Christmas, 1605-6 ; for the Masque of Beauty, given on Jan. 14, 1607-8, from which he printed five songs in his book of 'Ayres'; for the Masque written for the marriage of Lord Haddington, Shrove Tuesday, 1607-8 ; and for the Masque of Queens, Feb. 2, 1608-9. The printed description of the ' Hymenæi,' in which he seems to have appeared as singer as well as composer, contains an interesting testimony to the warm friendship existing between him and Ben Jonson at this time :—

And here, that no mans Deſervings complain of iniuſtice (though I ſhould have done it timelier, I acknowledge), I doe for honours ſake, and the pledge of our Friendſhip, name Ma. ALPHONSO FERABOSCO, a Man, planted by himſelfe, in that divine *Spheare*; & maſtring all the ſpirits of *Muſique* : To whoſe iudiciall Care, and as abſolute Performance, were committed all thoſe Difficulties both of *Song* and otherwiſe. Wherein, what his Merit made to the *Soule* of our *Invention*, would aske to be expreſt in Tunes, no leſſe raviſhing then his. *Vertuous* friend, take well this abrupt teſtimonie, and thinke whoſe it is: It

---

[1] P. 159 of *The Musician* periodical, not of this volume.—ED.

cannot be Flatterie, in me, who never did it to *Great ones*; and leffe then Love, and Truth it is not, where it is done out of *Knowledge.*

The omission of this passage from the Folio Edition of 1616 might be taken to show that Jonson's friendship with Ferrabosco was no more permanent than his friendship with Inigo Jones.

In the year 1609 Ferrabosco published two books. The first was a volume of Songs with accompaniment for lute and bass-viol. It is entitled 'Ayres: | By | *Alfonso Ferrabosco.* | London: | Printed by T. Snodham, for Iohn Browne, | and are to be sould at his shoppe in S. | Dunstones Church-yard | in Fleetstreet. | 1609.' It contains twenty-eight songs, of which a large proportion are from Jonson's Masques, and is dedicated to Prince Henry in the following terms—

To the most equall to his birth, and above all Titles, but his owne Vertue: Heroique *Prince Henry.*

That which was wont to accompany all Sacrifices, is now become a Sacrifice, MVSIQVE: And to a Composition so full of *Harmony* as yours, what could bee a fitter Offring? The rather, since they are the Offerers *first fruits*, and that he giues them with *pure hands*. I could, now, with that solemne industry of many in *Epistles*, enforce all that hath beene said in praise of the *Faculty*, and make that commend the worke, but I desire more, the worke should commend the *Faculty*: And therefore suffer these few *Ayres* to owe their Grace rather to your *Highnesse* iudgement, then any others testimonie. I am not made of much speach. Onely I know them worthy of my Name: And, therein, I tooke paynes to make them worthy of yours.

Your Highnesse
most humble Servant
ALFONSO FERRABOSCO.

This is followed by the commendatory verses by Ben Jonson, beginning 'To vrge, my lou'd *Alfonso* that bold fame' printed among his Epigrams; after which come some lines 'To the Worthy Author' by Thomas Campion, addressing him as

> '*Mvsicks* maister, and the offspring
> Of rich *Musicks* Father
> Old *Alfonso's* Image liuing.'

There is also a set of Latin Alcaics 'Amiciss. et Præstantissimo in re Musica, Alfonso Ferrabosco' signed N. Tomkins.

One of the songs out of this book was printed by Rimbault in his Ancient Vocal Music of England (1847), and five of them by Burney in his History (Vol. III., pp. 141, 142, and 354). He speaks of them very disparagingly, and indeed they are of no great interest to modern ears. But it is rather unfair to Ferrabosco to present them for our disapprobation, as Burney does, shorn of their lute accompaniment.

The other publication of this year has the following title-page :—'Lessons |·for | 1. 2. and 3. Viols. | By *Alfonso Ferrabosco.* | London : | Printed by Thomas Snodham, for Iohn Browne, | and are to be sould at his shoppe in Saint Dunstones | Church-yard in Fleet-street. | 1609.' These Lessons consist of short pieces, dances, etc., for the Lyra Viol, and are printed in Tablature. The Dedication is

To the Perfection of Honovr, My Lord Henry, Earle of South hampton.

Whilst other men study your *Titles* (Honourable Lord) I doe your *Honours* ; and finde it a nearer way to give actions, then words : for the talking man commonly goes about, and meetes the iustice at his errours end, not to be beleeu'd. Yet if in modest actions, the circumstances of singularitie, and profession hurt not; it is true, that I made these *Compositions* solely for your Lordship, and doe here professe it. By which time, I have done all that I had in purpose, and returne to my silence :

Where you are most honor'd

by

ALFONSO FERRABOSCO.

After this comes an address ' To the World.'

> Least I fall vnder the *Character* of the vaine glorious Man, in some opinions, by thrusting so much of my industrie in Print ; I would all knew, how little fame I hope for, that way : when beside his, for, and to whom they are, I aym'd at no man's suffrage in the making ; though I might præsume, that could not but please others, which I was contented had pleased him. But, as it is the errour, and misfortune of young Children, oftentimes to stray, and loosing their dwellings be taken vp by strangers ; and there lou'd and own'd : So these, by running abroad hauing got them false Parents ; and some, that, to my face, would challenge them ; I had beene a most vnnaturall Father, if I had not corrected such impudence, and by a publique declaration of them to be mine (when other meanes abandon'd me) acknowledg'd kind. This is all the glory I affected, to doe an act of Nature and Iustice. For their seale, they had it in the Mint, or not at all : Howsoeuer, if they want it, I will ease my selfe the vice of commendation.
>
> ALFONSO FERRABOSCO.

There is also a poem by Ben Jonson, 'When we do giue, *Alfonso*, to the light' (which is to be found among the Epigrams in his published works), followed by an Italian Sonnet signed Gual. Quin.

These two volumes contain all the music by Ferrabosco that was published in his lifetime, excepting three Anthems, or sacred part-songs, contributed by him to Leighton's 'Teares or Lamentacions' in 1614.

The early death of his pupil, Prince Henry, in 1612, made no apparent change in Ferrabosco's position, for (as will be seen) he retained his pension of £50, and transferred his services to the new Prince of Wales. From a warrant[1] dated Dec. 5, 1623, granting him as 'one of his Maties musicõs' a sum of £20 'for a new lyra and violl de gambo by him bought,' it appears that

---

[1] See a communication from Mr. Peter Cunningham in *Notes and Queries*, 3rd Series vol. iv.

he had received an appointment as one of the King's
Musicians, which probably brought him a salary of £40.
Besides these sources of income, on Oct. 14, 1619, he
obtained a share in what must have been a valuable
property.[1] (*State Papers, Domestic, James I., Docquet.*
14 Oct. 1619.)

A Graunt for 21 years to Alfonso fferabosco, Innocent Laneir
and Hugh Lydiard for cleansing the River of Thames of flats
and shelfes wh^ch annoy the same to the prejudice of Navigacõn,
wth a grant of such fynes and forfeitures as shal be forfeited to
his Matie vpon the statutes of 27° and 34° of K. Henry the
eight by anie persons for annoying the said River wth power to
them to sell the sand and gravell they shall take out of the
Thames to brickmakers or others at usuall prices, there is an
allowance to them of one penny p tonne of strangers goods and
merchandises to be imported and exported into or out of the
Port of London in ships or other vessles done by order from
Mr. Secretary Calvert Subscr by Mr. Attorney gnrall.

[Endorsed] 14° Octobris, 1619.

On the death of James I., the different musicians were
kept on in their places by Charles, and the arrears of
wages were paid. A quarter's salary, or £12, 10s., was
due to Ferrabosco. His salary of £40 as one of the
King's Musicians was also secured to him, and his yearly
livery; and on the death of John Coperario he was
appointed Composer of Music in ordinary, with a further
salary of £40 a year. The following documents in which
some of these details are found have not been printed in
full.

---

[1] Ferrabosco afterwards sold the Patent, or his share in it, 'for a great
sume of money' to one William Burrell. It was the cause of some dispute,
as will be found in the State Papers, Dom. Charles I., Vol. 303, n. 112
(Dec. 11, 1635), and Vol. 344, n. 86 (Jan. 25, 1638), whence it appears that
Burrell's 'Materialls' (engines, lighters, etc.) were valued at £2100, and for
the Patent £200 a year for five years was to be paid.

State Papers, Domestic. Docquets. Chas. I. 4 January 1625-6.—

A Warrant under the Signett to the Master of the great wardrobe for delivery of certaine parcells unto Alphonso fferrabosco one of his Ma^{ts} Musicõns for his yearly livery during his Ma^{ts} pleasure. Subscr by the Clerk of the Wardrobe upon signification of his Ma^{ts} pleasure by the Lord Conwey and procured by his Lordship.'

State Papers, Domestic. Docquets. Chas. I. 7 July, 1626.

Alphonso
Ferabosco
composer of music.

A Graunt to Alphonso Ferabosco during his lyfe of the roome and place of Composour of Musick in ordinary wth the fee of 40^{li} by the yeere from the death of John Copreario. His Ma^{te} pleasure signified by the Lo. Chamberlaine.

WINDEBANK.

State Papers, Domestic. Chas. I. Vol. XXXI., n. 36.

Grants and warrants stayed at the signett by the Lo. Conway. 8 July 1626.

A grant to Alphonso Farabasco during his life of the place of Composer of Musicke in ordinarie wth the ffee of 40^{li} by the yeare from the death of John Capreario.

His Ma^{ts} pleasure signified by the lord Chamberlaine.

The long document, dated July 11, 1626, which secures the different musicians their salaries, was printed in *The Musician* in an abbreviated form from Rymer's 'Fœdera.'

Ferrabosco died at Greenwich, where he had probably lived all his life, certainly from 1619 onwards, as appears from the Parish Registers. He was buried in the parish church there on March 11, 1627-8. His numerous appointments[1] were distributed after his death, Thomas Tomkins taking his place as Composer in ordinary, while

---

[1] The Ferrabosco family was evidently in high favour with the King. It looks very much as if these places were sinecures intended solely to provide salaries for favourite musicians.

his son Alfonso succeeded to the pension of £50, which he enjoyed as music-master to the Prince of Wales, and also (according to Mr. Cunningham's communication to *Notes and Queries*, 3rd Series vol. iv.) to his place of Musician for the Viols and Wind Instruments, and his son Henry succeeded to his salaries as Composer of the King's Music and as one of the King's Musicians. The following are the documents which relate to these different appointments—

State Papers, Domestic. Warrant Book. Vol. XXVI., No. 53.

CHARLES R.

Charles by the grace of God etc. To all men to whom etc. greeting. Knowe yee that we for certeine good causes & consideracŏns vs heerunto especially moving of oʳ especiall grace certeine knowledge & meere mocŏn Have given and granted and by theis presents for vs oʳ heires and succʳˢ doe give and grant vnto oʳ wel beloved Thomas Tomkins the roome and place of Composer of our Musick in ordinarie. And him the said Thomas Tomkins composer of oʳ musick in ordinary we doe make nominate and appoint by theis presentes. Wᶜʰ said roome and place Alfonso Ferabosco deceased late had and enjoyed. To have hold & enjoy the said Roome and place of Composer of oʳ musick in ordinary to the said Thomas Tomkins during his naturall life. And further of our more ample grace we have given and granted and by theis presentes for vs oʳ heires and succʳˢ we doe give and grant vnto the said Thomas Tomkins for his attendance in the exercise of the said Roome and place the wages and fee of fforty poundes by the yeere, To have receive and take the said wages and fee of ffortie poundes by the yeare to the said Thomas Tomkins and his assignes from the time of the death of the said Alfonso Ferabosco during the naturall life of him the said Thomas Tomkins out of the treasure of vs oʳ heires and succʳˢ at the receipt of the Excheqʳ of vs oʳ heires and succʳˢ by the handes of the Treasurer and Under-treasurer of vs oʳ heires and succʳˢ for the time being, At the fower vsual feastes or termes of the yeare, that is to say at the feastes of the annunc of oʳ blessed

O

virgin Mary, the nativitie of St. John Baptist, St. Michaell th'archangell and the birth of o^r Lord God by even and equall porcŏns quarterly to be paid together wth all such other interteynem^{tes} as the said Alphonso Ferabosco late had and enjoyed or ought to have had and enjoyed for the same. Although expresse mencŏn etc. In witnes etc. witnes etc.

This conteyneth yor Ma^{tes} Grant to Thomas Tomkins during his life of the roome and place of Composer of Musick in ordinarie wth the fee of fforty pounds by the yeare from the death of Alfonso Ferabosco.

And is don by order of the Lo : Bp. of Bathe and Welles.

WINDEBANK.

[Endorsed.]   Tomkins Warrt
15th March 1627.
March 1627-1628.

Exp^r apud Westm̃ decimo quinto die Martii Anno RR Caroli Tertio.   WINDEBANK.

State Papers, Domestic. Warrant Book. Vol. XXVII., n. 12.

CHARLES R.

Charles by the grace of God etc.   To all men to whom theis presentes shall come greeting.   Knowe yee that wee of o^r especiall grace certaine knowledge & mere mocŏn have given and graunted and by theis presentes for vs o^r heires & Successors we doe give & graunt to o^r wel-beloved servant Alfonso Ferabosco one of o^r Musitians one Annuity or yeerely fee of fiftie poundes by the yeere lately enjoyed by Alfonso Ferabosco father to the said Alfonso deceased as Instructo^r to vs in the arte of Musick when wee were Prince of Wales.   To have and yeerely to receave and perceave the sai𝖉 Anuitie or yeerely fee of fiftie poundes to the said Alfonso Ferabosco and his Assignes from the tyme of the death of the said late Alfonso Ferabosco during the naturall life of him the said Alfonso Ferabosco, out of the treasure of vs o^r heires and Successors at the Receipt of the excheq^r of vs o^r heires and Successors by the handes of the Treasurer and Under-treasurer and other the officers of th'excheq^r of vs o^r heires and Successors for the time being quarterly by even porcions at the fower vsuall feastes or Tearmes of the yeere, that is to say at the ffeast of th'Anunciacŏn of the blessed virgin Marye the Nativitie of St. John Baptist St. Michaell th'archangell and the birth of o^r Lord God in such manner and forme as the said Alfonso Ferabosco deceased had and receaved the same. And further of o^r like especiall grace certaine Knowledge and meere mocŏn wee have given and graunted and by theis presentes for vs our heires and Successors wee doe give & graunt to o^r wel-beloved servant Henry Ferabosco one of o^r Musitians the severall yeerely fees and wages following, vizt the fee and wages of fortie poundes by the yeere which said fee and wages the said Alfonso Ferabosco deceased lately hadd and enjoyed as one of o^r Musitians, and likewise the fee or wages of fortie poundes by the yeere more, which the said Alfonso Ferabosco lately enjoyed as Composer of o^r Musicq. To have and yeerely to receave and perceave the said severall fees and wages as well of fortie poundes by the yeere which the said Alfonso Ferabosco lately enjoyed as one of o^r Musitians as of the othe fortie poundes by the yeere lately likewise enjoyed by the said Alfonso Ferabosco as Composer of our Musicque to the said Henry Ferabosco and his Assignes from the time of the death of the said Alfonso Ferabosco deceased during the naturall lyfe of him the said Henry Ferabosco out of the treasure of vs our heires & Successors by the handes of the Treasurer Under-treasurer and other the officers of th'excheq^r of vs our heires & Successors for the time being by even porcŏns quarterly at the fower usuall ffeastes of the yeere, that is to say at the ffeast of th'Anunciacŏn of the blessed virgin Marye, the Nativitie of St. John Baptist, St. Michaell th'archangell and the birth of o^r Lord God in such manner & forme as the said Alfonso Ferabosco deceased formerly receaved the said severall wages & fees. Although express mencŏn etc. Ĩn Witnes etc. MONTGOMERY.

This Conteyneth yor Ma^{ts} Graunt of the severall wages and ffees yeerely in manner & forme following, vizt. vnto Alfonso Ferabosco one of yor Ma^{ts} Musitians 50^{li} p annum lately enjoyed by Alfonso Ferabosco deceased as Instructo^r to yor Ma^{te}, being Prince of Wales during his naturall life and unto Henry Ferabosco 40^{li} p annum as one of yor Ma^{ts} Musitians and 40^{li} p annum more as Composer of yor Ma^{ts} Musicke during his naturall lyfe from the decease of the said Alfonso Ferabosco theire father deceased whoe formerly held and enjoyed the said severall wages & fees for the services aforesaid. And is donne vpon significacõn of yor Ma^{ts} pleasure by the Lo : Chamberlaine of yor Ma^{ts} household. WINDEBANKE.

[Endorsed.] 28th March 1628.
Mr. Ferabosco's Graunt.
March 1627-1628.
Exp^r apud Westm̃ vicesimo octavo die Martii
Anno RR Caroli quarto
p WINDEBANK.

With regard to the character of Ferrabosco, there is nothing to add to what can be learned from the dedications of his two books. He obviously piqued himself on being a plain man of few words ; and it is equally obvious that he had a very good opinion of his musical powers, which is, perhaps, excusable in a musician highly esteemed in his day.

It only remains to say a few words about his family. The Greenwich Parish Registers form the chief authority for what we know about his children, but they do not go back earlier than 1615 for the Burials, and 1616 for the Marriages and Baptisms. In these Registers, it will be observed, there is no mention of the baptism of Alfonso and Henry, who must have been born some years before the existing Baptismal Register began. The following are the entries relating to the Ferrabosco family, arranged according to the dates.

Sept. 1. 1619. Susanna Pharabasco, Daugh^r of Alfanso Pharabasco—Baptized.

Nov. 27. 1621. Susanna Pharabasco—buried.

[Presumably these entries refer to the same Susanna. She was doubtless named after her grandmother, the wife of the elder Alfonso.]

Sept. 22. 1623. Katherine Farabasco, Daugh of Alfanso Farrabasco—Baptized.

Oct. 9. 1626. John Pharabasco, Sonne of Alfanso Farrabasco—Baptized.

[This, no doubt, is the John Ferrabosco who afterwards became organist of Ely Cathedral.]

March 11. 1627. Alfanso Farrabasco—buried.

November 9. 1631. Mary Farrabasco. Daugh of Alfanso Farrabasco—buried.

January 7. An° Dom (1635). George Bunckley, of St. Martines in the fields, Musiconer, & Elizabeth Phorabascoe, of East Greenew^ch in the countie of Kent, Maiden, married by lysence out of the faculties.

Aug. 5. 1638. Mrs. Ellen Pharrabasco—buried.

[This was presumably Alfonso's widow.]

Dec. 3. 1640. Elizabeth Farrabasco. Daugh of Henry Farrabasco—(baptized).

[This might very likely be the Mrs. Ferrabosco whom Pepys thought of engaging as gentlewoman for his wife, and who, he says, 'sings most admirably.' Diary, Sept. 4, 1664. She was afterwards in the suite of the Duchess of Newcastle. Diary, May 30, 1667.]

With regard to the Buncley or Buncle family, the following curious note is found in the *State Papers. Chas. I., Vol. CCCLXXV., no.* 80—

East Greenw^ch. The childe of George Buncle is pretended to be baptized by the father in his verbis, (the father beinge a recusant) Besse I baptize thee (pullinge out a glasse of water out of his pockett) In the name of the father of the sonne and of the holy ghost.

M^ris ffarrabasco grandmother to the childe complayneth and desireth, that the said childe may be christned accordinge to the rites of the church of England.

[Endorsed.] Dr. Woodes note.

his gr. would have Buncle called into ye high Com. & uppon his answere it may be seene what is further to be done.

It may be as well to add here that the son Alfonso (the third of the name) appears among the King's Musicians in 1628, 1635, and 1641. He died before the Musicians were re-established at the Restoration, as is evident from the Historical Notes that appeared in *The Musician*. Henry is named among the Musicians in 1628, 1631, and 1645. On June 10, 1658, the Report of the Jamaica Committee recommends a pension of £290 for the children of Robt. White and Col. Henry Ferribosco, 'slain in the service.' This may be taken to be the same Henry Ferrabosco, who would seem from this entry to have served abroad in the army, after losing his place as Musician.

With the death of John Ferrabosco at Ely in 1682, the musicians of the English branch of the family came to an end, though the name survived down to the time of Hawkins, who in his History (1776, vol. iii. p. 316) mentions a Mostyn Ferabosco, a lieutenant in the Royal Navy.

André Maugars

J. S. SHEDLOCK

OF this celebrated performer on the Viola da Gamba
little is known, but that little is interesting. The dates
of his birth and death are not given. He was a musician
in the service of Cardinal Richelieu, who made him Prieur
de Saint-Pierre Eynac. He came to England about 1620,
and remained about four years, and on his return to Paris
in 1624 published a translation of Bacon's *Advancement
of Learning*. In the dedication to Messire Henry Auguste
de Loménie, Maugars informs us that during his last journey ('dernier voyage,' as if, indeed, the visit of 1620 were
not actually the first) he thought he should best spend
his time by observing 'ce qui s'y treuve de plus excellent
et de rare.' In 1621 Lord Bacon, to quote the words of
Henry Morley in his Preface to the *Essays*, 'touched the
highest point of all his greatness,' and it is therefore not
surprising that both the man and his works appeared to
our learned musician well worthy of observation. In
1638 Maugars went to Italy. He appears indeed to have
fallen about that time into disgrace at the French court.
The story runs that he was accompanying some singers

in presence of the Grand Monarch, who suddenly complained that the Viol was drowning the voices. 'Curse the ignorant fellow!' said the accompanist, *sotto voce*, 'I will never play again before him' ('Maugré bien de l'ignorant, je ne joueroy jamais devant luy'). King Louis heard of this, and hence his displeasure.

Now in 1639, or early in 1640, there appeared at Paris a *Response faite à vn curieux sur le sentiment de la Musique d'Italie.* An editor's note to this first edition reads thus :—

'Ce sentiment a esté trouvé si judicieux, et si véritable par les Amateurs de la bonne Musique, et par des personnes d'honneur qui ont cogneu l'Autheur à Rome, qu'ils l'ont jugé digne d'estre communiqué au public à son insceu.'

This *Response* from the pen of Maugars was reprinted in 1672, 1697, and 1700, but with certain modifications. Bayle, in his *Dictionnaire*, under the article 'Baroni,' quotes from the edition of 1672, in which, indeed, it is described as a *Discours*, the passage relating to Léonora. This passage, translated into English, is also given in Hawkins's *History of Music*, the only place, in fact, in that history in which the name of Maugars occurs. Burney, apparently, makes no mention of him.

In 1865 the well-known writer M. Ernest Thoinan, having discovered the original edition at the Bibliothèque Mazarine, reprinted it, with notes, and an interesting introduction, in which he tells the story of Maugars's life, so far as he was able to glean it from the *Historiettes* of Tallemant, the Preface of Maugars to the translation of Bacon, already mentioned, and another Preface to a pamphlet of Bacon's, *Considerations touching a War with Spain*, also translated by Maugars. On the title-page of the latter Maugars describes himself as 'conseiller, secrétaire, interprète du Roi en langue anglaise.' In 1879 the *Response* was translated into German in the

Monatsheft für Musik-Geschichte, edited by R. Eitner. It will be given below in English, and, so far as I am aware, for the first time. Of the interest of this document, written by one who heard at Rome and admired the great Frescobaldi, there can be no question ; it speaks for itself. It is not known whether Maugars ever composed any music. Of his wonderful ability as a performer on the Viola da Gamba there is more than one record. Mersenne, who died in 1648, writes thus in the first book of his *De Instr. harm.* :—

'No one in France equals Maugars and Hottman, men highly skilful in this art, and who excel in diminutions [1] and in bowing of incomparable delicacy. There is nothing in harmony but what they can express perfectly, especially when accompanied by some one on the clavichord. But the former executes alone, and at the same time, two, three, or more parts on the bass viol, with so many ornaments, and with such swiftness of finger which seems scarcely to trouble him, that nothing of the kind has ever before been heard from performers on the viol or on any other instrument.'

Jean Rousseau also, in his *Dissertation sur l'Origine de la Viole* (Ballard, 1687), speaks of the improvisations of Maugars, of his taking a theme of five or six notes, and 'le diversifiant en une infinité de manières différentes, jusqu'à épuiser tout ce que l'on pouvait y faire, tant par accords que par diminutions.'

Tallemant says : 'Qu'il estait un joueur de viole le plus excellent, mais le plus fou qui ait jamais esté.'

I now give the translation of the *Response*, written at Rome, October 1, 1639 :—

'MONSIEUR,—You ought not to be astonished if I have

---

[1] This term, which occurs more than once in the *Response*, implies ' florid divisions of principal notes into rhythmically smaller and melodically differentiated notes' (Niecks, *Dictionary of Musical Terms*).

taken so long time in replying to you. You wish me to express my opinion concerning music, for which, however, I am little fit, seeing that it caused me to make a fugue so incoherent and so discordant, driving me from that sovereign object which alone can cheer my spirit and set my pen in motion. Nevertheless, the hope which you give me that yet once again that benign art will look favourably on me, and that a ray of its accustomed goodness, spread over my innocence, will dissipate all those dark vapours which calumny had raised against my honesty—this hope, I say, begins to restore my courage.

' Now, to acknowledge in some degree the good opinion which you have conceived of my musical knowledge, I am determined to write you frankly the feeling I entertain towards Italian music, and the difference which I find between it and ours ; imploring you, by the love which you have always had for this divine art, and by the desire which I have to please you, to criticise with all sincerity this little *Raisonnement Harmonique.* I therefore undertake to relate to you, without prejudice and without disguise, what hope taught me concerning it during the twelve or fifteen months I spent in Italy mixing with excellent artists, and listening attentively to the most celebrated concerts given at Rome. First of all I find that their sacred compositions display more art, science, and variety than ours ; yet on the other hand they contain more licence. For myself, as I cannot blame such licence, when discreetly taken, and with an artifice which insensibly deceives the senses, neither can I approve of the obstinacy of our composers, who cramp themselves up too much within narrow pedantic categories, and who fancy they are committing solecisms against the rules of art if they write two consecutive fifths,[1] or if they depart ever so little from their Modus.

[1] Stefano Landi in his Preface to ' S. Alessio' (Rome 1634) speaks of

It is no doubt in pleasant digressions of this kind that lies the whole secret of Art; music, as well as rhetoric, has its figures which all tend to charm and unconsciously to deceive the hearer. To speak truth, it is not necessary to amuse oneself by observing closely these rules so as thereby to miss the argument (suite) of a fugue or the beauty of a melody; for the rules were only invented in order to bridle in young scholars and prevent them from emancipation before they had attained the age of reason. It is for this reason that a judicious man, master of his subject, is not condemned by a fixed decree, to dwell always within these narrow prisons; he may skilfully take wing, according as his imagination prompts him to some fine research, and as the force of the words or the beauty of the parts may suggest. This the Italians thoroughly practise; and as in music they are more refined than we are, they laugh at our regularity, and so they compose their motets with more art, science, variety, and agreeableness than our composers theirs.

' In addition to these great advantages which they have over us, they bring better order into their concerts, and arrange their choirs better, assigning to each a small organ, which unquestionably enables them to sing in better tune, and thus render their musical performances more pleasant.

' The better to explain this order, I will give you an illustration, by describing a most celebrated, and further, most excellent concert which I heard in Rome on the eve and on the day of St. Dominicus, in the Church of Minerva. This church is fairly long and spacious; two organs are placed in it, one on each side of the principal altar, where had been placed two bodies of musicians. Along the nave there were eight other choirs, four on one

---

Ritornelli for violins with a bass part moving purposely in fifths and octaves with one of the parts, for the sake of the beauty of the effect.

side and four on the other, raised on stages eight to ten feet high, and facing one another at equal distances. Each choir had an *orgue portatif*, according to custom ; and this need not create astonishment, seeing that more than two hundred can be found in Rome, whereas in Paris it would be difficult to find two in tune. The *maître compositeur* beat time for the principal choir, which included most beautiful voices. Each of the other choirs had a man whose sole business it was to watch this chief conductor, so as to conform to his beat ; thus all the choirs sang to the same measure, without dragging. The counterpoint of the music was figured, and filled with beautiful themes (*chants*) ; there were also many agreeable *récits*. Sometimes a soprano (*un dessus*) from the first choir sang a *récit*, which was answered by one from the third, fourth, and tenth. Sometimes two, three, four and five voices from different choirs sang together ; at other times portions of all the choirs recited, each in their turn, as if in emulation one of another. Sometimes two choirs contended one against the other ; then two others answered. Another time they sang three, four, or five choirs together, and afterwards only one, two, three, four, or five voices ; at the *Gloria Patri* all ten choirs joined in. I must confess I had never been so enchanted ; but especially so in the Hymn and in the Sequence, in which the *Maistre* generally makes special effort, and in which I really heard some wonderfully fine melodies, variety of the most *recherché* kind, excellent invention, and some very pleasing and well-contrasted movements. In the Anthems there were some very good symphonies of one, two, or three violins, with organ, and of some archlutes playing certain airs in ballet [1] measure, and answering the one to the other.

[1] In France about 1670, as M. Thoinan remarks, minuets and other dance music were played in the churches.

'Let us, sir, place our hands on our conscience, and judge sincerely whether we have any such compositions; and even if we had, it seems to me we have not many voices who could perform them straight off. They would need a long time to practise together, whereas these Italian musicians never study together (*ne concertent jamais*), but sing all their parts from sight. And what I find still more admirable is this, that however difficult the music, they never break down; also that one voice from a choir will often sing with another voice from another choir which it may never have heard or seen. And I beg you to notice that they never sing twice the same motets; again, that scarcely a day in the week passes but what there is a festival in some church where good music is performed. Thus one is sure of hearing something new every day. In this consists the pleasantest diversion I have had in Rome.

'But there is another kind of music, by no means in vogue in France, and for that reason it will be well worth my giving you a detailed account. It is called *style récitatif*. The best I heard was at the oratory of St. Marcellus, where there is a congregation of the Brothers of the Holy Crucifix, composed of the chief noblemen of Rome, who consequently have the power of collecting together the rarest Italy can produce; in fact the most excellent musicians pride themselves on being there, and the most competent (*suffisans*) composers solicit the honour of having their compositions performed there, and try to show in them the best results of study. This admirable and delightful music is only given on the Fridays of Lent, between the hours of three and six. The church is by no means as great as the Sainte-Chapelle at Paris, at the end of which there is a spacious *Jubé*, with a medium-sized organ of soft tone, and most suitable for the voices. On both sides of the church here are still two little galleries in which were placed the best instrumentalists. The voices commenced with a Psalm in motet form, and then all the instruments played an excellent symphony, after which the voices sang a story from the Old Testament (*Histoire du Viel Testament*), in the form of a sacred play (*Comedie spirituelle*), such as that of Susannah, of Judith and Holofernes, or of David and Goliath. Each chorister represented a personage of the story, and expressed to perfection the energy of the words. Then one of the most famous preachers made exhortation, and when that came to an end, the music recited the Gospel of the day, as, for instance, the story of the Samaritan woman, of the woman of Cana, of Lazarus, of the Magdalen, or of the Passion of Our Lord ; the singers represented perfectly the different personages mentioned by the Evangelist. I could not overpraise this *musique récitative* ; to judge of its merits it must be heard here on the spot. As to the instrumental music, it consisted of an organ, a great *clavessin*, a lyre, of two or three violins, and of two or three archlutes. At times one violin sounded with the organ, and then a second answered. At another time they all three played together different parts, after which all the instruments joined in. At times one archlute varied some ten or twelve notes in a thousand different ways, each note consisting of five or six beats (*mesures*) ;[1] then another took up the same theme, only in different manner. I remember one violin which played entirely in chromatics (*de la pure chromatique*), and although at first this shocked my ear I grew gradually accustomed to this new style, and took great pleasure in it. But it was specially the great Friscobaldi who displayed endless invention on his *clavessin*, the organ continuing all the while (*l'orgue tenant toujours ferme*).

---

[1] Tantost un arciluth fasait mille varietez sur dix ou douze notes, chaque note de cinq ou six mesures.

'This famous organist of St. Peter's well deserves his European reputation, for, although his printed works testify sufficiently to his ability, still, to judge properly of his deep science, he must be heard in his improvisations of *toccades*,[1] full of admirable research and invention. You ought, therefore, to point him out as an original genius to all our organists, so that they may be anxious to come and hear him at Rome. Since I have happened thus unconsciously to fall into praise of that excellent man, it will not be out of place for me to give you my opinion of the others.

'The performer on the harp who holds the first place is the renowned Horatio, who, living at a time favourable to harmony, and having found Cardinal de Montalte impressed by his strains, got on rather by means of his income of five or six thousand crowns, which that *esprit harmonique* liberally bestowed on him, than by his *bien-joüer* and ability. I do not, however, wish to weaken the praise which he has deserved, since we cannot always be what we have been. Age gradually dulls our senses, withdraws from us insensibly those graces and delicacies, and especially that agility of the fingers which we only possess while young. The ancients were right when they painted Apollo always young and vigorous.

'Besides these two, I have not seen any here in Italy who could be compared with them. There are some ten or a dozen who perform marvels with the violin, and five or six others with the archlute, making no difference between the archlute and the theorbo, except higher tuning of the two highest strings; they use the theorbo for singing and the archlute in combination with the organ, with every possible variety and nimbleness of finger.

'The lyre is also in high favour with them; but I have

[1] Old French spelling.

heard none who could be compared with Farabosco in England.

'There are other excellent performers on the harp, like Signora Constancia, who plays it perfectly. There, sir, is the list of those who excel on instruments. It is true I have heard some who know how to develop a fugue on the organ (*qui suivent fort bien une fugue sur l'orgue*), but not in so pleasant a manner as our performers. I do not know if it is because their organs have not so great a variety of stops as those which we have nowadays in Paris; it seems that most of their organs are only for the purpose of accompanying voices and supporting the other instruments.

'As for the *espinette*, they play it in a very different manner from that to which we are accustomed. I have seen some curious folk who have had some made with two keyboards; the one, proper, for the Dorian mode, and the other for the Phrygian; they divide the note into four strings (*le ton en quatre chordes*) so as to try and play in purest manner the chromatic and enharmonic genera, and to pass easily from one semitone to another. I assure you that produces a fine effect; but as these two genera have not yet been properly treated in our tongue, I hope, if God grant that I return one day to Paris, to give a lecture on this subject, by drawing from the best ancient authors, and modern Italian and English, who in their writings have endeavoured to restore for us these two genera, of which the ancients made such marked use; only the diatonic has remained to us, which at the present day has been truly developed to a high degree of perfection.

'As to the viol, no one now excels on that instrument here in Italy; it is, indeed, little played on in Rome. This surprises me, seeing that formerly they had an Horatio de Parme who did marvels with it, and who bequeathed to posterity some very good pieces, of which some of us have made good use for other instruments, and as if they were our own productions. The father of the great Farabosco, an Italian, made known the instrument to the English, who since then have surpassed all nations.

'You would scarcely believe, sir, the esteem in which those who excel on instruments are held by the Italians, and how much more they value instrumental than vocal music, saying that one man can produce finer effects than four voices combined, and that it has charms and licences not belonging to vocal. But I should not be quite of that opinion, provided one could have four voices in perfect tune, equal, well-agreeing, and not any one overpowering the other. In support of this opinion they state that instrumental has produced mightier effects than vocal, as it is easy to prove from ancient histories, celebrating the force and *vertu* of the lyre of Pythagoras : *Pythagoras perturbationes animi lyrâ componebat*; of the harp of Timotheus, which moved, as it willed, the passions of Alexander and of many others. As, however, these other examples have been related by poets, in whom I have never placed much confidence, I leave them alone, making use only of two or three illustrations from sacred story, so as not to exceed the limits of a letter. David drove away the evil spirits by which Saul was possessed, and quieted the soul of the latter by the melodious chords of his harp. St. Cecilia forced Tiburtius and Valerian to renounce Paganism, and made them embrace the Christian faith, *cantantibus organis*. And St. Francis, in the fervour of his meditations, asking of God that he would let him partake of one of the joys of the blessed, heard a concert of angels who played on viols, as being the softest and most charming of all instruments. This concerning instrumental music will suffice for the present.

P

There remains now, according to my scheme, to speak to you about vocal music, choristers, and the method of singing in Italy.

'There are a great number of *castrati* for the *dessus* and for the *haut-contre*, very fine natural *tailles*, but very few deep basses. They all know their parts well, and sing the most difficult music at sight. In addition, they are nearly all comedians by nature; and it is for this reason that they succeed so well in their *comédies musicales*. I saw them perform three or four last winter, and I must frankly confess that they are incomparable, inimitable in this *musique scénique*, not only as regards singing, but also as regards the expression of words, postures and the gestures of personages whom they naturally represent well. Their mode of singing is more animated than ours; they have certain inflections of voice which we do not possess; it is true they sing passages much more roughly, but now they are beginning to cure that fault.

'Among the excellent, the Chevalier Loretto and Marco-Antonio hold highest rank; but, so it seems to me, they do not sing airs in so captivating a manner as Léonora, daughter of the beautiful Adriana, a native of Mantua, a marvel in her day, and one who has produced a still greater by giving birth to one of the most perfect of singers.

'I should do injustice to the talent of this illustrious Léonora if I did not speak of her as of a marvel of the world; but I do not pretend to improve on those powerful intellects of Italy who, in order worthily to celebrate the merits of this incomparable lady, have filled a volume with excellent poems in Latin, Greek, French, Italian, and Spanish, which have been printed at Rome under the title: *Applausi poëtici alla gloria della Signora Leonora Baroni.*

'I will be content to tell you that she is endowed with

fine parts; that she can well distinguish between good and bad music; that she understands it perfectly well, and even composes, so that she is absolute mistress of what she sings, and she pronounces the words well and expresses to perfection their sense. She does not pride herself on being beautiful, but she is neither disagreeable nor a coquette. She sings with frank, generous modesty, and with sweet gravity. Her voice is of high compass, pure, sonorous, harmonious; she tones it down, or reinforces it without making any grimaces. Her raptures and her sighs are in no way lascivious; there is nothing impudent in her looks, and in her gestures she displays virgin modesty. In passing from one tone to another she expresses the divisions of the enharmonic and chromatic genera, yet so skilfully and pleasantly, that every one is charmed by this beautiful and exceptional method of singing. She needs no assistance with the theorbo or the viol, without one of which her singing would be imperfect, for she herself plays the two instruments perfectly. Finally, I had the good fortune to hear her sing several times more than thirty different airs, with second and third couplets, which she composed herself. I must tell you that one day she was gracious enough to sing, together with her mother and sister, her mother playing the lyre, her sister the harp, and herself the theorbo.[1] This concert of three fine voices and of three different instruments so ravished my senses that I forgot my

---

[1] Maugars's account recalls the concert given by Cardinal Barberini, at which Milton was present, when he heard Léonora sing, accompanied by her mother on the lute. Milton, by the way, celebrated the genius of Léonora in three fine Latin epigrams, very possibly, as has been suggested, for the *Applausi poëtici* mentioned above: the first is entitled ' Ad Leonoram Romae canentem.' In the second there is a special reference to the singing of Léonora, and of her mother's accompaniment, in the beautiful lines:

' Et te Pieria sensisset voce canentem
Aurea maternae fila movere lyrae,'

mortal state, and thought myself among the angels, enjoying the felicity of the blessed. Thus to speak to you as a Christian : [1] music ought by touching our hearts, to raise them to God ; since it is a foretaste in this world of eternal joy, and not to lead them to vice by lascivious gestures to which we are only too naturally inclined.

'In that virtuous house, pressed by these rare beings, I was first compelled to display that talent which it has pleased God to bestow on me, in presence of ten or twelve of the most intelligent artists of Italy, who, after listening attentively to me, spoke some words of praise, yet not without jealousy. As a further test they forced Signora Léonora to retain my viol, and begged me to return on the next day. This I did ; and being warned by a friend that it was said I performed very well pieces which I had studied, I played to them this second time all kinds of preludes and fantasias, so that they really held me in greater esteem than they had done the first time. Since then many honourable persons, out of curiosity, have been to see me, as my viol is only willing to go out of my room for the Purple, to which it has been accustomed for many years to obey. Though I had gained the esteem of honourable persons, it was not sufficient to win absolutely that of professionals (*gens du métier*), somewhat too refined and too *retenus* in applauding strangers. I was informed that they acknowledged I played very well alone, and that they had never heard music on the viol in so many parts ; but that as I was French, they doubted whether I was

---

[1] Maugars was a Catholic ; his father tried to convert him to Protestantism, but, to quote Maugars's own words :—

'ny jamais les menaces d'un père en ma plus tendre jeunesse (à qui Dieu fist la grâce de cognoistre son erreur deux ans avant sa mort) ny le désir d'acquérir des richesses, ny mesmes la crainte dés perils dont tant de fois on s'est efforcé d'intimider ma conscience, lorsque j'étois aux pays estrangers, n'ont pu en aucune sorte destourner mon esprit, n'y l'esloigner tant soit peu de la foy de l'Eglise Catholique.'

capable of treating and developing a theme *à l'improviste.* You know, sir, that that is not my weakest point. These same words were repeated to me on the eve of the festival of *Sainct-Louys* in the French Church, while I was listening to a performance of excellent music which was going on.

'The next day I therefore decided, animated by this holy name of Louys, by the honour of my nation, and by the presence of twenty-three Cardinals who were assisting at the Mass, boldly to mount a *tribune,* where, having been received with applause, I was given, after the third *Kyrie eleison,* fifteen or twenty notes to play on a small organ, and these I treated in such varied manner that I created great satisfaction, and was requested by the Cardinals to play again after the *Agnus Dei.* I considered myself fortunate in being able to render this small service to such an eminent company. I was given a fresh theme, more lively than the first, and this I developed in all sorts of forms, with changes of movement and rate, so that they were much astonished, and came at once to pay me compliments; but I withdrew to my room to rest.

'This performance procured for me the greatest honour I ever received; the news of it spread all over Rome and came to the ears of His Holiness, who, some days later, graciously sent for me, and among other words addressed to me the following : *Noi habbiano sentito che lei ha una virtu singolare, la sentiremmo volontieri.* I will not speak about the satisfaction expressed by His Holiness, after he had honoured me by listening to me for more than two hours. One day you will meet with trustworthy persons who will relate the interview to you in detail.

'The friendship which you have for me convinces me, sir, that you will not look upon this digression as a sign of vanity; it has been made for no other purpose than to prove to you that a Frenchman who desires to acquire fame in Rome must be thoroughly well versed in his art; especially as they do not think us capable of developing a theme *à l'improviste*. And certainly every man who plays an instrument does not deserve to be considered excellent unless he can do so; this is especially the case with the viol, which, being in itself ungrateful on account of its few strings and on account of the difficulty of playing on it in several parts, is specially fitted for a lively presentation of themes, for the production of. beautiful *inventions* and agreeable *diminutions*. But for this two natural qualities are most essential—a lively and strong imagination, and a rapidity of hand to carry thoughts quickly into effect. That is why cold natures will never succeed well. But to conclude this *raisonnement*, my opinion is that if our choristers would take a little more pains to study, and to hold intercourse with foreigners, they would equal them in good and agreeable singing. Of this we have had an example in a French *gentilhomme*, to whom the Muses have not denied special favours. He adjusted so well Italian with French method, that he was generally applauded by all honourable folk, and in addition to other good qualities which he possesses, has deserved the honour of serving the most just and most intelligent monarch of the world.

'If our composers would only emancipate themselves somewhat more from their pedantic rules, and travel a bit to hear music of other countries, I am of opinion that they would meet with greater success. I know well that we have some very capable ones in France, and, among others, that illustrious *Intendant de la Musique du Roi*, who interprets so beautifully and judiciously his charming motets and his ravishing airs, and whose manner of singing is so excellent that all the music of Italy will not avail to make me lose the esteem in which I hold his merit and his *vertu*.

' And, finally, to extract something profitable from this *Discours*, I have observed generally that we sin through lack, and the Italians through excess. It seems to me that *un bon esprit* might easily write compositions with all their beautiful varieties, yet without their extravagances :—

" Nec verò terræ ferre omnes omnia possunt."

Every country has its speciality. We compose admirably *airs de mouvement*, and the Italians marvellously well *la musique de Chapelle*. We perform very well on the lute, the Italians very well on the archlute. We play the organ very agreeably, and the Italians very learnedly. We play the *espinette* in most excellent manner, and the English play the viol to perfection.[1] I confess that I am somewhat indebted to them, and that I have imitated their chords, but those only. Birth and French food have given us advantage over all other nations, for they cannot equal us in beautiful movements (*beaux mouvements*), in agreeable *diminutions*, and particularly in the natural melodies of *courantes* and *ballets*.

' I was here going to finish, but I perceive a crime which my memory was going to allow me to commit, by forgetting the great Monteverde, *Maistre Compositeur* of St. Mark's, who discovered a new and admirable way of composing, for instruments as well as voices. I must, therefore, name him to you as one of the first composers in the world, and whenever God permits me to visit Venice I will send you his new works.

' There, sir, is what you were so eager to know concerning the music of Italy ; but I foresee that in satisfying your curiosity I shall not satisfy the vanity of some of our boasting musicians, if you communicate this letter

---

[1] Hubert le Blanc, a century later, in his *Défense de la Basse de Viole* (1740), is, however, of different opinion. He says : ' Le violon était échu en partage aux Italiens, la flûte aux Allemands, le clavessin aux Anglais, et aux Français la basse de viole.'

to them, for you will thus make me lose their good graces. Nevertheless, if they will open their eyes and cast aside prejudice, as I am detached from all kinds of interests, and if they will well weigh this *Raisonnement*, bearing in mind their over-formal music—unless, indeed, they wish to be held obstinate enemies of reason—they will find my judgment sincere and true, and they will, no doubt, profit by my observations. If that happen, well and good ; I shall esteem myself fortunate to have opened up in some measure the way towards greater progress in music. But if they persist in their obstinacy, I care not. At any rate they cannot prevent me from feeling that satisfaction in my soul which results from having rendered faithful testimony to the truth, while acting as a friend. I thus hope to gratify persons of merit and of knowledge, and not to become unworthy of the profession I have always made of being in all sincerity, your most humble and most affectionate servant, M.'

This letter, as I have said above, speaks for itself. One may not agree with the whole of the *Raisonnement*, yet there is much in it well worthy of attention. The account of the playing of the great Frescobaldi, not on the organ, but on the *clavessin*, the arrangements of principal and sub-conductors for the ten choirs in the church, the allusions to Ferabosco (note the spelling of that name —also that, by the way, of Frescobaldi—different from the usual one) in connection with England, are of special interest.

Reference is made in a footnote to Milton, who was in Italy at the same time as Maugars. It would be interesting to know who the Frescobaldi was whom the poet met there, and to whom, in his letters after his return to England, he sent friendly messages. His Christian name was Pietro ; that of the composer, Girolamo.

Letters from Weber to the

Abbé Vogler and to Spontini

J. S. SHEDLOCK

AT the beginning of the year 1810, Weber, unjustly suspected of borrowing money under false pretences, was banished from Stuttgart, where for several years he had been a kind of secretary to Duke Ludwig, brother of Frederic, king of Würtemberg. He went straight to Mannheim, where he struck up friendship with his namesake, Gottfried Weber, the theorist. The latter, who had been in this city since the year 1802, held a Government appointment, and was a man of considerable influence. A society of musical amateurs (vocalists and instrumentalists) named the 'Museum' had been formed, and of this Gottfried was appointed conductor. With Alexander von Dusch, the brother of Gottfried's second wife, Carl Maria also became great friends; he is, indeed, named in the letter written by the composer presently to be mentioned. Weber gave two very successful concerts at the 'Museum' in March and April; at the second, his Cantata *der Erste Ton* was produced. Of the happy, merry days spent by him at Mannheim, surrounded by art-loving friends, Max Maria has given a graphic account in his life of his father.

At the beginning of April—immediately, in fact, after his second concert—Weber went to Darmstadt to study under the Abbé Vogler. He had already met this remarkable musician at Vienna in 1803, and had received some instruction from him. At Darmstadt Weber found Gänsbacher, an acquaintance of those Vienna days, and a pupil of Vogler's; also Meyerbeer, 'son of a rich banker,' who had been placed under the same master. Weber and Gänsbacher became much attached to each other; they lived together in the house of a widow lady, and at very moderate cost. Gänsbacher in his autobiography tells us how many, or rather how few, kreutzers they paid for their midday and evening meals; breakfast was a luxury which they could not afford. Vogler gave his pupils the German Psalms of Moses Mendelssohn to set to music in four parts, and they went every day to the master, who criticised, and sometimes corrected, their work; only sometimes—for we read that, as a rule, the Abbé took his midday meal with the Grand Duke, and at the lesson, which followed immediately afterwards, frequently fell asleep, pencil in hand!

In May, Weber paid a visit to his favourite Mannheim, where shortly afterwards he was joined by Gänsbacher. They gave concerts there and in other places. They enjoyed themselves much, especially at Heidelberg, where they chatted, drank coffee, smoked pipes, and made music, finding life far pleasanter than in 'God-forsaken, Luther-possessed Darmstadt,' as, indeed, Gänsbacher describes that city in his autobiography. At length, however, they had to return back to work, and we hear of them analysing the works of Handel and Bach under Vogler's direction.

Now, on the 10th of June, Weber wrote the following letter to his namesake at Mannheim :—

'DEAR BROTHER IN MUSICAM,—That is a confoundedly pleasant piece of trash, which even the devil himself could at first make nothing of. With your pen you have counterpointed in fine fashion against (one another and against) me, poor *cantus firmus*. God forgive you for having disturbed me just in the midst of a great and important work ; for the scribbling (as indeed anything from you) has given me no end of pleasure, and now I shall not rest in peace until that sea-dog Johnnie has read the thing. You must know, dear Weber, that at the request of Vogler I have undertaken something which may win for me *great reputation*, but may also set many cursed dogs on to me. (That I forgot to write a part to the variation which I composed for you, torments my soul like an unresolved ninth.) He has improved and revised twelve *Chorales* of Sebastian Bach (You cursed fellow, why did you go away just as Vogler's Pastoral Mass, which Simrock is going to publish, was to be performed ? I really think it too bad of you !), and to this work I have to furnish a comparison plan and analysis ; my part is, indeed, all ready, and I would like to show it you. It is now striking half-past nine, and at ten o'clock Vogler *plays the organ for us*, so good-bye until the afternoon.

'[I have spoken with Vogler, and you know he is a funny fellow ; in short, he will *not* come to you just now, as Schönberger appears here as guest in several *rôles*. He was annoyed at having known nothing about the performance of the Past. Mass ; he would have gone to it. I took the opportunity to impress upon him your request, but he has not as yet given any definite reply, so, for God's sake, give *der Erste Ton* ; as soon as he has decided to travel, I will let you know immediately. Restless spirit !

he can never come to a decision long beforehand. You, however, come over *here*. The address at Leipzig is to the Editor of the *Zeitung für die Elegante Welt*. I beg you to do it soon. I have not yet read the article in the *Corresp.*, but will look it up. Write me definitely the day of the 'Museum,' perhaps Vogler may then quickly decide to come. I am already half-dead here. Do answer my questions in my letter.]

'Now the trash has so increased, that I must make a wrapper for it. Hence I would like still to scribble down what occurs to me.

'I shall *perhaps write Vogler's biography* (let that be between us), that is if I have enough perseverance. I have made acquaintance with Schönberger, because I would much like to get her for my concert at Frankfort, whither she is returning at the end of August for the autumn fair; as in summer, without this, there is nothing to be done, I will also put off my concert to the autumn fair, and then, in the favourable season of the year, I will go on my way. Meanwhile, I will compose this and that. It seems, however, as if one could not hit upon a single decent thought here in Darmstadt; I feel downright stupid.

'[*A propos*, you might say something in your article in your *Eleg. Z* about my striving to accomplish something in a literary way; it would give me great pleasure, only soon. What would I not have given for you to have been here to-day, and to have heard Vogler's playing, and his lecture with practical examples concerning his system of acoustics! Gänsbacher is writing a wee little operetta; the music is thoroughly neat and pleasing. And *Beer* is counterpointing on Psalms.] If I should travel with Vogler, Gänserich is already instructed to seize hold of some hymns. Now I know of nothing else, except that I love thee heartily, [that I hope to receive something from Vogler for the "Museum," and that I heartily greet thy wife and brother Dusch, together with the Huths.   Write soon again to thy Semper idem   WEBER].'

In this remarkably interesting letter there are several allusions which invite comment. The opening remarks were intended merely to give readers an outline of Weber's life and surroundings at the time when he wrote this letter.

And first comes Weber's reference to Vogler's *improvement* (*sic*) of Bach's *Chorales*, and to his own analysis, etc., of that extraordinary piece of work. It was published at Leipzig (about 1810, says the Rev. J. H. Mee in his interesting article 'Vogler,' in Sir G. Grove's *Dictionary of Music and Musicians*), under the title :—

Zwölf Choräle von Seb. Bach, umgearbeitet von Vogler, zergliedert von Carl Maria v. Weber.

(12 Chorales of Seb. Bach, arranged by Vogler, analysed by Carl Maria v. Weber.)

This is not the moment to discuss this curious and, I might add, audacious publication.   Yet I cannot refrain from noticing an article on the subject written by the devoted pupil.   Weber says that it is a bold undertaking to call in question (*antasten*) the fame and knowledge of a man of world-wide recognition.   And so, probably, say all of us.   He, however, trusts that impartial minds will justify him.   Further on he remarks : ' A well-known writer names Bach the greatest harmonist of his and of all times.   Vogler, who is always most ready to honour the services of others, recognises Bach as a rare, great genius, and marvels that without knowing a system of inversions (*Umwendungen*) he should have discovered such rich harmonic progressions, and displayed variety in which he surpassed all his contemporaries.   But that he exhausted the knowledge of harmony is, indeed, a bold assertion, and one which has been sufficiently re- futed by Vogler.'

Weber, it must, however, be said, was not solely responsible for this patronising recognition of Bach's transcendent genius ; the original sketch of the article shows that the writer was to some extent influenced and guided by other hands. At the head, as a kind of motto, stands the following, signed Vogler :—

> 'Recensere errores minimum—
> maximum est emendare opus,
> perficere inceptum.'

Vain Vogler! To try to *improve* Bach was bad enough; to bolster up his *Bearbeitung* with such a sentence was still worse!

The words 'good-bye until the afternoon,' and the con- tents of the remainder show that Weber only finished his letter after Vogler's recital and lecture.

The Pastoral Mass, according to the Rev. J. H. Mee, 'was both popular and impressive.'

Weber speaks of his having to put his letter in a 'wrapper.' In those days, a half sheet, written on one side, was folded, closed with wax or wafers, and the address written on it. Weber writing on both sides (the 'Now the trash,' etc., commences on the other side of the sheet) had to enclose his letter in a wrapper.

Weber's enthusiasm after hearing Vogler's organ recital seems fully justified by all the accounts which have been handed down respecting the Abbé's performances. He played on all the great organs of Europe, and visited London in 1790, where his performances were highly appreciated. In the one season he made from one thousand to twelve hundred pounds. Of the Darmstadt recital I shall have something more to say presently.

The reference to *Beer* (Meyerbeer) is amusing. Counter-point and fugue were daily studies with Vogler's three pupils, and the works written by Meyerbeer during those student days bear traces of severe *régime*. A portion of the above letter is printed in Max Maria v. Weber's 'Carl Maria v. Weber, Ein Lebensbild,' vol. i. pp. 208-9. The passages omitted are enclosed in the above translation, also in the original text given below, in brackets. The reasons for these omissions are by no means obvious; they form, indeed, the most character-istic portions of the letter. The first one is indicated by lines, thus, — — —; but there is nothing afterwards to show that anything has been left out, except an *etc.* at the end, which might be taken to stand for the usual winding up of a letter. It will, however, be seen that, in the lines omitted, there is another reference to Vogler, also to Dusch, the brother-in-law of Gottfried, and to, apparently, some family of the name of Huth. This last name is clearly written, otherwise I should have thought the Hout family, who lived in a paradise of a place near Heidelberg, was meant: with them Weber had spent many happy hours. There are also some strange *verbal* alterations in the published text: *e.g. Simrock* in place of *Kühnel* in the reference to the Pastoral Mass; *als wenn* in place of *als ob*, etc. etc.

The whole of Weber's letter has been given in transla-tion, yet not the whole of the contents of the half sheet of paper on which that letter was written. Besides Weber, Gänsbacher, and no doubt Beer, had attended the lecture-recital. The first two had apparently returned home together, and probably Gänsbacher, after Weber had finished the letter to Gottfried Weber, which had been interrupted in the morning, asked his fellow-pupil whether he might scrawl down a few lines to Gottfried; for a few lines from his pen, of which a translation will

be given, appear *between* those written down by Weber
after his return from the recital—between the lines,
in fact, commencing 'I have spoken with Vogler,' etc.
Weber, as we have seen, had been deeply impressed,
while Gänsbacher's *Unus est Deus, unus est Voglerus,*
speaks volumes. The reference to the organ thunder
makes one think that Vogler's programme included
Knecht's 'Pastoral Festival interrupted by a Storm,' a
piece much admired—or at any rate his rendering of it—
when Vogler visited London in 1790.

Here is what Gänsbacher wrote :—

'Post prandium dupplex. That was a feast for the
ears! To-day, for the first time, I heard the organ
thunder ; truly a god, when alone he sets the thousand
throats sounding. It will be long before anything stirs
me so powerfully ; *unus est Deus, unus est Voglerus* ; was

the whole theme. We jotted down

notes, each in his own way, diligently ; and so the
beautiful remembrance of Mannheim was often repeated.
The latest news is that Weber, summoned to Court

this moment from his has

gone thither with wise despatches. Apart from our little
circle this is the most interesting (event) in Darmstadt.'

Gänsbacher was himself an accomplished organist,
and at the time of the recital in question was thirty-two
years of age, and therefore able to appreciate what was
good. His enthusiastic notice of Vogler's playing—a
notice written, too, while the sounds of the organ were

still ringing in his ears—is most welcome. We now listen eagerly to any one who gives reminiscences, say of Paganini's or Liszt's playing forty, fifty, and even sixty years ago. Despite the knowledge that imagination often unconsciously helps failing memory, stories commencing 'I remember once, many years ago,' always find attentive listeners. But here, in Gänsbacher's hastily scrawled lines, we have, as it were, a photograph of his feelings, taken almost at the moment in which they were so violently stirred. It is, indeed, extraordinary that this Gänsbacher description of Vogler's playing should not have been mentioned by Max Maria v. Weber.

Weber in his letter speaks of his literary attempts. Like Schumann, he was something more than a composer. He was interested in his art generally, and it was in this very year (1810) that he, Gottfried Weber, Alexander von Dusch, and Meyerbeer founded the so-called 'Harmonischer Verein,' in order to further the cause of art, and to promote thorough and impartial criticism.

This little society was founded towards the close of the year, but Weber and his friends had already, before that, contributed articles to various periodicals. Early in the year 1810 Weber had published a first article entitled *Ueber Mannheim,* and other articles.

Weber says : 'I shall perhaps write Vogler's biography.' We know from a letter that he still entertained the idea up to 1818—an idea, however, which was never carried out. But if he did not write a biography of his master and friend, he at any rate contributed an article entitled *Ein Wort über Vogler* to the *Morgenblatt* in 1811. He opens thus :—'It is a recognised fate of great men to be ignored during their lifetime, may be to die of hunger, and after death to be extolled to heaven by hungry publishers. . . . So will it be in the world with Vogler.'

I have already said that to promote impartial criticism

was one of Weber's aims. Here, from the same article, is what he thought, not only of Vogler, but also of the critics of his day :—

'Vogler, who was the first to set to work at music in a thoroughly systematic way, certainly differs in many points from the opinions of other great men. His system, however, is not presented in the most intelligible form. But of all those gentlemen critics, is there one who has taken the trouble to learn it? or who modestly seeks explanation from the author? who, in regard to his willingness to communicate his experience and his knowledge to others, shows himself a truly great man, one who works for the sake of art and of humanity?

'No!—they read hastily, find a few expressions sounding somewhat strange, etc., and, in order to appear witty, or to display a *bon mot*, write criticisms ; and that they may have the laughers on their side, lay hold of any mortal thing which lends itself to ridicule (and in what work even recognised as perfect is such not to be found ?). Thus, as said, there is nothing left to the composer but to die.'

Mr. Mee says that had Weber carried out his intention of writing a life, 'his representation of Vogler might perhaps have altered the universally unfavourable verdict of modern times.' Weber was much attached to Vogler. When, in 1814, the latter died, Weber wrote to his friend Gänsbacher, 'He will ever live in our hearts.' Now, whether he would have written, or perhaps it would be better to say, whether it would have been possible for him to write, a thoroughly impartial biography, may be open to question ; in any case it would have been a thoroughly interesting one.

I now give the German text of Weber's letter, with the Gänsbacher addition. The passages left out of his father's letter by M. M. v. Weber, are enclosed in brackets. There are many small differences in words, spelling, etc., which can be seen by comparing this letter with the published version. One of the most curious changes is the already mentioned substitution of Simrock for Kühnel in regard to the publication of Vogler's Mass. The publisher may have been changed to Simrock, but this might have been explained in a footnote.

'10 *Junÿ* 23.

'AN GOTTFRIED WEBER,

LIEBER BRUDER IN MUSICAM.

'Das ist ein verflucht angenehmer Wisch aus dem anfänglich kein Teufel klug wird, ihr habt ja ordentlich mit euren Federn gegen [einander und] gegen mich armen *cantus firmus* contrapunctirt. Gott verzeihe [es] euch dass ihr mich eben an einer sehr grossen wichtigen Arbeit gestört habt, denn das Geschreibsel hat mir, so wie alles von euch, ludermässige Freude gemacht, und nun habe ich kein Sizleder mehr bis der Seehund der Jörgel das Dings gelesen hat. Du musst wissen, lieber Weber, dass ich eine Arbeit auf Vogler's Verlangen unternommen habe, die mir *viel Ruf,* aber auch verflucht viel Hunde über den Leib hezen kann, dass ich auf Variation Stimme zu schreiben vergessen, dass Sie (?) für dich componirt, quält meine Seele wie eine unaufgelöste None. Er hat nämlich 12 Choräle von Seb : Bach verbessert und umgearbeitet, warum reisst denn du verdammter Kerl just weg, wenn man Vogler's Pastoral Messe aufführt? die bey Kühnel herauskommen, weisst du dass ich dir das sehr übel nehme? und wozu ich einen Vergleichungs Plan und Zergliederung bey der Arbeit schreiben soll, der auch schon fertig ist, und den ich dir gar zu gern zeigen möchte—jetzt schlägt es ½ 10 Uhr und um 10 Uhr spielt Vogler *für uns Orgel,* daher valet bis Nachmittag.

'[Ich habe mit Vogler gesprochen, und du weisst er ist
ein curioser Kauz, daher kurz dass er vor der Hand *nicht*
zu euch kommen wird, da die Schönberger noch mehrere
Gastrollen giebt. Er war böse dass er nichts von der
Aufführung der Past. Messe gewusst, er wäre herüber
gekommen. Ich habe ihm bey der Gelegenheit Euer
Anliegen ans Herz gelegt, er hat sich aber noch nicht
bestimmt darauf erklärt, gebt also den *ersten Ton* in
Gottes Nahmen, sobald er sich entschliesst zu reisen,
erfährst du es augenbliklichst sein unruhiger Geist, daher
kann er nie lange voraus Entschlüsse fassen. Kommt
Ihr doch *herüber.* Die Adresse nach Leipzig ist *an die
Redaktion der Zeitung für die Elegante Welt.* ich bitte
dich es bald zu thun. Den Aufsaz im *Corresp.*: habe
ich nicht gelesen, werde ihn aber aufsuchen, so was eignet
sich nicht recht für eine Zeitung. Schreibe mir doch den
Tag des *Museums* bestimmt, vielleicht entschliesst sich
dann Vogler schnell zu kommen. ich sterbe schon
beynah hier. antworte mir doch auch auf meine Fragen
in meinem Briefe].'

Over the above lines, in enclosed brackets, Gänsbacher
wrote :—

' Post prandium dupplex. Das war ein Ohrenschmauss!
Zum erstenmahle hörte ich heute die Orgel donnern ; ein
wahrer Gott, wenn er die tausend Kehlen allein anstimmt ;
nicht bald ergriff mich etwas so mächtig ; unus est Deus,
unus est Voglerus.

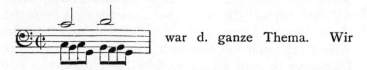   war d. ganze Thema.   Wir

dupten und stupten, jeder nach seiner Art fleissig ; dabey
ward die schöne Erinnerung an Mannheim oft wiederholt.

Das neueste ist, dass Weber diesen Augenblick von seinem

nach Hof abrufen, mit weisen Depechen dahin abging. Ausser unserm kleinen Kreis ist dies eigentlich das interessanteste in Darmstadt.'

Weber's letter continues :—

'Nun ist der Wisch so angewachsen, dass ich ein Couvert darum machen muss. Daher will ich lieber noch hersudeln, was mir einfällt. Ich werde *vielleicht Vogler's Biographie* schreiben (unter uns gesagt) wenn ich nämlich so viel Sizleder behalte. ich habe mit der Schönberger Bekanntschaft gemacht, weil ich Sie gern in mein *Concert* in Frankf. haben möchte, wo sie Ende August wieder hingeht, zur Herbstmesse, da im Sommer ohne diess Nichts zu machen ist, so will ich mein *Concert* in Frankfurt auch bis zur Herbst Messe sparen, und dann in der günstigen Jahrszeit meinen Stab weiter setzen. Unterdessen *componire* ich noch eins und das andere. Es ist aber als ob man in dem Darmstadt gar keinen ordentlichen Gedanken kriegen könnte. Ich bin wie vernagelt.

'[*apropos* wenn du in de Aufsaz de Eleg. 2. etwas davon erwähnen könntest, dass ich auch in litterarischer Hinsicht etwas zu leisten strebe, wäre es mir sehr lieb, aber nur bald. Was hätte ich drum gegeben wenn du heute da gewesen und Voglers Spiel und Vorlesung mitt praktischen Beyspielen über seine Akustik gehört hättest. Gänsbacher schreibt ein kleines Operettchen. sehr artige liebe Musik, und *Beer* contrapunctirt an Psalmen.]

'Wenn ich mit V. verreisen sollte, ist Gänserich schon *instruirt* einige Hymnen zu *capern*. Nun weiss ich nichts mehr, als dass ich dich herzlich liebe. [dass ich hoffe von Vogler etwas für das Museum zu erhalten, und dass ich deine Frau und Bruder *Dusch* nebst Huth's herzlich grüsse. Schreib bald wieder an deinen semper idem

WEBER.

'DARMSTADT, d. 23 *Juni* 1810.'

In 1811 Weber left Darmstadt, and on March 14 he arrived at Munich, where he remained five months, and appeared at several concerts. In the same year he visited Leipzig, Gotha, and Weimar. In 1812 he conducted his *Silvana* at Berlin. In 1813 the post of Capellmeister of the Prague Theatre was offered to him, and he accepted it. 'If God will only bestow on me some post without cares, and with a salary on which a man can live!' exclaimed Weber to his friend Gänsbacher in a letter written August 4, 1816. Such has been the prayer of many great musicians, yet one to which very few have received a favourable answer. Weber had remained at Prague since 1813, but in spite of the salary being a good one, the composer was not satisfied; and, although he had nothing definite in view, resigned the post September 30, 1816. Count Brühl, Intendant of the Court theatres, tried, though in vain, to procure for Weber the appointment of Capellmeister at Berlin in Himmel's place. In that same year, however, he was summoned to Dresden by the King of Saxony to undertake the direction of the German opera. Here again he found a post with a comfortable salary, though certainly not one 'without cares.' He met with much opposition from the Italian company, with the famous Morlacchi at their head. Now, on the 18th of June 1821 *Der Freischütz* was produced at Berlin, and Weber, like one of our poets, suddenly found himself famous. At that time Spontini was the 'ruling spirit in operatic matters' in that city, so that also here poor Weber had to contend against Italian

influence. Spontini had been appointed Capellmeister
in 1820. His relations with Count Brühl, to whom he
was nominally subordinate, were never friendly; and,
moreover, as mentioned above, the Count was favourably
disposed towards Weber. The triumph of *Der Freischütz*
was all the more galling to Spontini, since, to a certain
extent, it eclipsed the success which he had obtained
only a few weeks before with his *Olympia*, originally
produced at Paris in 1819. In March 1822 Count Brühl
proposed a performance of *Der Freischütz*, but Spontini
proposed instead *Le Nozze di Figaro*, and declared that
the means which the Count was taking to attain his
end with regard to his favourite opera did credit neither
to his taste nor to his impartiality. An unpublished
letter, of which a translation will now be given, gives a
vivid idea not only of the unfriendliness of the Italian
composer, but also of the generous spirit and modest
demeanour of Weber. The letter, written from Dresden,
and bearing the date February 7, 1822, is not even noticed
in the life of the composer by his son. In that work a
letter is mentioned, written by Weber to his wife three
days later. It is a private one, in which reference is
made, in case of his death, to his will. The letter of
February 7 runs thus :—

'WOHLGEBORENER HERR GENERALDIRECTOR
UND RITTER.

'MOST HONOURED SIR AND FRIEND,—In conformity
with your wish, I have handed your honoured letter of
January 12 to Herr Hoff-Rath Von Könneritz, and
pointed out to him how particularly unpleasant, especially
to *me*, must be the delay on his part in writing to you.
Before I answer the other points of your letter, allow me
to say a few frank, well-meant words. Surely my letters
cannot be properly translated to you. In yours prevails

a marked irritation, a mistrust in my uprightness, which contrast only too forcibly with the other friendly things which you are kind enough to say to me. My dear, most honoured sir and friend, do not let this discordant tone arise between us. Our respective positions are of such a kind that there is no need for us to say flattering things to each other, if we do not feel thus disposed. You are a man of world-wide fame, an artist beloved and justly held in high honour by your great monarch, and with full liberty you exert a wide influence. So far as I am concerned, I have had opportunity to show by deed my honest appreciation of your works, and that, too, before I enjoyed the pleasure of your personal acquaintance.

'I opened the Opera at Prague in 1813 with *Cortez*, and placed anew on the stage *Die Vestalin*, removing all the insertions and restoring the passages cut, with the care and respect due to such a work.

'And I did the same here in Dresden shortly after my arrival. Why, then, should I now only *appear* to take interest? I know of no outward cause which could determine me to feign an interest to which my inmost heart was a stranger.

'*You* have *no need whatever* of me : I entertain the conviction that you, even if you were my enemy, would not oppose any hindrance to the performance of my works. So let us act together in full confidence, and I beg that you will receive in kindly spirit what, from the bottom of my heart, I feel obliged to say to you. Besides, an artist in his career meets with quite enough petty annoyances; let us not render life still more bitter. And now to your letter.

'I do not think my second letter could have contradicted the first. It is natural that the more one tries to give a work in the best possible manner, it is impossible to free oneself from a certain anxiety in the selection of means;

for one does not wish to have to reproach oneself for anything, nor for the composer to be able to say, thus and thus it would have been better. The splitting up of our forces into German and Italian opera causes that feeling of anxiety more here than elsewhere.

'Cantù holds a high position, and is stronger than Bergmann. Nevertheless he is better suited for *coloratura* than for declamatory singing. The difficulties which I am now enumerating to you must not lead you to believe that the work is not to be given; they are mentioned rather to prove to you how I am considering the matter on all sides, so as to discover what is for the best.

'With regard to the translation, I regret that Valentini has neither time nor musical knowledge, nor are you inclined to have it made under your supervision. Montucci has certainly written Italian libretti, but never made any *translations*, and this is a very different matter. Herr Wagner, however, is master of music and of languages; this he has already shown in *Die Vestalin* and *Cortez*, and it is therefore quite natural that he should be thought of first.

'The establishment of an Italian Opera at Vienna is still uncertain, and, on the whole, this exchange is a subordinate matter. As regards the feeling of the public here in Dresden towards your music, the ever-warm sympathy shown for years towards your *Vestalin* and *Cortez* is sufficient proof that it knows how to appreciate works of this kind.

'The *Königl. Kapelle* thanks you, through me, most respectfully for your permission to allow the Overture of *Olympia* to be performed. It was given on the 1st of February. I was present at the rehearsals, and the public bestowed the enthusiastic applause which must everywhere follow this fiery stream.

' Accept the renewed assurance of my deep respect and friendship, and believe me always, your true, devoted

C. M. V. WEBER.'

The spirit of this interesting letter is clear enough. For its fuller comprehension one would naturally like to be in possession of the Spontini letter to which it is an answer. I have tried above to give in brief form an account of Weber's position at the time at which the letter was written, and of the attitude of Spontini towards him generally. But with regard to the latter I will make one addition. Spontini went to Dresden on June 11, 1822. Weber went to meet him on his arrival, but, as his son tells us, there were no manifestations of warm friendship between them. Spontini gave to Weber a cutting from the *Journal des Débats* of May 2, in which mention was made of Beethoven as occupying one of the highest positions among composers past and present. 'L'auteur de *l'Invitation à la Valse*,' it went on to say, 'commence la sienne en France.' The sting was in the piece mentioned, considering that with his *Freischütz* Weber had already achieved immortality. There now only remains to make one or two short comments with regard to certain names mentioned in the letter.

Cortez was, in fact, the first opera which Weber gave at Prague. The performance took place on September 10, 1813. The work was originally produced at Paris, November 28, 1809.

Cantù, Giovanni (1799-1822), was a distinguished tenor vocalist, 'unser trefflicher Cantù,' as a Dresden paper of the time named him, who sang in Italian Opera at Dresden from 1818 until his death.

Bergmann, Johann Gottfried (1795-1831), was also a tenor singer of note. He was appointed 'königl. sächs. Hofopernsänger' at Dresden in 1816, where he remained until his death. He played the part of Max in *Der Freischütz* and that of Adolar in *Euryanthe*.

The libretto referred to was probably that of *Olympia*, which was given in Dresden in 1822.

Three days after Weber wrote this letter he started on a journey to Vienna, where on the 18th of the same month he attended a performance of *Der Freischütz*. Of that performance he made the following entry in his diary: *Der Freischütz! ach Gott!* He wrote a letter to his wife complaining that all the *tempi* were wrong, either too fast or too slow. This journey accounts for the already mentioned 'will' letter to his wife.

The Letters of

Theodor Billroth

ROBIN H. LEGGE

I

'To be one of the greatest surgeons of his time, as Theodor Billroth was, is quite sufficient to arouse interest in his letters,' says the editor of a volume of these delightful letters, published originally a few years ago in Vienna. These letters range over a wide field of subjects; but it is only from those that refer to matters musical that I intend to extract the honey. Besides being a fine surgeon, Billroth (who died in 1894) was an acute critic. He, the intimate friend of Brahms, Joachim, Hanslick, and many other famous musicians, had had his critical faculty sharpened by contact with these men, and the result is found here and there in the letters. From his youth up he had a passion for music, and was a skilful amateur pianist.

The first of the 553 published letters was written from Göttingen in 1850 (when Billroth was barely one-and-twenty years of age) to his mother, wife of the Lutheran minister at Greifswald.

'When I went on the evening of the 30th January 1850 to Wehner,[1] he had just received from Jenny Lind, who had recently given a concert in Hanover, a reply to his invitation to her to give a concert at Göttingen. Jenny Lind replied that " I would like very much to sing to the youths, and will come with pleasure if they want to hear me." These words impressed me so that I rejoiced all the more at recognising the Queen of Song in that charming girl.

' Do not, dear mother, ask me to describe our joy, our delight and our enthusiasm. It is impossible. One's feelings of rapture for what is great and sublime cannot be described—they can only be felt. Yet I will try to give you an idea of the days we lived with the one and only Jenny Lind. I only fear that when I read what I write I shall find once again how cold and dead is everything black on white, which yet was so warmly felt !

' As the orchestra here is very bad, Wehner invited Bähr, Hambruch and myself to play with him an overture arranged for eight hands at the concert. You will easily understand that we did not need to be asked twice, for the honour of taking part in such a concert seemed very great to us.

' In order that Wehner should meet with as little difficulty as possible in the arrangements for the concert, a committee of the best known of his pupils was formed to receive orders and issue tickets. Wedemeyer was his private secretary, and Breul, Becker, Behr, and I were members. The concert was to take place in the theatre —the largest hall in the place—which would hold some 800 souls. Stalls and seats in the boxes cost 4s. 6d., gallery and pit 3s. Within an hour or two of the opening

[1] University musical director at Göttingen, and subsequently conductor of the Royal Choir at Hanover.

of the ticket-office every available seat was sold, and many people had to go empty away—to our great regret.

'*The* evening came at last ; we were busy practising the overture. *She* had arrived at the Crown Inn, but immediately changed this abode for Wehner's house. (Wehner had met her previously in Leipzig at Mendelssohn's, his teacher, and again at Ems through Mendelssohn's widow.)

'I was very anxious to see her as soon as possible, and so hurried as soon as we heard that she had come to Wehner's house, where Bähr and I hid in a little room that we might see without being seen. The impression which her outward appearance made upon me was unimportant ; I thought her plain rather than pretty, but I was struck by her uncommonly deep and sonorous voice. When she had gone into her room we slipped out quickly, happy at being the only students who had seen her. She was simply clothed in a travelling dress of black silk, a grey hat and brown cloak. Somewhat calmed we went to Breul's, ordered wine, and busied ourselves until late at night with writing out the tickets, and were so overjoyed at the prospect of what was in store for us, that I slept very little from excitement.

'On the following evening, Saturday, Feb. 2, the concert was to take place. In the morning from 10 to 12, and afternoon from 2 to 4, we issued tickets, which gave us a good deal of trouble, since the whole place was in a ferment, and the crowd was so great that I still can hardly understand how every one got away safely. We sat in a small room in Wehner's house, in the doorway of which we had put a table to keep ourselves from being carried by storm by the crowd. Never before had I wallowed so in money as on this day, for I was told off to count it. The receipts were 1009 thalers, among which a roll of twenty-five double louis looked fine. I forgot to mention that this morning a very pretty poem to Jenny Lind was written by my acquaintance, Seiffert, and handed to her by Wehner. It is said to have amused her greatly.

'At last seven o'clock arrived. The theatre was crammed to overflowing; our pianofortes were on the stage. We went up and played the overture to *Jessonda*, which sounded quite exceptionally well on the fine instruments by Rothmüller, for of course each of us was on his mettle. When we were once more off the stage Jenny came to meet us and to thank us. She impressed us so by her words, her grace and her sweetness, that we stood fixed to the spot, quite unable to speak one single word, so that the situation came perilously near to being ludicrous. A moment later she went up, led by Wehner.

'But it strikes me I have said nothing yet of her appearance. Difficult as it is to describe any one, it is infinitely more difficult to describe Jenny Lind. She is of medium height and physique. Her countenance makes a very charming, pleasant impression, although she is not at all pretty. Scarcely, however, has she opened her mouth to sing or to speak, than she enchants every one and moves even the most phlegmatic. She has blonde hair, which she usually wears in " elf-locks " or waved, blue eyes, a very pretty mouth, broad nose and rounded chin. This evening she was dressed in pink, and wore in her hair beautiful green grapes over the coil; in her bosom were more grapes, which suited her admirably, although this may be hard to believe from a mere written description. Except for a couple of rings on her fingers she was quite without jewels. Every one of her movements, her smile, her whole demeanour, is bewitching.

'We scarcely saw her enter before she was at the front of the stage. The applause that greeted her entrance was so terrific that for a moment I feared the house would come down. She was overwhelmed with bouquets and wreaths. The art and grace with which she accepted

these offerings, and her movements roused the audience
to further applause. At last the public quieted down and
all awaited what was to come.

' My own expectations were the highest man can derive
from man as I went to the concert; but after the first
few bars of the aria from *I Puritani* I saw that my idea,
which was by no means a lowly one, was nothing in comparison with such singing. Do not ask me, dear mother,
to describe how she sang. Only those can realise it who
heard her. Her *coloratura* is of such beauty and roundness
that you, when you hear the greatest artist play a scale on
the most perfect of instruments, can have hardly an idea
of the loveliness of her scale. I can realise a singer
singing more brilliantly, but that it is possible that one
can sing more beautifully—*that* none can believe who has
heard her. When she sings ornaments, they are so easily
executed that one cannot believe them difficult. And
her shake! that is indescribable, and only comparable
with the nightingale's song. She executes it so quickly,
that it is hard to realise that one hears more than a single
note ; yet one does hear the two. What am I prattling
about her singing? Were I to write you whole volumes
about it, you would still be unable to gain an idea of what
it really is.

' She sang an aria from *La Sonnambula*, then " Und ob
die Wolke" from *Der Freischütz*. Great is she in aria!
Lovely, bewitching on the stage. But when she sings a
song—then ! The public were stirred to such a pitch of
excited enthusiasm by her singing of songs by Mangold,
and Taubert's "Ich muss nun einmal singen," that some
actually wept, others smiled, and from very adoration
would not let her go. We were, of course, on the stage
all the time, so as to be close to her. Wedemeyer and I
hugged ourselves in admiration, and writhed like worms ;
we were in such a state of fearful excitement as to be

capable of anything. With boundless shamelessness the public demanded everything *da capo*, and with angelic patience and good-naturedness Jenny sang three songs twice. Since some of the more reasonable of the audience thought it rude to exact everything *da capo*, and said so, so to speak, by hissing, this hissing created a very unpleasant impression, for it seemed as if there were some who did not want to hear more. Although there was no question of this she appeared to fret, and at the end of the concert was not so light-hearted as at the beginning, for which I cannot blame her.

'When we had opened the second part with the *Masaniello* overture, she spoke most charmingly to us. This time we were rather more courageous, and made some sort of a reply, although I forget now precisely what it was.

II

'As I have already said, dear mother, the individuality of Jenny Lind's singing is indescribable. I can only tell you this, that she sings with greatest ease from the

deep A flat to the high F , and

one note is as clear and full as the other. The most effective and peculiar in its kind is her *crescendo* and *diminuendo* to the quietest *pianissimo*, so that one hardly knows whence the tone comes; it is so light, that one hardly knows if one hears anything or not; yet one hears it clearly, and it is neither thin nor fine-drawn, but full and round. Her *fortissimo* is never shrieking, but always, beautiful, never sharp nor shrill, but always powerful and such as makes one's blood run cold.

'One moment the tears steal down one's cheeks, another

R

one almost laughs aloud for very pleasure. Her German pronunciation when she sings is pure and perfect, so that one never notices that she is a Swede. When she speaks one observes that she is a foreigner, although she rarely makes a mistake. The arias she sang from memory, yet without the least theatrical manner. Her singing, and indeed her whole bearing, is Nature itself. Every movement is beautiful and picturesque. There is nothing lovely in her appearance, but her manner is so womanly, even girlish, that she seems angelic. She has retired from the stage ; for this, however, she is far too great.

' There—I have produced a picture of a kind of my dear Jenny, yet you can have no idea how charming she is.

'When at the end of the concert she sang by request a Swedish song to her own accompaniment (in which she showed us by her originality as a Swede another new and delightful side), she left the theatre amidst the shouts of the public and a perfect tumult in the street ; for the excited people, filled with wild enthusiasm, followed her carriage, and were only prevented with some trouble from taking her horses out. As to the impressions of the concert which I took home with me, I am not very clear ; I dreamed waking and wandered eternally in the magic garden of heavenly music. As it was quite impossible for any of us to sleep who had been with her, we went to a friend's and there sat dumb and silent. No one smoked, ate, or drank. Each was buried in thought. But in this we all agreed, that anything more beautiful in music was inconceivable, or at least could not be borne by an ordinary mortal. With the pacifying hope of seeing and speaking with her on the morrow, when we had to present our account, we went home, not thinking that this was the small beginning of many happy days.

'On Sunday morning she went to church, and is said to have put ten *louis* in the offertory. Although I take this to be an exaggerated rumour, it is not impossible, for in England she is said to be very pious. But that her piety is not of the common order, but real devotion without hypocrisy and without exaggeration, not pharisaical nor condemnatory of all other men—that you will see from what I have still to say of her.

'At 12 we went to Wehner's to pay our respects to her. There we met Wedemeyer, Breul, Becker, and Seiffert, as well as many others who wanted to see and speak to her. Among them were the Syndic Œsterley, Frau Von Siebold, etc. In order to avoid these visitors she had gone for a walk ; and we left, too, as there were so many folk still awaiting her. She had stated her determination to see no one else but us, since she had come here on our account, not on theirs. We students had open, honest hearts; our love for music was pure and youthful. We went away, then, determined to return in the evening to see if we could speak to her.

'At 1, when she returned home, a deputation from a *corps* waited on her to invite her to give a second concert. This invitation she accepted in a most friendly manner, adding that it would give her great pleasure if they wished it. Just as they were on the point of taking leave, she called them back and sang to them two lovely songs by Schumann, and Mangold's "Zwiegesang," whereby their enthusiasm was considerably increased. As soon as we heard the news, we met again in Committee, and within an hour every ticket was once more disposed of. The second concert was fixed for Monday, February 4, at 12 o'clock in the hall of the Crown Inn, and once more 1½ thalers went to benefit the poor. She did not want to sing again in the theatre, partly because the actors had rights by contract to seats, and partly because the music was not altogether suitable there. We took 530 thalers, and could have taken twice as much had there been room for the people. For not only Göttingen, but the neighbouring towns, were on their legs.

'On Sunday evening I went to Wehner's, happily alone. She and Wehner were busy arranging the programme and seemed very happy. I entered quite unconcernedly and spoke with them of what she should sing. I implored her to sing a couple of Mendelssohn's songs. To this she acquiesced in the most friendly way. Unfortunately our quiet happiness was short-lived, for visitor after visitor was announced: Count Winzingerode, Professor Zachariæ, Rector of the University—every one wanted to see her and speak to her, and waited for that purpose in the hall. As I went out from her room to fetch some more music, you should have seen their long faces, for they were very cross at my having free access, while they, to whom generally everybody bowed the knee, stood outside and waited. Through the incautious good-naturedness of Frau Wehner, who wished every one to know her, more and more came into the house, until at last Jenny Lind became quite annoyed. She said to Wehner that she wanted to know none of the false old men who were nothing but hypocrites. As Baum was among the crowd I pushed my way through to him and told him that he must not come in as Jenny would receive no one. . . .

'When I came back to Wehner's and found that something like peace was restored, most of the long-nosed fraternity having retired, Bähr and I smuggled ourselves into the room unobserved, and immediately busied ourselves with lists, concert programmes, etc., and had the felicity of apparently pleasing her by our presence. After tea she seated herself at the piano and extemporised for us; she was an excellent pianist. Then Wehner played, and she took a volume of Schumann's songs, which at that time were quite unknown, and sang them through. Seated at the piano, resting one arm upon it, she made a lovely picture. As only she, Wehner, Bähr and I were present, she was quite unreserved and was so happy and charming that we hardly realised that the natural, simple girl was Jenny Lind, one of the most famous women in Europe. Although she only sang with about one-eighth of her voice—that is quite *pianissimo*—and only passages which especially appealed to her were given with full force, yet even then her singing was so divine that I, seated comfortably in a big arm-chair, thought I was but dreaming. These hours spent in her company I still count among the very happiest. When at ten o'clock we took our departure, and she had thanked us again for our trouble, and shaken us by the hand, I felt mad enough to do anything. I crawled home, her songs still buzzing in my ears, more dreaming than waking.

'On the following morning after distributing the tickets between 9 and 11 to a huge crowd, we went at 12 to the concert, where Bähr and I were permitted to sit in her room, because we could not find a seat in the concert-hall. But I forgot to mention before that Prince Schwarzenberg, Prince Radali, Adami and Beaulieu-Marconnay (no relation to the other Beaulieu), who were students here, had given her a morning serenade with a military band from Northeim.

'At 12 the concert began. Great as was the enthusiasm at her first concert, at the second the public were quite beside themselves. And I must confess that I cannot find words to express what I felt that day. It seemed as if the host of heaven had come down to make us mortals happy. She sang the aria from *Der Freischütz*, "Nie nähte mir der Schlummer"; and the Rhenish folk-song by Mendelssohn, " O, Jugendzeit," which had to be repeated. This she sang in a wholly inspired

manner. I can never forget in a lifetime her singing of
the words:

> " Der Himmel steht offen
> Man sieht die Engelein,
> O! Konnt' ich, Herzliebste,
> Stets bei dir sein ! "

'This song she selected expressly for us students.
When she appeared there was a fearful hullabaloo, hats
and caps were waved, and we shouted ourselves hoarse.
In fact, we all lost our heads, I among the rest. She also
sang Mendelssohn's " Spring Song " from the posthumous
book, then the great " Queen of the Night " aria from *Il
Flauto Magico*; and lastly a song by Taubert, which she
repeated. How she delivered the words " Weiss nicht
warum ich singe," cannot be described. When enthusiasm
had reached its height and bouquets and wreaths surrounded her so that one could almost believe that every
hot-house in Göttingen had flown to her, she sat down
again at the piano and sang a Swedish song. But I was
already so overcome that I could bear no more. When
the concert was over and she went with Wehner into a
room, she told him she felt so happy she could kiss the
whole world !

'When we were all refreshed, Frau Wehner said to me
that Jenny Lind had told her that she loved dancing, but
never had an opportunity to dance, and that she was
going to arrange a small *thé dansant* for the evening,
to which I was invited. At 7 I was at Wehner's, with
a number of others, about ten couples. One of the
gentlemen played the piano. The matrons were left at
home, and only a few old dames admitted as chaperones ;
and even these were quite unnecessary, since on such a
day both gentlemen and ladies were on their best
behaviour. In order to avoid worrying Jenny Lind with
too many dances, we arranged with Wehner which dances

we would have with her; I seized the second valse.
This evening and the following morning are among the
happiest in my life. Through the kindness of Frau
Bartling I was the owner of a lovely camellia, of which
I made a bouquet which I laid on Jenny's table before
she came in. When most of the guests had arrived and
she entered, she immediately saw my bouquet and asked
Wehner who had put it where it lay. When he told her,
her eyes sought me out, and immediately every one between
us vanished. As I was too agitated to approach her, she
came and thanked me, giving me her hand in the kindest
way. Naturally I blushed crimson and seemed ridiculous
even to myself, though her hand-shake permeated every
bone and muscle in my body. If ever I have enjoyed
myself on any one evening I did then. We were all so
happy; Jenny Lind so delighted, and danced so well
and so willingly. Her every movement was full of grace!
Ay! those were happy hours!

III

'When I or Bähr played either too quickly or too slowly
she came to the piano and gave us the right *tempo* by
tapping on the instrument or playing the melody—so
while playing close to her I felt as happy as when I was
dancing with her. But the pleasures of the dance were
temporarily interrupted by a *corps* of students, who
honoured her with a torchlight procession. The oldest of
the students, who were mounted on horseback, carried
decorated poles and small swords, and wore jack-boots
and caps, represented the ancient glory of the *corps*.
When she looked from her window and called out " Long
live the Göttingen students!" the enthusiasm was general,
and torches and caps were waved about.
'She was as delighted as a child, clapping her hands,

and saying to Wehner and me, who were standing beside her: "I have seen many torch processions, but none has ever seemed so lovely as this!" And I must say, too, that this made a brave show, with its four hundred torches and all the brilliant pomp of the students' costumes. The deputation from the *corps*, all of whom were dressed in costume, were invited to stay on, and as a sign of her everlasting kindliness, I may tell you that she arranged an extra dance, in which the ladies had to seek their own partners. Of course she chose first the deputation who could not dance with her later, because she was already engaged. Thus the evening flew. Wedemeyer danced the cotillon with her. In the "bow" tour the whole company was stirred up with excitement to see who could first obtain a bow from her. She, for fun, made the tour twice, and then ran over to me. You can realise the astonishment of the princes and aristocrats who were sitting behind me, who believed they only had the right to such honours; yet in the second tour again it was not they, but Wehner, who was honoured, so that he and I were the only pair who received bows from her hands. When the dance was over, everybody wished to have a souvenir. So Wehner had the idea of cutting off from her dress two long blue ribands, which were distributed piece-meal. The ladies already had a pleasant souvenir in the bouquets which they had brought with them from the concert to the cotillon.

'At last we bade her adieu. One or two of us shook hands with her once more, saying that should we meet again elsewhere we should not forget to bring her greetings from Göttingen. About one o'clock we went home intoxicated with admiration and full of happiness at the thought of seeing her on the morrow.

'The Hanoverian *corps*, to which Breul and Bähr belong, and with whom I had already become intimate, wanted to accompany her to Northeim, and invited me to go with them. On the following morning, at eight o'clock (February 5th), we set forth, she in her carriage with twenty riders for bodyguard. The eight handsomest folk and best horsemen were selected as outriders, dressed in student's festival garb. They wore blue and yellow sashes—the Swedish colours. When Jenny Lind was on the point of getting into her carriage, [accompanied by Wehner and her maid, one of the riders (Marcard) said to her: " We students have an ancient custom of accompanying those we love when they leave us. Permit us, then, dear lady, to accompany you." These few words pleased her mightily because, though brief, they were heartfelt.

' So the brilliant procession set forth, the twenty riders blazing forth their trumpet signals. Often on the journey she would sit perfectly still while a rider pointed out the objects of interest by the roadside ; then, too, she would look through the window from her corner at us, when the whole company would burst into a terrific " hurrah ! " It was easy to see that she accepted all our homage from no motives of vanity, but that it gave her real, hearty happiness. In ecstasy she said once to Marcard, who rode constantly by her side : " You 've no idea how lovely you all look ! "

' The road to Northeim has never seemed to me so short as then. When we were arrived at that place, and her carriage was at a standstill, many carriages passed her, whose occupants one and all greeted her heartily. When we had descended we all went into the " Sun " Inn and took our places at a long table in the dining-room, at the end of which sat Jenny Lind and Wehner. Champagne was ordered, and at her request we all sang a number of student-songs. In the chorus of the song, " Mein Lebenslauf ist Lieb und Lust," she joined, accompanying us with shakes and turns in the highest part of her compass. Our enthusiasm was tremendous. Every one wanted a souvenir of to-day also. At last Wehner got a piece of blue riband which she cut into pieces, one for each of us to make into a bow. After we had drunk her health and she had toasted Wehner (of course with constant interruptions of hurrahs), one of the riders (Brande by name) delivered a short speech to her, in which he said that we should never forget this day or this happiness, and he ended by toasting Sweden. Whereupon Jenny Lind stood on a chair and spoke such beautiful and moving words of thanks and adieu that we could hardly restrain our tears. Her tears actually were flowing. She said she felt herself unworthy the honours we had offered her; she had already seen many great and stirring scenes, but last night and this morning had left an absolutely indelible impression in her memory. She ended with the words: " I speak badly— I *feel* better! God bless you all, my student friends! "

'With these words she and Wehner went out, we following in pairs to see her to her carriage. One more hurrah! and away she went. I shall never forget how she leaned from the carriage and gave us a last farewell! When she was lost to sight we began with one accord to sing "Ist kein schöneres Leben als Studentenleben." For my whole life long will those days be unforgotten. Oh, could I but tell you, dear mother, how moving was all this! Words are too weak and too lifeless to express lively feelings. I cannot write more. For she is indescribable. I can only sing her song—

> " Wie der Gesang zum Herzen drang,
> Vergess' ich nimmer mein Lebenlang."'

IV

Scattered here and there throughout other of these letters are innumerable sentences and paragraphs of

interest and value, historically and critically. Dr. Billroth, in a letter to his wife, written at Stuttgart in 1870, says:—
'Yesterday evening we were established at Stockhausen's. . . . It was a delightful evening. Stockhausen sang "Die Lorelei" and Schumann's "Rheinlied" more beautifully than ever. . . . Everything is warlike. Stockhausen is an enthusiastic German, and is busy *composing patriotic songs.*'

Stockhausen has long been known as probably the finest interpreter (male) of Schumann's, Schubert's, and Brahms's songs; but who has seen his compositions? I once heard a story of Stockhausen to the effect that his *one* composition, a German patriotic song, written while the great singer was engaged at Paris, led to his expulsion from the French capital; but I have always regarded it as more or less apocryphal.

The letters descriptive of scenes witnessed by Dr. Billroth during the Franco-German war are of great interest, but are outside the scope of this article.

The learned doctor shared with many others, notably Eduard Hanslick, the distinguished Viennese musical critic, a strong antipathy to Liszt's music. In a letter written to Hanslick in 1873, Billroth says:—

' Herr Dessoff,[1] whose energy has raised our Viennese musical life from the lowest to the highest, has conceived the original, if not very happy, idea of sandwiching a piece by Liszt in between two of Beethoven's works. This is called the "Mephisto-Walzer" and seems to have been inspired by Heine's poem *Faust.*[2] . . . To be musically impotent is, for a man like Liszt, a misfortune; but yet it behoves us not to point out that impotence. It is, however, downright rude of us to offer to the public music which it is flattery to describe as "ordinary." Had a

---

[1] Then conductor of the Opera at Vienna.
[2] It was after Lenau's *Faust.*

reproductive artist of such calibre as Liszt no organ for differentiating between the " hateful in music" and the good ?   Every morsel of Offenbach is gold compared with this arsenic of musical ingenuity.   I devoutly hope that a musical institution like the Philharmonic Society—of which Vienna is proud—will never again defile itself with such " Brocken pitch ! " '

Of Brahms's string-quartets in C minor and A minor (Op. 51), which the composer dedicated to Billroth, and which, like the majority of Brahms's chamber compositions, were first heard at Billroth's house, Billroth wrote in November 1873 to Lübke of Stuttgart :—

' A couple of evenings ago Brahms's new quartets were played at my house.   There is much in them of real beauty in a very concise form ; they are not only extremely difficult technically, but not easy to understand at first.   If they are played in Stuttgart let me recommend you to study them before hearing them either in the score or in a four-handed pianoforte arrangement ; otherwise a great deal that is lovely will be lost.   Hardly a concert takes place here now without some work or other by Brahms figuring in the programme.   As a chorus-director and conductor he is developing quite an unexpected schoolmasterly talent.'

In another letter, written in 1874, to Lübke, Billroth says that—

' Brahms is now become so popular, and is made so much of everywhere (if not always with the greatest intelligence), that it would be easy for him to become a rich man through composition, if he were silly enough to wish for this—which, happily, he does not.'

Although the following extract does not refer to matters musical, I cannot refrain from quoting it as an excellent instance of Billroth's humour—a humour by no means common among German scientists and pedagogues :—

'At Easter I spent five weeks in Italy, and am much inclined to regard Italy as a gross swindle. In Naples and neighbourhood it was deadly cold ; never have I been so frozen. Fick, whom I met there, is slowly recovering from a four-weeks' catarrh of Siberian intensity. Hanslick, my delightful travelling companion, is recovering from typhoid. In Rome it rained like string for ten days and nights; in Florence, ditto, for three days. I saw little enough that was new in Italy. Places, pictures, statues are much better seen in pictures, panoramas and ballets, where the lighting is better and there's no rain. In Rome the Viennese beer-house on the Corso was the place most sought after. Of Italians there are not many in Italy; German professors and students, architects, Viennese more than in Vienna, form the principal part of the population. When the sky is overcast one happily can see nothing at all of the ancient smearings on the walls of the Sistine Chapel.'

From which it may be seen that though Billroth shared with the majority a want of appreciation of the art of fresco-painting, he had what the majority have not —the honesty to say so.

But humour bristles in many of the letters, in most of those written at holiday-time :—

'In Carlsbad I mean to give myself over to doing nothing and to music, and have an idea of arranging for my own benefit Brahms's string-quartets for pianoforte —(have no fear that I will publish my arrangement !)— and then I'm ready for anything.

'Brahms I have seen once or twice. His quartets—and a shocking bad one by X.—were played at my house a day or two ago. He has ready a new book of "Liebeslieder"; some of them are lovely, but almost too much in the same *genre*. In manuscript he has a new pianoforte quartet which I like immensely.'

By Schumann's *Manfred* Billroth was obviously affected, since he wrote thus of it :—

'*Manfred!* Oh! that you had seen it and heard it! . . . The scene with Astarte's spirit always brings the tears to my eyes; even now when I think of it I shiver again. This music!—"Verzeihst du mir?" "Manfred, lebe wohl," "Morgen wird dein Leid zu Ende gehen!"— When Astarte here sings the notes precisely as they should be sung—warmly, feelingly!—and then—the Manfred (Lewinsky) so sympathetic to the audience—the orchestra, and Herbeck's conducting! I tell you it makes one mad. Is it well to feel such things—or ill?

'Yet everything else new that we have had I forget promptly. Beethoven's Mass in D, for example. I heard it for the third time and had previously studied it. For me such music is much deader than the weakest in Bach and Handel. Not that it is especially abstruse. No! dull, unimportant in invention it is—vexatious, top-heavy music. Beethoven cannot write for chorus, it all sounds ineffective. His fugue themes, too, are ineffective; one is always glad when the worrying noise is over. If men were honest the majority would agree with me. For musicians by profession this is what Michael Angelo's Sistine Chapel is to painters. Yet for an artistic musical ear it is worn-out music. . . . Among Brahms's new songs (Op. 62-3, 64-6), published by Peters, a few are of exceptional value. . . . The string-quartets I have heard several times this winter. When we played them as duets we took all the *tempi* much too fast. Brahms will have but moderate *tempi* everywhere, because his music cannot "speak clearly" in quick *tempo*, owing to its numerous changes of harmony; this applies equally well to a great deal of modern music. Beethoven, Schumann, Wagner, Brahms in all their riper works show a preference for *andante*, which Wagner describes as specifically

German. Through Mendelssohn rapid *tempi* had become too fashionable ; yet therein is less of true inward passion than used to seem.'

A little light on Brahms as a song-composer is shed by Billroth's remark *à propos* of Daumer, the author of the text of the ' Liebeslieder,' that

' Several verses might have been written by Wagner, so incomprehensible are they. On this point Brahms is very touchy. If the feeling of a poem, its depth of expression, or its popular character holds him, he cannot resist it. A month ago Frau X. sent Brahms a " Cantata for use at Cremations," with the request that he would set it to music.'

Of Dvoràk Billroth said in 1881 to Lübke :—

' A gigantic talent. . . . He, it is true, often works hurriedly, lazily, but lazily *à la* Schubert. He is paid such high terms now by publishers that he tears along almost at scribbling pace. Had he been younger when discovered he would have done great things ; what he does not get at first he cannot get any better by grubbing. Dvoràk's nature is similar to Schubert's, if the former has not obtained the height of the other, more especially in song.

' Brahms, on the other hand, grows daily nearer Beethoven. His latest work, the " Tragic Overture," is grand, though one must hear it several times before taking it in. A joyful pendant to this is the fantasia-overture on student-songs, the Academical festival overture composed for Breslau.'

Again, in writing of a performance of Brahms's *Nänie* in Vienna, Billroth throws a curious light on the state of music in the Austrian capital in 1883. Billroth wrote :—

' More than once such serious works are never given. Conductors and choral societies produce them once from a sort of vanity when they are quite new ; but the singers don't attend these rehearsals, for they know beforehand that there is nothing to be made by them out of such pieces. . . . Once things were better; now everything is going downhill—Philharmonic, choral societies, quartets, none will have serious music. Now opera and ballets are at a premium—even the Burg Theatre is doing well. But all other theatres are bankrupt.'

In a letter of extreme interest to Brahms, written the year before Billroth's death, the latter said:

'You agree with me that modern man is inclined to prefer things in a minor mode; to this can be compared such a fact as that duller, softer colours are preferable in our immediate surroundings to those which are inclined to be hard. When you and I were boys it was different. Modern folk object to a bright light in their rooms; they like coloured glass windows. Sharp, shrill voices are unpleasant. In the drawing-room one talks in the minor. . . . My impression, speaking generally, was that the Major period began with Handel and Haydn, and that before them in the time of the oldest folk-songs the Minor was the rule. But that this is wrong in regard to folk-songs you have already shown me; nevertheless the Scottish and Swedish folk-songs are more often minor than those of any other people. My sole source of information in regard to old French dance measures is the three volumes of *Echos du temps passé.* It is, however, not unlikely that the Editor sought for songs in the minor mode, giving them the preference. . . . All major folk-songs, ancient as well as many that are modern, sound to me more or less trivial, while those in minor are often distinguished. An ancient melody in minor seems to me less antiquated than one in major.'

But all things must have an end. I have quoted (in translation) a good deal from these letters, but not one-hundredth part of what is of interest in them. Few volumes of letters of wider interest have come before me in recent years, and none in which a layman speaks so well upon music and musicians. Billroth learned much from his constant intercourse with Hanslick and Brahms, but he had a wonderfully acute natural gift for criticism, a sense of humour uncommon among Germans, and a dignified and telling style.

The Art of Pantomime Ballet

STANLEY V. MAKOWER

WAGNER'S position as an artist has become merged in
that of the social reformer, and in England, at all events,
it will take him some time to emerge into his normal
rank as a musician. Before this can happen, the young
ladies of England must have ceased to confuse their daily
emotions with those of Isolde, just as they have practically ceased to disguise themselves any longer as the
Burne-Jones woman.

That theatrical art should develop rather in the
direction of ballet than opera in the immediate future, is
a possibility hinted at by Wagner himself in one of his
speeches, and suggested by a significant passage of *Die
Meistersinger*, in which Beckmesser performs a scene in
dumb pantomime, closing with the theft of the manuscript
written by Hans Sachs for Walther and the entry of the
Master Cobbler himself.

Until the time of Gluck the ballet was simply a dancing
interlude in opera. Thus it was treated by Lulli,
Couperin, Rameau, and others, who used it as a commercial
trap in which to catch big audiences, just as to-day big

audiences are decoyed into the theatre by the bait of rich
costume and elaborate scenic effect.   It was M. Noverre,
*Ancien maître de ballets en chef de l'académie impériale
de musique,* who represented the great classical revival of
the time in this department of musical art.   His letters
to Voltaire are full of theories of the dance, of constant
allusions to the corrupt state of the ballet, in which he
notices a total lack of intelligence both in the choice and
management of the subject as well as in that of the
gestures.   The ballet of that time must have been as
senseless an exhibition of gymnastics as that which we
may witness any evening at the Empire or, to a less
exquisite degree, at the Alhambra.

M. Noverre has left two volumes of letters and a
number of scenarios for ballets.   He was born in 1727,
and died in 1810.   His *Lettres sur la danse,* first published
in 1760, were soon translated into almost every European
tongue, but the first English edition of them that we can
find is dated 1783.   This is prefaced by a brief history
of dancing, written by the English translator, who hides
himself under the cloak of anonymity.   A pity; for he
must have been a considerable person, to judge by his
catalogue raisonnée of the dances of the ancients, beginning
with that performed by Moses and his sister after the
passage of the Israelites through the Red Sea, passing
through the Astronomic or Egyptian period spoken of by
Plato and Lucian, when dancers moved in the order of the
constellations, up to the time when Pylades and Bathylus
introduced the *ballet d'action* at the time of Augustus.
He tells us that the ballet died on the accession of Trajan,
that it was not revived until the fifteenth century, when
an Italian nobleman re-introduced it on the occasion of
the marriage of Galeas, Duke of Milan, and Isabella of
Aragon.   He rushes us up to the time when the Dau-
phiness (the Princess of Conti) and other ladies of the

Court of Louis XIV. danced in *Le Triomphe de L'Amour*, by Quinault, the music by Lulli, this being the first occasion on which women acted upon the stage in ballet. He reminds us that Queen Elizabeth would often dance a ballet with her guests after dinner. In about twenty-five pages he suggests enough to fill as many volumes.

M. Noverre was the pioneer of a new school in the ballet. To him dancing meant more than an elaborate gymnastic feat; it was inseparable from an intention both intellectual and emotional. The ballet-master had to be at once a painter, a poet, and a historian. The *ballet d'action* presented a series of pictures as carefully composed as those put on his canvas by the painter; each picture had to illustrate a situation, each situation a variety of real emotions. There was to be none of the conventional symmetry (ten irresponsible arms waving in one direction on one side of the stage, ten equally irresponsible waving in another direction on the other side) which had made the ballet a corrupt and unreasonable exhibition of limbs that waggled and hopped and twirled to the rhythm of meretricious music.

M. Noverre took his subjects from Corneille, Racine, and Voltaire, using their plays merely as Shakespeare used Holinshed—to build his own conceptions out of their facts. The process would consist in the compression of the drama into a set of scenes in which the characters acted, and in which they were moved by strong emotions as a result of their action, all the quiet and explanatory dialogue being discarded as incapable of translation into the ballet form, as well as all those speeches and scenes which depended for their interest on allusions to the past and the future, such being, again, outside the scope of illustration by gesture.

The ballet-master met with all the opposition and opprobrium that fall to the lot of those whose mission it is to lead a new movement. Superficial wits, whose bowing acquaintance with his theories was on a footing with their capacity for understanding them, declared with a contemptuous shrug, that the next thing this maniac would attempt would be to dance the maxims of La Rochefoucauld. But the twenty years that elapsed between the first edition of the letters in 1760 and their republication in 1782 witnessed a complete and triumphant change in the treatment of the ballet. If Mimes no longer wore masks, had not M. Noverre given point to the necessity of their abolition in the following picture?—

' Imagine to yourself a table surrounded with a number of gamblers, all wearing more or less grotesque masks, but masks that smile. If you look only at the faces you will find all the players wearing a look of contented satisfaction; you will say that they are all winning; but fix your eyes upon their arms, their attitudes, their gestures, and you will see on one side the motionless attention of uncertainty, of fear or of hope; on the other the impetuous movement of fury and of anger; here you will see a smiling mouth and a clenched fist menacing heaven; there you will hear terrible imprecations issuing from a mouth convulsed with laughter,—in a word, this opposition between the face and the gesture produces an astonishing effect easier to conceive than to describe. So with the dancer, whose face tells us nothing, while his gestures or his feet express the feeling by which he is overborne.'

Amazing is the vision of the world as a *mise en scène* for the ballet revealed to us in these letters—the vision of a man absorbed in his art. In every aspect of life he seeks the most imposing pictorial summary. He observes the workshops of different artisans with scrupulous attention, notes the different attitudes of the men with their relation to the movements and positions forced upon them by their work. He dwells with contempt on the want of artistic conception which characterised the decorations in celebration of peace after the Revolution. Listen to what he says *à propos* of the allegorical figures of Liberty reared on a low and insignificant piece of ground in Paris :—

'Moses, who knew more about such matters than the late Directoire—to whom may God grant peace and mercy!—did not stand upon a little plain on the day of an august and mysterious celebration. No, he was much too great a master in the art of effect. He took up his position upon Mount Sinai, and from an eminence like this he bestowed his code of laws upon the Hebrews.'

M. Noverre's experiences in England were coloured with a peculiar grace owing to his warm admiration for Mr. Garrick. The actor met this with an equally warm appreciation of the ballet-master, whom he called 'The Shakespeare of the Dance'; nor can we doubt the sincerity, though we may smile at the Gallicism, of M. Noverre, when he called Shakespeare 'The Corneille of England.'

The text of pantomimes was no more distinguished in Mr. Garrick's day than it is now. No wonder then that it inspired the French Master with a healthy contempt. But stage contrivances in the pantomime even at that primitive period of their development gave him acute pleasure ; and a mechanical fountain, in which silver gauze was made to represent water with much success, fascinated him so completely, that he offered the management twenty guineas to part with the machine ; yet they would not consent to the exchange.

'If the water had remained motionless, nothing would have astonished me ; but these sprays moved rapidly and continuously.'

The reforms of M. Noverre were not limited to the dancers nor to the abolition of masks, hoops, and other

superfluous accessories which had become encrusted into
the traditions of the ballet. Sir Henry Irving himself
could scarcely dwell more earnestly on the importance of
accuracy in costume and scenery, and what is more,
of discriminating use of light and a skilful manipulation
of figures and perspectives. Away with the footlights,
and let there be a careful graduation of the heights of the
performers and of the colours of their costumes. Jupiter
seated on Olympus, or Apollo on Parnassus, by reason of
their supposed distance from the spectator, should be
made to appear smaller than the divinities and Muses
assembled at the base of these mountains. This is to be
managed by having two people to play Jupiter or Apollo,
one a young boy for the top of the mountain, the other
a man dressed in the same costume, and made similar
in every aspect, for the bottom of the mountain. An
excellent illustration is provided in the scene of a party
of hunters and huntresses defiling out of a wood along a
path running down the centre of the stage and ending in
a bridge. About six relays of people of diminishing size
were employed, so that every time the party reappeared
from behind the stems of trees they looked smaller, and
so it was contrived to give the illusion of distance.

Among other subjects with which M. Noverre deals in
his correspondence is the art of chorography, or committing elaborate dances to paper by a scheme of notation.
He compares the system with that of musical notation,
making this trenchant distinction between the two : that
where a good musician will read two hundred measures
in one second, an excellently good chorographer will not
be able to read two hundred dance measures in two hours.
Moreover, he reminds us that what is most worthy of
preservation in the dance is the emotion expressed by
the limbs and by the eyes of the dancer, and in one of
his later letters he suggests that Boucher should be

commissioned to paint on a series of panels the greatest dancers in their successive poses throughout a ballet, by which means future generations would be able to study them as the sculptor studies his Michael Angelo.

He devotes one long letter to the subject of anatomy—a science with which every master of the ballet should be familiar, for without it he will be unable to teach successfully; and he adds that the tutor should study the anatomy of each pupil, so that he may not lose time in trying to make a man fitted by his physique to the *haut-comique*, for instance, an exponent of tragedy. He gives us examples of three different types of dancers from the works of painters—Van Loo having immortalised the *danse sérieuse*, Boucher the *danse demi-caractère*, and Teniers the *danse comique*.

In another passage these letters deal with the use of the *bâton* in orchestral performances, declaring it a useless instrument where intelligent musicians are concerned. Dr. Richter recently confirmed this view in a performance of the second movement of Tschaikowsky's *Symphonie Pathétique*, which was played without the conductor once having recourse to what the ballet-master called 'the sceptre of ignorance.'

M. Noverre not only reformed the ballet, but he showed in his letters that the profession of a great dancer could be made as dignified as that of a great lawyer. For the meretricious side of dancing he had no more sympathy than for the meretricious side of dancers. To follow a great art and serve it nobly required, according to him, a great devotion and an untiring energy; it left no time for the practice of follies. When he was not engaged in dancing, the dancer's business was to be reading—studying other forms of art, lifting his mind to a plane of thought which should constantly grow higher.

His own letters display a wide and varied knowledge

which could only have been gained by the closest study ;
but the vastness of his attainments never interfered with
the simplicity, even *naïveté*, of his nature. In one of his
later letters he is writing to an English lady about a
famous *danseuse* :—

'When I seek, madame, to tell the praises of Madame
Gardel the pen slips from my hand, words fail me. . . .
From her feet springs a shower of diamonds, if you will
pardon me the exaggeration. . . . Her arms are very
agreeable. . . . You have only to see her to become
enchanted with her candour, her propriety, her wit, her
admirable smoothness of manner.'

A few of Voltaire's replies are bound up in the volumes
of Noverre, published in 1807. They express a deep
admiration for the ballet-master, whose friends were
numerous. Among them were Frederick the Great and
his brother Prince Henry of Prussia, Marie Antoinette,
Alembert, Diderot, David Garrick, Sir Joshua Reynolds,
the Duchess of Devonshire, and many other celebrated
people of the time. He visited Vienna, Berlin, Milan,
Stuttgart, London, Lyons, and finally settled down in
Paris. He collaborated with Gluck, Mozart (in *Les petits
riens*), Piccini, and Sacchini. The English translation of
his letters has never been republished since 1783. He pro-
jected a *Dictionary of the Dance*, but never lived to finish it.
It is idle to hope that the fragments which he wrote are
in existence, but it is certain that they were full of interest.

Scarcely a passage of M. Noverre seems antiquated
to-day, unless it be the repeated assertion that Art is a
copy of Nature—a definition which we have long ceased
to accept. Yet M. Noverre was none the less an artist,
because the little truth in his definition of Art lay mutilate.
Any definition of Art will in all likelihood be false, because
it will exaggerate a partial truth in order to declare itself
uncompromisingly hostile to the current fallacies of the

age in which it is made. Thus appeals were made to
Nature in the eighteenth century in order to combat a
sentiment prevailing among audiences of the day that Art
was something which excluded Nature.

But for this, you may listen in vain through these
letters for the sound of a note purely contemporary.
Nay, the writer's instinct is rather on the verge of pro-
phecy; so that as we read of those silent moments in his
ballets when the music is suspended and the figures, mute
and of a sudden motionless, grow strangely expressive,
the fancy leaps nimbly from M. Noverre, the poet of
dumb pantomime a hundred years ago, to M. Mæterlinck,
the dramatist in silence of our own day, and is glad at
the discovery that the conceptions of both are fired by
the eloquence of inaction where action ceases to express
anything, and of silence where speech is inadequate.

The further development of Noverre's theories was
temporarily arrested by the continuous rise of Opera, to
which Meyerbeer and Halévy again made the ballet a
very subordinate thing, so that it was introduced in perfectly irrelevant fashion whenever people grew tired of
the tragic action of the play. The complacence of the
ballet in these operas is marvellous. The corps stood
at the wings in perpetual readiness to flutter on when
wanted; they were wanted at most extraordinary moments
and under the most extraordinary circumstances; they
frisked about the palaces of kings and the precincts of
convents with equable impropriety. But Wagner sent
them scurrying into oblivion, and the rush of their dresses
no longer has power to send a thrill through a fashionable
audience.

Traces, however, of an enthusiasm for a saner and more
dignified form of the ballet are to be found in certain
dumb pantomimes which, within the last few years, have
been favourably received in London.

The mysteries of success on the stage in opera, drama, or a combination of both, are often more than Eleusinian, but when the brilliance of such success as attended the performance of Giuglia Ravogli in the part of Orfeo on the one hand, and of Egidio Rossi as Pochinet on the other, is followed by almost total obscurity, the phenomenon defies even the resources of speculation. It would almost seem as if the singer had in one stroke committed herself to a posterity from whose grasp no subsequent effort during her lifetime could restore her to contemporary fame. So with Rossi. Time may narrow the truth of so wide an assertion, but that two such artists have been permitted to retire unquestioned, for so long a period, from the scene of such triumphant achievement as was theirs, is a fact entirely impenetrable.

In the case of M. Rossi at least, this very impenetrability turns us back into the main stream of our subject. To-day the ballet in England may be compared to a hot-house in which every variety of imbecility is nursed into rare perfection. The eye that selects the costumes, poses the figures and directs their movement is the eye of a tired debauchee ; the pen that traces the music of a ballet score is guided by the hand of a skeleton ; the spirit that pervades the air of the theatre is sold behind the bar for sixpence a glass. Night after night the painted figures of the ballet hurry in tumultuous ineptitude across a stage that is everywhere ablaze with a fierce vulgarity. The sceptre of the irrepressible stockbroker governs the theatre of the arts no less than the theatre of South African politics. It is in the ballet that London drama may be seen on its last degenerate legs, dancing ignobly into the dawn of a new century.

M. Rossi disturbed the uniformity of this impression by his performance in *L'Histoire d'un Pierrot* during one brief season. Being neither a stockbroker nor the friend of a stockbroker, but only a man passionately devoted to the art of expressing emotions in silent gesture, and gifted with a singular ability ennobled by hard work and uncompromising sincerity, he was suffered to leave England robbed of ambitions, the fulfilment of which would have brought about a complete regeneration of the art of dumb pantomime in this country.

Believing himself to be Pochinet, the wine-merchant, who befriends Pierrot and his abandoned wife through all their domestic tragedy, with the simple, imaginative illusion of a child believing itself to be the mother of the dolls with which it is playing, M. Rossi attained heights in his impersonation which give the enthusiasm of M. Noverre a modern interest.

The last act of *L'Histoire d'un Pierrot* is so admirable that a quotation of the scenario falls into agreeable relation with what has been said before to constitute the essence of dumb pantomime. The story is presented by three typical figures: Pierrot, the idle, irresponsible husband; Louisette, his faithful wife; and Pochinet, the old friend who edges the border of the dark tragedy with a thread of silver. Pierrot steals money from his wife's money-box to run away with a Spanish dancer. Pochinet is too drunk to arrest his flight, but just succeeds in stopping the seduction of his wife by an unscrupulous lover. A musical interlude precedes the opening of the third act.

Scene—A small square. At the back a street; on the right the house of Louisette with door and ground-floor window sloping gently towards the spectator. On the left, similarly posed, the wine-shop of Pochinet with signboard. On the left of the door of the shop, a seat against the wall; on the right, a few paces from the wall, a drinking-fountain.

I. It is early morning. Pochinet fat and round, a fresh colour in his face, wearing a serious expression, opens his shop. He sweeps the pavement. Next he enters his shop to fetch a pitcher and a wine-jar. He goes to the fountain, fills the pitcher, and places it by his side; then, after looking to see if any one is passing down the street, he takes the wine-jar and indicates to the spectator, that with the wine in the jar and the water in the fountain he is going to make a profitable mixture. He fills the jar with water, and stirs it conscientiously with the stick of his broom. He tastes it, dipping his finger into the mixture. Excellent! And it will harm nobody. Then he re-enters his shop, removing the jar and leaving the pitcher beside the fountain. The scene is empty for a moment.

II. Pierrot appears on the right, emerging from the bottom of the stage; he is a piteous figure, his clothes soiled and torn; an old faded waistcoat replaces the white one worn in the days of prosperity; his mandoline is slung across his shoulder. He can scarcely support himself, and he is terribly hungry. Faint with weariness he can go no further.

He sees the fountain, and goes to drink a few drops from the palm of his hand. He feels better. But on bending over the basin, he sees his image reflected in the water. God! How changed!

Ah, yes! he remembers the miserable story. The little brunette, to follow whom he abandoned his wife. One day a handsome soldier came and carried her off from him. Since then he has had to beg his bread with his mandoline.

He sees the wine-shop. Ah! Perhaps he can get a mouthful here. Timidly he approaches, while tuning his mandoline, whose worn strings jar horribly. Never mind. He begins a serenade. Suddenly one of the strings breaks. No luck! Seeing the door half open, with bowed head and a look of shame, he stretches his hand. But the door shuts. Pierrot is in despair!

How happy they are inside there. They are eating, while he is dying of hunger. He draws his belt tighter, then seeing the seat, 'If I were to sleep,' he thinks, 'I should perchance forget my hunger.' So, after putting his hat and his mandoline on the ground by his side, he stretches himself upon the seat and gradually sinks into sleep.

III. Louisette comes out from her house on the right, leading the child Pierrot by the hand. She gives him a ball: 'There, go and play for a while in front of the house. Be a good boy.' Then she re-enters and reappears at the window which she opens. She hangs out the cage containing the two pigeons, and beckons to the boy Pierrot, who has thrown aside the ball, to come and have a cake which she offers to him. The child takes the cake, breaks off a fragment, and standing on tiptoe gives a few crumbs to the pigeons through the bars of the cage. Louisette retires. The child goes on playing, and sends his ball near the seat upon which lies Pierrot asleep.

He runs after the ball, but stops, amazed, before the poor man. Softly he pulls his arm to wake him. Pierrot does not stir. The child begins again, and slowly Pierrot opens his eyes, rises and gazes dreamily at the boy before him, who offers him a share of his cake. Pierrot takes it, rubs his eyes. Is he still dreaming? Then his eyes fall on the clothes of the child, white like his own.

Bewildered, scarce daring to believe: he takes him upon his knee, kisses him frantically. Tears come into his eyes, when of a sudden the door on the right opens again and Louisette reappears. Pierrot sees her, and covered with shame hides himself, shrinking up against the wall, and putting up the collar of his coat to disguise his face the better.

Louisette pays no attention to him, but calls the boy Pierrot, who runs to his mother, asks her for a penny to give the poor man lying there and crying. Louisette without looking at the man gives him the penny, happy in noting the generous heart of the child, who returns to Pierrot and offers him the money. But Pierrot does not dare face him. The child drops the penny into Pierrot's hat, and then rejoins his mother, who takes his hand, and the two go off on the right, the boy turning his head frequently to have another glance at Pierrot.

Pierrot, when they are both gone, rises quickly and runs forward to follow them as long as he can with his eyes.

IV. This is his wife, and the little Pierrot there must be his son! Tears of mingled grief and joy rise to his eyes. But of a sudden the sight of his own clothes recalls him to reality. Who

can care for him now in his present miserable condition?
Hiding his head in his hands, he returns to the seat upon which
he sinks, overwhelmed with pain.

Pochinet comes out of his shop, and goes to fetch the pitcher
which he had forgotten. He sees Pierrot and does not recognise
him. 'Another beggar,' he thinks to himself. 'I'll get rid of
him.' He taps him on the shoulder, and signals him to be off.
Pierrot rises slowly. The eyes of the two meet. They recognise
each other. Pierrot falls into the arms of Pochinet.
'What! You!' thinks Pochinet, 'and in such a plight!'
'Alas,' replies Pierrot, 'if you only knew!' But suddenly he
stops; he is dying of hunger; he totters, and once again
Pochinet holds him in his arms and places the unhappy Pierrot
exhausted, almost fainting, upon the seat. Pochinet runs to his
shop, and reappears immediately with a plate of food, a bottle of
wine, and two glasses, which he puts on the seat by the side of
Pierrot. He makes him eat. 'More! More!' Then filling
his glass with wine he offers it to him. 'Drink now, comfort
yourself, my poor friend.' Pierrot, about to drink, stops. 'And
you? Will you not drink with me?' 'Yes,' answers Pochinet,
'we will drink together. Wait a moment!' And he goes to
the fountain and fills his glass. 'See here! By drinking
nothing but water, I saved enough to buy my shop, for I had
taken an oath. Do you remember the terrible scene? I was
drunk. You were gambling with a friend. Suddenly I saw
him cheat. I wanted to warn you. But it was impossible, I
grew sleepy—so dead sleepy, that after you had gone, your
friend wanted to profit by my sleep and take away your wife.
Luckily I roused myself in time to save her. From that day I
swore never to drink again. And I have kept my promise.'

Pierrot remembers too well, but interrupting him brusquely,
'The little boy I saw there with my wife. Is he—?' 'Your son,'
replies Pochinet. 'Your wife lives there. All will be well. Go
in and ask for pardon.'

But Pierrot shakes his head sadly. 'Impossible.' Louisette
will never pardon him all the wrong he has done her. 'Ah,
perhaps not,' echoes Pochinet. 'Stay, do you recognise this,'
and he shows him the cage hanging at the window of Louisette.
'Yes,' replies Pierrot remembering the past. 'Well then, look

at it and listen to me,' says Pochinet. 'In this cage there were two creatures who loved each other, until one day one tired of his love, and took flight upwards towards the sky, leaving the other desolate. In vain she begged him to come back. But one morning the pigeon who had flown far—ever so far—came back, his wing broken, dragging his claws one after the other to the cage. He tapped at the door with his beak, and implored the solitary pigeon to pardon him, which was done in a single kiss.'

This is what Pierrot must do. Let him throw himself at the feet of his wife, and a kiss will seal their reconciliation. Pochinet pushes him towards the door. Pierrot shakes his head doubtfully. Has he not seen his wife go away from him with the child? But Pochinet looking behind him sees Louisette and little Pierrot returning. An idea strikes him. 'Quick! In there with you! Hide yourself,' he says to Pierrot; 'I will call you,' and Pierrot disappears behind the door of the wine-shop, while Louisette and the child advance.

V. The child runs to Pochinet, who knows him. Then the wine-merchant takes the hand of the young woman, 'Are you to be always sad,' he asks, 'are you never to smile again?' Louisette tries to smile, and makes towards the house. Pochinet holds her back. 'But, but, but—Pierrot?' he says, 'do you never think of him?' 'Never,' says Louisette, remembering all she has suffered. 'Well, but if he were to come back—by chance—one day—to implore your pardon, would you not see him?' 'No,' and the tears came into her eyes at the thought. But Pochinet pursues his idea. Unperceived by Louisette, he signals to Pierrot to come and throw himself at the feet of his wife.

Pierrot comes slowly, and, folding his hands, kneels. Louisette turning round beholds him. Terrified, and fancying she is in a dream, she recoils. Pierrot supplicates her, and Pochinet persuades Louisette to pardon. But, horrified, she withdraws the hand taken by Pierrot. No, she cannot forgive. He has torn out her heart and trampled it under foot. Pierrot rises. He expected this. Now nothing remains for him but to go on with his vagabond life, until the day shall come when he will die forgotten in an obscure corner of the world. And he goes to the bottom of the square while Louisette cries. Then Pochinet, bending down to the ear of the boy Pierrot, who is looking on all the while in mute astonishment, bids him take first his father by the hand, then his mother, and bring them together. The child does simply what he is bidden. He takes Pierrot's hand and draws him gently towards Louisette; then taking his mother's hand, he puts the one in the other, and seals this union with a kiss. Pierrot and Louisette fall into each other's arms.

Pochinet, almost more moved than either of them, lifts up the child in his arms, and placing him between both of them, indicates that on the head of the dear little one is the burden of forgetting and forgiving.

The simplicity of this story as set forth by M. Fernand Beissier may raise a smile, but regarded from the technical point of view as the scenario of a pantomime ballet, it is entitled to the highest consideration. We have only to note the exquisite use of objects to illustrate the situation, the sunlit square in which the drama is focused, the wine-jar, the pitcher, the mandoline, the cake, the child's ball, the pigeons. From all these the action is precipitated with an eloquent economy. We may smile as we read this story, but when it is quickened with the suggestive music of M. Mario Costa, and thrilled with the incomparable gestures of M. Rossi, the smile is undone, the lips are dragged at the corners, and the tears come as irresistibly as at the bidding of the best spoken drama. Pochinet relating the fable of the pigeons, Pochinet striving to break to Louisette the news that Pierrot is close at hand, and failing twice, thrice, to open his lips because the pain of the situation seals them, and lastly, Pochinet at the end of the drama dropping into total isolation, suggesting in a single helpless quiver of the hand that the rest of life is for him thrown into shadow by the light of an action, entirely beautiful because supremely human, and carrying with it the human penalty of isolation which falls on

T

those whose nobility of conduct is disinterested—all this was expressed by M. Rossi with a poignance that remains a sentiment in us long after the play is over and the curtain has fallen.

The lesson taught by genius to incompetent mediocrity is too truthful to be easily pardoned.   Every gesture of M. Rossi was an eloquent condemnation of the corrupt condition of the ballet in England; while it created an emotion in the spectator, it criticised his tolerance for inferiority.   The performance of *L'Histoire d'un Pierrot* was followed by the engagement of M. Rossi to perform in a ballet at the Alhambra.   Here the artist encountered enemies armed with the invincible weapon of stupidity. His personation of the Merchant in *Beauty and the Beast* was marred by a powerful combination of the vanity of the other actors with the inanity of the musician who composed the score.

M. Rossi has not visited England since this occasion. Very likely no one else could be of such service in the regeneration of the ballet, but the feet of our pantomime actors are not willing to be guided by any such consideration.   They naturally prefer pirouetting against time and capering to the tune of those in whose hire they pursue their trade.   M. Rossi could only discountenance the abuse of an art for whose integrity no sufficient number of champions could be found, and so, after one admirable lesson, he left us.

The result of his visit cannot be traced in any immediate change in the conditions of ballet upon the English stage; but, for those who were privileged to see his performance, the meaning of the word 'ballet' was enlarged into a new and hitherto unsuspected significance. Fashions in art are fickle, but the principles underlying artistic conception have always been the same, so that there is nothing uncommon in the spectacle of a corrupt habit in the practice of an art, side by side with the growth of the very idea that is most hostile to such a habit. Only when the strength of the idea outgrows that of the habit does regeneration make itself externally manifest.

We may have to wait long for an outward sign of the influence of M. Rossi on English pantomime ballet, but his achievement is none the meaner for this. He revived thought in a region of art that had almost passed outside the notice of English-thinking people. He awoke an enthusiasm of which this article is but a faltering attempt at commemoration. No trumpet-blast of notoriety heralded his coming. Yet he won a brilliant if brief success, and retired almost in the full tide of victory. By the poetry of his gesture he left an impression which, in its process of incorporation with other tendencies in the dramatic thought of the time, must inevitably be taken into account, and to which much that is good in the future history of pantomime ballet will have to be ascribed.

Supposing the soul of the ballet to be a flower that only blossoms once in a hundred years, we may profitably indulge the fancy that M. Rossi has given us the first warning that the time for this rare and beautiful appearance is at hand, so that we may look in the direction from which it is expected and not postpone our arrival on the scene until the miracle is over and the petals of the wonderful flower again lie withered on the ground.

Walter Pater on Music

ERNEST NEWMAN

READERS of Walter Pater's volume of essays entitled *The Renaissance,* will remember the article on 'The School of Giorgione,' in which Pater puts forward the thesis that music is the typical art, the art in which form and idea are blended so inseparably that we cannot even picture to ourselves the one without the other; and that all the other arts, in so far as they draw near to perfection, become more and more like music in this respect, inasmuch as their appeal to us becomes so subtle, so undivided and indivisible, that they begin to resemble music in their fusion of the form and the idea. 'All art,' he says, 'constantly aspires towards the condition of music. For while in all other kinds of art it is possible to distinguish the matter from the form, and the understanding can always make this distinction, yet it is the constant effort of art to obliterate it. That the mere matter of a poem, for instance—its subject, namely, its given incidents or situation—that the mere matter of a picture, the actual circumstances of an event, the actual topography of a landscape—should be nothing without the form, the spirit, of the handling—that this form, this mode of handling, should become an end in itself, should penetrate every part of the matter—this is what all art constantly strives after, and achieves in different degrees.' He proceeds to give a concrete illustration of his meaning in connection with the art of painting; and of poetry he remarks that 'the ideal types . . . are those in which this distinction (between the matter and the form) is reduced to its minimum; so that lyrical poetry, precisely because in it we are least able to detach the matter from the form, without a deduction of something from that matter itself, is, at least artistically, the highest and most complete form of poetry. And the very perfection of such poetry often appears to depend, in part, on a certain suppression or vagueness of mere subject, so that the meaning reaches us through ways not distinctly traceable by the understanding, as in some of the most imaginative compositions of William Blake, and often in Shakespeare's songs, as pre-eminently in that song of Mariana's page in *Measure for Measure*, in which the kindling force and poetry of the whole play seems to pass for a moment into an actual strain of music.' And he sums up thus: 'In music, then, rather than in poetry, is to be found the true type or measure of perfected art. Therefore, although each art has its incommunicable element, its untranslatable order of impressions, its unique mode of reaching the "imaginative reason," yet the arts may be represented as continually struggling after the law or principle of music, to a condition which music alone completely realises. . . .'

Now it seems to me that Pater goes astray at the outset by making any reference whatever to the 'idea' of music. The word is wholly inadmissible. One can see how Pater has arrived at his position. In an art such as poetry it is frequently possible to separate what the artist is saying from his particular mode of saying it—possible, that is, to separate the idea from the form. ›We can, for example, turn many a poem into prose, without the reader losing any portion of what the poet actually says—the loss of course being on the side of emotion, of æsthetic pleasure, not on that of intelligence, of understanding, of reality. Take, as a simple illustration, the well-known verse of Landor (which I am compelled to quote from memory):—

> ' I strove with none, for none was worth my strife ;
> Nature I loved, and, next to Nature, Art ;
> I warmed both hands before the fire of life,—
> It sinks, and I am ready to depart.'

Of the actual attitude towards life which Landor is here assuming, we can give any one an accurate notion simply by saying, ' I contended with no one, for no one was worth contending with. I loved Nature first, and Art next. I lived as completely as I could, and now that my capacity for strenuous life is departing, I am ready to die.' That is the *idea* of the poem, an idea easily distinguishable from the particular manner in which Landor has chosen to express it. Finding himself able, then, ′to separate the idea from the form in such a case as this, Pater has too readily assumed that since he cannot view the form and the idea of music in separation, it must be because in music they are completely, indissolubly blended and interfused. But his conclusion is wrong. If we cannot say of music, ' Here idea ends, here form begins ; this is the thing said, this the manner of saying it,'—that is because music voices nothing that can be said to answer to the term ' idea,' used as Pater uses it in reference to the arts of poetry and painting. One comes at the first step upon the old, insoluble problem, ' What *is* music ? What are the mental processes by which a composer's experiences find expression in pure sound, and

what the processes by which this sound achieves its effect
in us, the hearers?' Whatever music may be, it is
certainly not an expression of anything answering to
what we understand by an idea when speaking of the other
arts. When Pater, for example, writes that 'in its consummate moments, the end is not distinct from the means,
the form from the matter, the subject from the expression,' and that towards this condition 'all the arts may
be supposed constantly to tend and aspire,' one has to
ask him, 'What *is* the end of a strain of music, what *is*
the matter of it, what *is* the subject?' And if it be
replied that Pater's argument insists that no answer can
be given to this question, for the reason that the end, the
matter, the subject, are blended inseparably with the
means, the form, the expression, the rejoinder is that in
that case we have no right to speak of the *subject* of music
at all, and still less right to speak of the other arts as
aspiring to the condition of music. It is evident that the
utmost we can say is, not that form and idea are interfused in music, but that these terms, drawn from other
arts, are here quite inapplicable ; that they have, in fact,
no meaning.

The reason of this is easily discovered. In all the
other arts we can roughly trace two factors—a reference
to actual life, actual experience, and an emotional thrill at
the presentation of this experience in a particular way. In
the case of music we cannot see any direct reference to
actual life. It seems to take certain emotional *impressions*
left in us by the contact of actual life, and, by the employment of sounds in certain relations, to recall, not the
emotion *and* the piece of life that generated it, but the
emotion alone. For this reason it can necessarily evoke
only the broader, the less specialised, emotions. The
fact that more people are susceptible to music than to
any other art, and the fact, insisted on by its enemies

that music is the only art which makes any impression
on animals, the only art which stimulates them, in however low a degree, to some such mood of sadness or
excitement as ours—these facts in themselves show that
music deals with the broadest organic sensibilities of our
being. Man cried before he spoke, and even, as the music
of many savages will show us, found expression for his
moods in rudimentary musical sounds before he had learned
to express in the language of the understanding all that his
organs of sensation may be supposed to have taught him.
It was only when the brain had become more highly
specialised that sensations and emotions passed from the
vague to the clear, from the indefinite to the definite, and
that man learned to think as well as to feel. It is, of
course, in this direction that the great mental development of mankind has gone on.   Contact with other things
has gradually led to something more than a blunt
sensation, such as we may imagine a jelly-fish to feel
when a tuning-fork is made to vibrate near it. The
whole impress of an object did not terminate simply with
the sensation of the moment ; there remained in the
primitive brain a memory of the sensation, and this, upon
the revival of the external impress, would lead from mere
feeling to knowledge, to increased self-consciousness.
Thus man gradually passed beyond the stage in which
all his being could be expressed in a cry, or even in
music. Emotions and ideas began to take upon themselves finer and subtler characters, derived from the more
specialised, the less primitive fibres of the brain and
nerves ; and for these the form of expression of the vague
primal organic sensations was found to be insufficient.
Thus arose the other arts, the essence of which is that
they give voice to aspects of the world with which we
have been made familiar through our later developed
nerves and brain.   In poetry and painting there is always

a reference to actual life which is absent from music. What converts these references into art seems to be the touch upon those same organic sensibilities to which music addresses itself—the words in poetry, for example, having not only the property of reproducing scenes and experiences for us, but the further property of stimulating, through the medium of this reminiscence, the great deep fountains of organic feeling, of joy and sorrow, of anger, love, hatred, despair. And only in so far as the words have this quality of leading us through them, through and beyond their actual meaning, to the point where, by some mysterious magic, they thrill as well as inform us, make us feel as well as think, do they become art.

Here it may seem as if Pater might easily have turned this statement to the account of his own theory, by saying that if the sole function of the words of a poem, or of the subject of a painting, is to attune us to a state of exquisite æsthetic feeling, the less they stand forward on their own account the better ; and that on these terms it may quite justifiably be said that, since for this evocation of the mood without undue prominence of the medium that calls forth the mood we have to go to music, then in proportion as a poem or a picture draws near to this condition it really approaches perfection. The answer to that must be that in the vast majority of poems—in all, in fact, except a few small lyrics that aim only at stimulating a fugitive emotion—the function of the words is something more than to be merely the glass through which we look at life. The glass has an interest of its own. The words, that is, apart from their artistic power to cause the great primal waves of feeling to surge up in us, have the further power to awaken our interest by recalling actual life to us in its concrete forms, just as painting recalls actual life by means of imitation. This is an element of æsthetic pleasure that is wholly

ignored in Pater's theory. We are interested, as I say,
not only in the emotion aroused, but in the suggestions of
experience by which the emotion is stimulated ; it is, in
fact, the later-developed parts of our nature demanding
their due. Hence the art that approaches most nearly
to music in that it recalls no concrete, specialised experience, but simply sends through us a pulse of organic
generalised emotion, as music does, must, from the very
nature of the case, be exceedingly rare. It can only be
the lyric, and the lyric only at its very tiniest, for it is
impossible to handle words for more than a very few
lines without passing beyond words that are employed
simply to crystallise a mood, to words that have the
effect of adding a reminiscence of the concrete—thus
departing from the ' musical ' condition. Pater's ' perfect '
poetry, then, could be counted on the fingers of one hand,
while the great mass of poetry that moves men, lacking
this ' musical' quality, must be held to be relatively imperfect art—a position which outrages the æsthetic judgment of the world, placing, as it would do, a beautiful
morsel like Rossetti's *An Old Song Ended* above the
bulk of Shakespeare, and certainly above *The Ring
and the Book*. When we have arrived at this point it
becomes clear that Pater was led into such a fallacy
partly by his thoughtless use of the word ' idea,' and
partly by the bias of his own nature, which leaned
towards the musical, and was more at home among
exquisitely attuned sensations than among the pathos
and interest of the rough-hewn facts of life. One sees
this even in the passage in which he illustrates from
painting his contention that the perfect art tends
towards music. ' In an actual landscape we see a long
white road, lost suddenly on the hill-verge. That is the
matter of one of the etchings of M. Alphonse Legros :
only, in this etching, it is informed by an indwelling

solemnity of expression, seen upon it or half-seen, within
the limits of an exceptional moment, or caught from his
own mood, perhaps, but which he maintains as the very
essence of the thing, throughout his work. Sometimes a
momentary hint of stormy light may invest a homely or
too familiar scene with a character which might well have
been drawn from the deep places of the imagination.
Then we might say that this particular effect of light,
this sudden inweaving of gold thread through the texture
of the haystack, and the poplars, and the grass, gives the
scene artistic qualities, that it is like a picture. And
such tricks of circumstance are commonest in landscape
which has little salient character of its own ; because in
such scenery all the material details are so easily
absorbed by that informing expression of passing light,
and elevated throughout their whole extent to a new and
delightful effect by it. And hence the superiority, for
most conditions of the picturesque, of a river-side in
France to a Swiss valley, because on the French river-
side mere topography, the simple material, counts for so
little, and all being very pure, untouched, and tranquil in
itself, mere light and shade have such easy work in
modulating it to one dominant tone. The Venetian
landscape, on the other hand, has in its material conditions much which is hard or harshly definite ; but the
masters of the Venetian School have shown themselves
little burdened by them.'

One has only to read that passage critically to arrive
at the psychological genesis of Pater's theory. His
idealisation of music as the type of perfect art, and his
notion that landscape approached perfection as it became
vague and indefinite like music,[1] came from the swoon of

----

[1] I am not arguing, of course, against the painter's pure rapture in effects of
light and colour, as distinguished from the interest created by the ' subject ' of
the picture. What I do contend is that this hardly makes out Pater's main

his more specialised faculties in the presence of beauty.
The broad emotion, the gently diffused organic thrill,
were all he wanted, not the mood that also has its
artistic interest and its beauty—the æsthetic pain, which is
really a pleasure, that comes from the spectacle of the
strife, and torture, and frustration of life and of nature.
He seems to have been curiously like Wagner, in that
certain very vague and generalised emotions were sufficient to satisfy his æsthetic needs. Wagner's *Art Work
of the Future* touches Pater's theory of art where it
maintains the 'purely human' character of music, this
character distinguishing it from the other arts, which are
concerned with faculties whose main business is with the
world of actual life. It simply means that Wagner
despised poetry because it gave him no real æsthetic
pleasure; and Pater's theory, if pushed to a rigorous
logical conclusion, would be indistinguishable from
Wagner's. The theory loses sight of the fact that,
although the delight given by music is most continuous
and most homogeneous, human beings are content to
forgo this continuity and homogeneity of sensuous
pleasure in the other arts for the sake of other
qualities which they possess, other virtues by which
they appeal to organs that must also have their
æsthetic satisfaction. Even in music one sees the
same phenomenon. Look, for example, at the curious
sonata of Beethoven (Op. 31, No. 2), with the strange
descent, near the close of the first movement, into recitative. Music like this, many people would contend, has
no place in a sonata. Instrumental music must appeal
to us, in Gurney's words, as a ' self-justified succession of

theory. Refine the 'subject' of landscape away as far as you like, there must
always be *some* subject, some reference to actual nature, some reminiscence of
things concrete; and this kindling of memory is an essential part of the total
æsthetic pleasure. To this there is no parallel in music.

tones.' Recitative only finds its justification in the words which it accompanies; and the sensation of frustration, of perplexity, which many musicians feel when the recitative passage occurs in this sonata, is really most significant. Why does one tolerate, along with words, a musical sequence that is quite uninteresting apart from the words? Plainly because the words, or, at any rate, the words and music in combination, minister to a faculty which craves satisfaction; and some of the finest scenes of Wagner's operas—such as that between Alberich and Hagen, in *Götterdämmerung*—would be unmeaning and almost uninteresting if played simply as music. The final conclusion is that, just as instrumental music by itself cannot satisfy certain of our æsthetic needs, so there are other needs, other faculties, which no music can satisfy; which cannot be satisfied even by the poetry that approaches most nearly to music. And if Pater argues that the highest art is that which resembles music in its vagueness, we must attribute this judgment to the fact that Pater's brain was more susceptible to vague than to specialised artistic emotion.

Music and Race

ERNEST NEWMAN

IT is a good many years ago now since John Stuart Mill
laid it down that of all the methods of accounting for the
differences between one nation's characteristics and those
of another, the method of explaining everything by 'race'
was assuredly the most vulgar.   And if even yet we have
not learned to see the futility of these pseudo-explana-
tions in political history—if even yet, for example, we
attribute the defects of Irish civilisation or of the French
character to the 'instability of the Celt'—it is hardly
reasonable to expect sound science on the question of
race and music.   Here, of course, the wrong idea does no
great harm, such as is done by the kindred error in
politics; but it is, perhaps, worth while giving a little
attention to it for the mere sake of clearness and
correctness.   And so, having been much grieved at
heart, during a perusal of Dr. Parry's admirable volume
on *The Evolution of the Art of Music,* by the jaunty,
naked, and unashamed appearance of some of the
most dreadful racial fallacies, I am moved to express
my feeling about the matter here, in the hope that the

next edition of the work will be rid of what is almost its only defect.

The fallacies begin about the middle of the book. Dr. Parry is concerned to point out what he imagines to be the difference between the Italians on the one hand, and the Germans and English on the other. 'In respect of external beauty' neither English nor Germans are 'so keen in appreciation, or so apt in creative faculty, as Italians, and during the period in which beauty was the principal aim of art they had to follow the lead of the more precocious nation. . . . The late English phase of the madrigal period affords instructive illustrations of racial tendencies, for composers aimed at characteristic expression of the words far oftener than the great Italian masters had done' (p. 144). This is merely one of those half-truths that have sufficient conformity to facts to make them impose on us at first hearing, until we see that a number of other facts can be adduced to prove precisely the opposite. There is, of course, a certain amount of truth in the view that the Italians, as a whole, have leaned to what we may call linear or superficial beauty, while the Germans and the English have set store by a beauty that is more intensive and esoteric. But the danger lies in the looking upon this quality of the Italians as due to something in the 'Italian nature.' A moment's reflection will show us that we English have had composers, such as Balfe and Vincent Wallace, whose work was typically 'Italian' in point of stress upon linear beauty; while Palestrina and many of the older Church composers go far to upset the theory that mere 'external beauty' is the great characteristic of the Italians. Broadly speaking, as I have admitted, the Italians did lean towards external and the Germans towards internal beauty. As Dr. Parry puts it in another place: 'The Italians gravitated away from strong dramatic expression [in opera], and, indeed, from immediate expression of any kind, and endeavoured merely to illustrate situations as they presented themselves by the general sentiment of an entire movement or an entire passage of melody. . . . A certain native easy-going indolence seems to have directed them into the road they chose, while the development of melody of the operatic type (which in itself is equivalent to linear design) sprang from the gift and instinct of the nation for singing' (p. 146). But the main reason for the degeneration of operatic expression into mere luscious aria-writing was the political and social stagnation of the country, the so-called cultured and leisured class being at one with the uninstructed in the desire merely for an easy form of sensuous pleasure at the theatre ; while the absence of any good poetical drama left all classes without ideals of what true dramatic expression should be. The language, again, which, as Vernon Lee has remarked, tends by its very fluidity to singing rather than to virile rhetoric or drama, would assist the downward course of dramatic expression in opera. Clearly there are concrete local and temporal causes by which we can explain the facts, without having recourse to the pseudo-explanation of ' race '—to what Dr. Parry calls ' the peculiarities of the Italian disposition.' The Italian is by no means the only nation that has written ' Italian opera.'

So again with Dr. Parry's later comparison of Italians and Germans (p. 231). ' The bent of the Germans, on the other hand, was not so much towards beauty as towards expression and character. Their very type of beauty was different from that of the Italians. The Italians looked for beauty of externals, and the Germans for beauty of thought. The instinct for beauty of thought comes out analogously in their artists' work. To the eye there is not much beauty of externals in Albert Dürer

and Holbein, but of expression and thought there is
ample to engage the mind and the sensibilities again and
again.' But what of the vast strength of Michael Angelo,
and the refined, intellectual sensibility of Leonardo? I
can very well imagine Dr. Parry, if these two artists had
been Germans, contrasting them, as typical of the German
spirit, with Raphael or Titian. I can imagine him, for
example, taking a sensuous, blonde Magdalen of Titian
as typical of the Italian feeling for external beauty,
and calling attention to the quiet, intensive, meditative,
intellectual beauty of the *Mona Lisa* as typical of the
German's more 'inward' manner of conceiving life. And
if Adolf Jensen and Spohr had been Italians, would not
Dr. Parry have been able to quote them as examples of
the Italian thirst for sensuous, external, linear beauty?
The plain truth evidently is that German music became
deeper in content than the Italian, because the social
circumstances of the two nations were different. The
politically-emasculate society of Italy simply wanted
sensuous amusement from music. In Germany, the mere
impulse of the Reformation, tending as it did to make
life more serious for a time, had much to do with making
more serious the national manner of regarding the art
which was so useful a servant of religion. The explanation of the national difference may be sought along many
lines, but the explanation of 'race' is at all events
superfluous. No one contends, of course, that as a nation
the Italians' are not more sensuous than the Teutons *in
certain things*.[1] But remembering, as we must do, how
the culture of one nation can fertilise that of another, and
how a change in the social conditions or the means of
cultivating an art will lead to a radical change in the
methods and expression of art, it is clear that all

---

[1] In matters of eating and drinking the Teutonic nations are certainly very
much more 'sensuous' than the Latin.

formulas about the linear beauty of the Italians and the inward beauty of the Germans are hopelessly *à priori* and unscientific.

This becomes still more evident when, in a later chapter, Dr. Parry arrives at the position that, though Haydn and Mozart 'both were Southern Germans and Roman Catholics in religion,' Haydn 'is throughout as Teutonic in spirit and manner as it was possible to be in those times' (*sic*), while Mozart 'with more delicate artistic perception, more sense of beauty, a much higher gift of technique, and more general facility, is comparatively deficient in individuality, and *hardly shows any trace of Teutonism in style from first to last*' (pp. 242, 243). I do not know what Dr. Parry means by the extraordinary remark that a Teuton was as Teutonic as it was possible to be in his day, as if Teutons were more Teutonic at some times than at others. But when he speaks of Mozart, also a Teuton,[1] as showing few traces of Teutonism in style, and four pages further on, again, of Haydn acting 'with Teutonic impulse,' the theory of race is evidently becoming a little threadbare. And all the while Dr. Parry's pages themselves furnish the true explanation of the difference between the two composers. He has pointed out that Mozart's travels and constant association with high-class musicians and men of culture gave a quality to his music that was necessarily absent from the simpler Haydn, whose life was less varied, less open to the breath of foreign culture, and whose great model was Philip Emmanuel Bach, the serious German.

---

[1] Dr. Parry may, of course, reply that by 'Teutonic' he means belonging to Northern Germany. But an examination of the theory on these lines makes it still more absurd. Beethoven, I suppose, would be regarded as a typical 'Teuton.' Yet Mozart's birthplace, Augsburg, is considerably nearer Bonn (Beethoven's birthplace) than is Rohrau (Haydn's birthplace). If race goes for anything, then, Mozart ought to have been more Teutonic than Haydn.

Clearly (setting aside the constitutional difference in alertness and vivacity of temperament) it is to the different circumstances of the lives of the two men that we must trace their idiosyncrasies of style, not to any fancied difference in the amount of 'Teutonism' that was imparted by the gods to each of these Teutons.

For after all Dr. Parry's insistence on the great racial contrast between the German and the Italian, it turns out later on that 'Mozart and the Italians, *among whom he represents the highest type*, usually make long meandering passages of melody with no very definite articulation' (p. 291); so that the typical Italian is after all a German! Mozart, in fact, though a German, is not 'a true Teuton.' 'The true Teuton,' Dr. Parry remarks (*à propos* of Schubert), 'aiming at concentration of expression, compresses his thought into figures which are specially definite and telling.' It apparently does not occur to Dr. Parry that Schubert had a very different class of songs to set to music from those of Mozart, and that he was writing for a somewhat different audience. This, however, is by the way. The important thing is that of two Germans, one is a typical Italian and the other a true Teuton. What, then, is our astonishment upon discovering, a sentence or two later, that Schumann 'was gifted with more of the familiar Teutonic disposition to reflect and look inwards than Schubert, whose gaiety of the Viennese type generally kept him in touch with the outward aspect of things' (p. 292). That is, the true Teuton is *not* a true Teuton in comparison with a truer Teuton. It is charmingly symmetrical, but hardly scientific ; the upshot of it all being that by 'Teutonism' Dr. Parry simply means earnestness and depth. If a composer of any nation shows this spirit, he has the spirit of Teutonism ; if a German has not the spirit, he is not a 'true Teuton.' The formula is utter chaos.

But even worse than this elaborate fantasia upon Teutonism is Dr. Parry's little interlude upon Gallicism. He begins by saying that 'the French have never shown any talent for self-dependent instrumental music'—the historical reasons for this, such as the superior development of poetic art in France in the seventeenth and eighteenth centuries, and the strength given to opera by its early association with the King and Court, not being hinted at. It is all due to 'the French spirit.' 'The kernel of the Gallic view of things is, moreover, persistently theatrical,[1] and all the music in which they have been successful has had either direct or secondary connection with the stage. Berlioz was so typical a Frenchman in this respect that he could hardly see even the events of his own life as they actually were ; but generally in the light of a sort of fevered frenzy, which made everything—both ups and downs—look several times larger than the reality. Some of his most exciting experiences, as related by himself, are conceived in the spirit of melodrama, and could hardly have happened, as he tells them, except on the stage. This was not the type of human creature of whom self-dependent instrumental music could be expected ; and it is no wonder that when he took to experimenting in that line of art he made it even more theatrical than ordinary theatrical music' (p. 277). You have only to label the French 'theatrical,' and all the rest follows. On these lines, then, the drama of Kyd and his fellows in Elizabethan England was, by reason of its bombast and melodrama, typically French. It does not occur to Dr. Parry that Berlioz's delusions as to the events of his life were due not to the fact of his being born on the other side of the Channel, but to a cerebral disease which is as

---

[1] Bossuet, Massillon, Pascal, Vauvenargues, Condorcet, Flaubert, and Leconte de Lisle—to name only a few—were presumably *not* Gallic, then.

common among Englishmen as among Frenchmen. On
Dr. Parry's thesis, Swedenborg and Joanna Southcote
must both have been French. Do Frenchmen as a whole,
however, take so melodramic a view of their daily lives as
Berlioz did? Part of Dr. Parry's indictment of Berlioz's
'French theatricality' is, I suppose, based on the composer's very stagey letters to his old love Madame F....
But the lady's letters to Berlioz are models of calm and
sage good sense—although she was French, and might,
therefore, according to Dr. Parry's theory, have been more
likely to carry on the correspondence in the good old
theatrical manner. Even on Dr. Parry's own showing,
Berlioz was an abnormal case; yet this abnormal case
becomes, for the purposes of the argument, the 'typical
Frenchman'! Even Dr. Parry goes on to remark that
'the tendency to exaggeration is all of a piece with the
high tension of his nervous organisation.' Quite so;
only why not put his musical eccentricities down to his
abnormal organisation, instead of to a quite imaginary
'Gallic view of things'? And finally, Dr. Parry has, of
course, to point out, while referring to 'the dangerous
susceptibility of the French nature to specious show and
mere external effect,' that 'the most imposing result
obtained in the direction of French opera is strictly in
accordance with those characteristics of the nation which
have persisted so long that they were even noticed by
the conquering Romans' (p. 311). As a matter of fact,
there is not a grain of evidence that the Gauls spoken of
by 'the conquering Romans' were the ancestors of the
modern French, or that the Romans had made a very
profound study of the mental and moral qualities of the
Gallic tribes they came in contact with. These are
vulgar errors that will ultimately go by the board, and
with them, let us hope, all *à priori* theories about Gallicism
and Teutonism and the rest. The very latest thing in

the race-fallacy is the wild nonsense now current as to the 'Slavonic' brain and temperament; as if all Slavs were built upon the same mental pattern, and as if the countries occupied by them were no more than five miles square. The problems of national psychology are not quite so distressingly simple as this; but if otherwise intelligent and able writers have not yet cleared their minds of the more primitive fallacies that cluster round Saxon and Celt, it is perhaps too much to expect from them anything like a rational understanding of the complex being whom, with easy comprehensiveness, they term the 'Slav.'

The Libretto of the Future

W. BARCLAY SQUIRE

THE history of the development of the libretto remains
to be written. It would be an interesting and not un-
profitable task to trace the gradual evolution of the art
of writing words for stage-music from the curious be-
ginnings of the operatic form in those compositions in
which, like the *Amfiparnasso* of Orazio Vecchi, the
dramatic action was confined to a few characters, probably playing in dumb show, while the words they were
supposed to say were set as madrigals sung by an
invisible chorus, down to the complex works of Wagner,
in which music and words are so closely wedded that
neither can be properly understood apart from the other.
The influence of the Masque, surviving in its merely
spectacular displays down to the modern French Grand
Opera, the revolt against conventional forms which in
England gave rise to ballad opera, in Germany to the
Singspiel, and in France to the Opéra-Comique, the reaction on Grand Opera, giving rise in its turn to the
Romantic School of the first half of the present century—
these and a thousand other side-issues which at various

times have left their traces on operatic forms have never
yet been treated from the point of view of historic evolution
and development. At the present day, when the precise
form which the opera of the future is to assume is a
matter of so much doubt and uncertainty, a comprehensive
study of the whole question would be especially valuable,
and might point the way in a direction at present little
thought of, or at least but dimly perceived. One thing,
at all events, is certain : if opera is to retain its place as
a living form of dramatic art, the lines upon which it is
constructed—in other words, the forms of librettos—must
be cleared from the uncertainty of aim and vagueness of
method which characterise most of the productions of
the last ten or fifteen years. That we live in a period
of changing taste must be patent to the least observant
intelligence. Such revolutionary epochs are common to
all the arts. Opera, though it cannot be said to have
existed for much more than two hundred years, has
already experienced several crises of the kind, and the
past has proved that though the outlook has often been
as gloomy as it is at present, yet light has suddenly
appeared from an unlooked-for quarter, and new progress
has been made in a direction which at first seemed most
unpromising. Just now, doubtless, one of the great
drawbacks to anything like progress in opera is the
remoteness of the chance a composer has of getting his
work performed. This is especially the case in England,
where there is no permanent central operatic establishment ready to produce new works. On the few occasions
when there seemed a possibility of a national opera being
firmly established, there has been no deficiency in the
supply of new works, but in each case the experiment has
resulted in failure, and one after another the operatic
companies which appeared destined to form the nucleus
of a permanent establishment in London have either been

broken up or have drifted away into the provinces. In no instance has the experiment lasted long enough for it to be ascertained what really are the lines upon which English composers and librettists should work, and it is to a large extent this, more than the actual lack of subjects fit for operatic treatment, which occasions the difficulty composers complain of in finding good opera-books.

A librettist working for a permanent establishment, whether it be Grand Opera or Opéra-Comique, knows at once the public for whom he has to write, and the company he has to fit; but when, as, for instance, at Covent Garden, works written for production under the most widely divergent conditions, and destined originally for performance in theatres of utterly different dimensions, are performed side by side, it is almost inevitable that both librettists and composers should lose all sense of proportion and produce operas which are a jumble of the most incongruous ingredients. Not only is this the case in England, but in France also, where opera still flourishes more than in any other country, and also to a less extent in Germany, the same confusion exists, and there is the same breaking down of barriers which were formerly strictly maintained. The difference between works produced at the Grand Opera and at the Opéra-Comique is almost a forgotten tradition; subjects only suited for a small stage and for delicate treatment are handled with a heaviness of touch which is only fitted to the immense auditorium and vast stage of the largest opera-house, while works destined for the limited resources of a small theatre are brought forward in huge buildings where they infallibly lose half their proper effect. This difficulty of *locale* is, after all, one which can be remedied by operatic managers themselves. In the ideal opera-house of the future it could be met by having two theatres, either under one roof or adjoining, as in the case of the Residenz Theater and the Opera House at Munich, where the stage and auditorium of the former are precisely the right size for works of the Opéra-Comique repertory which would be practically ineffective on the large stage of the regular opera-house. More serious for librettists and composers are the questions of subject and construction—what subject is at present best fitted for opera-libretti, and in what form is the book to be cast in order to give the musician best scope for his talent, and to hit the public taste? If these questions could be decided definitely, the clouds which enshroud the future of opera would be dispelled, but it is precisely on these points that the greatest uncertainty at present seems to exist, and that both librettists and composers seem now to be groping vaguely in the dark. Just as in political science a careful and scientific study of past history may point the way to new combinations and new tendencies which should be fostered in the present, so it is not impossible that an examination of the various vicissitudes of opera in the past, treated in a broadly scientific rather than in a technical manner, might throw light upon these grave uncertainties which at present paralyse all efforts at the production of new operas of value. Such a task is beyond the scope of a mere news-paper article. For its proper accomplishment it demands not only a large practical knowledge of opera, but also an amount of antiquarian research which would yield what the ordinary reader would probably consider very dry results.

Without, however, attempting to enter upon so wide a field, or arriving at conclusions which would, in the circumstances, be only too misleading, it may not be out of place to draw attention to some of the broad lines which an historical survey suggests. In the first place, it is not a little remarkable that, for upwards of a hundred years, the only subjects considered proper for Grand Opera were principally classical. Gasparini and Domenico Scarlatti, indeed, produced operas on *Hamlet*, Handel brought out a *Riccardo Primo*, and the Cid legends and the works of Tasso were occasionally drawn upon, but on the whole the librettists of the Grand Operas of the last century went for their subjects either to classical history or mythology. The two men whose names are most intimately connected with the operatic stage throughout the eighteenth century—Apostolo Zeno and Metastasio—almost without exception drew their inspiration from these sources, and the influence they wielded on public taste was increased by the fact that their libretti were used, not by one composer only, but over and over again, often during a period extending to forty or fifty years. Looking back upon the changes and developments which have taken place in opera since the days of Weber, it is a little difficult to account for the permanence of public taste during the eighteenth century. The reason seems to be that until the rise of *Intermezzi* and their successors, *Opere Buffe*, opera was regarded entirely as the entertainment of the upper classes, depending for its very existence principally upon the small courts which swarmed throughout Italy and Germany. The formality of the ancient *régime* was reflected in the music of the men who set the libretti of Haym, Zeno, and Metastasio. Rules of etiquette extended to stage matters, and it was as much a matter of necessity that an opera should contain the regulation number of *Arie cantabile*, *Arie di portamento*, *Arie parlante*, and *Arie di bravura*, as that certain dignitaries should sit in armchairs and others only be entitled to stools without backs. In works so bound down by formality it is not to be wondered at that little attention was paid to dramatic fitness. The singers, indeed, wore costume, and a certain amount of gesture was expected, but no attention was paid to the story, and the recitatives probably gave a fitting opportunity for that conversation which always seems, down to the present day, to have been an inevitable accompaniment of opera before a fashionable audience. For this kind of work court-poets, like Apostolo Zeno and Metastasio, were admirably qualified. They never troubled themselves with the invention of dramatic plots, but all their talents were directed to writing smooth and singable verses, and in this they were both, and especially Metastasio, admirably successful. The reforms of Gluck, which it must be remembered were principally directed to the French Grand Opera, where there lingered the tradition of a more virile recitative, handed down from Cavalli through Lully, did not have any immediate effect in modifying the construction of the *Opera Seria* which ruled Italy and Germany, and it was not until the wave of Revolution swept over Europe that the old opera, with its conventionalities and classical absurdities, vanished in the train of the small courts, which had been its chief supporters. On the French stage, strengthened by Gluck's reforms, supported by the fashion of the Consulate and early Empire, and above all fortunate in having as its exponents musicians of such high artistic merit as Cherubini and Spontini, opera on classical subjects survived down to the third decade of the present century, when it was finally extinguished by the wave of Romanticism which originated musically in Germany, and in France with the dramas and novels of Victor Hugo and the elder Dumas.

The revolt against the pedantry of the older Italian opera gave rise to the *Intermezzi* of Pergolese, the *Opere Buffe* of Mozart, and the comic operas of Grétry. From these it was but a step further to the romanticism of Weber, Spohr, Marschner, Lindpaintner, and the early works of Wagner. In Italy, where the drama has never taken firm root in public taste, the decay of the old school was marked by no such strongly marked characteristics as are to be found in the development of opera north of the Alps. Librettos became more than ever the mere pegs upon which to hang a series of conventional airs and concerted pieces, and it is noteworthy that Rossini, perhaps the most gifted composer the country has produced for more than a century, ended his career as a writer of operas immediately he came in contact with the activity of the French Grand Opera. From the thirties down almost to the present day the one man who influenced the form of librettos in Northern Europe with undisputed sway was Scribe. For us, living at a period which has seen his method at its last gasp, it is difficult to do justice to his ability. In his best works, such as those he wrote for Meyerbeer, Halévy, and Auber, his talent lifts him high above any of his contemporaries; and if it is easy now to laugh at his conventionality and the poverty of his language, it should not be forgotten that he practically was the founder of a new school of opera, and had the insight to perceive what was required for the lyric stage at a time when the old methods were discredited and the operatic outlook seemed as forbidding as it does at the present day. But for him and Meyerbeer, Wagner could hardly have started upon his career; and though it pleased the Bayreuth reformer in after years to claim Gluck as the source of the innovations which have had so widespread an effect, the judgment of posterity, unbiassed by personal considerations which are still too close to the present generation to be seen in proper perspective, will probably look upon the German reformer as the artistic successor of a system which he attacked so violently by precept and example. The form of Grand Opera, as established by Scribe, has influenced alike operatic composers of all schools. Its power is to be detected in Donizetti's latest and best work; and the remarkable development in Verdi's later style dates from the time when he came in contact with the Parisian stage. Just now the reaction is making itself felt, and the French school seems daily becoming more and more under the influence of Bayreuth, and to be breaking loose from the traditions which for half a century have given it the leading place in the operatic stage. Unfortunately for the prospect of the immediate future, the secret of Wagner's power is so much more to be sought in the musical than in the dramatic side of his genius that, so far as the forms of librettos go, his influence has been principally destructive. His 'neue Kunst' remains still an unaccomplished dream, unless the isolated productions of his own brain are to be considered as a school, beginning and ending in himself. Until a composer arises possessing in an equal degree his extraordinary musical capacity, it seems hopeless to look for any one who will take up the sceptre where he laid it down.

With one exception, the consideration of which does not come within the scope of the present article, Wagner's works do not seem to point the way to any further developments, and it is in an altogether opposite direction that the 'neue Bahnen' of opera must be sought. It sounds almost a commonplace of journalism to say that anything may be proved by statistics, but though it is obvious that conclusions based upon such evidence are not to be accepted without a large margin of allowance for extraneous circumstances, the bent of popular taste can be undoubtedly gathered from a record of the number of performances of leading operas on the principal European stages during the last few years. Data for such a comparison are not to hand for a final and accurate result to be arrived at, but sufficient figures can be quoted to show that the public taste has latterly set in in a very definite and remarkable direction. Though productively Germany —including the Austrian Empire—must take a lower rank than Italy, and even France, the number of permanent operatic establishments where opera is sung in German is so much above that of any other country that it is safe to take, for our present purpose, the German operatic stage as an index of the opinion of the musical world. A Berlin critic has been at the trouble of tabulating the number of performances of different operas during 1894 at the various German opera-houses (including those of Austria and Switzerland). From this the following interesting particulars are selected of operas which were played more than a hundred times :—

> Auber : *La Muette de Portici,* 149.
> Beethoven : *Fidelio,* 149.
> Bizet : *Carmen,* 194.
> Donizetti : *La Fille du Regiment,* 103.
> Flotow : *Martha,* 217.
> Gounod : *Faust,* 204.
> Humperdinck : *Hänsel und Gretel,* 469.
> Leoncavallo : *Pagliacci,* 503.
> Lortzing : *Undine,* 129.
>   „   *Czaar und Zimmermann,* 145.
>   „   *Der Waffenschmied,* 143.
> Mascagni : *Cavalleria Rusticana,* 515.
> Mozart : *Le Nozze di Figaro,* 122.
>   „   *Don Giovanni,* 116.
>   „   *Die Zauberflöte,* 123.
> Nessler : *Der Trompeter von Säkkingen,* 197.
> Nicolai : *Die Lustigen Weiber von Windsor,* 123.
> Rossini : *Il Barbiere di Siviglia,* 112.
> Smetana : *Die Verkaufte Braut,* 193.
> Thomas : *Mignon,* 107.

Verdi: *Il Trovatore*, 206.
Wagner: *Der Fliegende Holländer*, 118.
    „   *Tannhäuser*, 223.
    „   *Lohengrin*, 270.
    „   *Die Meistersinger von Nürnberg*, 113.
Weber: *Der Freischütz*, 275.

Looking over this curious list, which may be taken as representing the most popular works in the general operatic repertory during the year in question, it is noteworthy that it consists almost entirely of operas which are marked by strong national characteristics. Can anything be more German than *Hänsel und Gretel*, Lortzing's *Undine* and *Waffenschmied*, Nessler's *Trompeter*, Wagner's *Tannhäuser* and *Meistersinger*, and Weber's *Freischütz*? National characteristics of Italy are the basis of Auber's *Masaniello* and Leoncavallo's and Mascagni's operas; French militarism inspired Donizetti's *Fille du Régiment*; Bohemian village life Smetana's *Verkaufte Braut*; Bizet's *Carmen* lives through its Spanish local colour, and even Flotow's *Martha* and Nicolai's *Merry Wives* owe something to the fact that the scene of each work is laid in England. It would be interesting to see if this feature of a taste for operas on strongly marked national subjects has increased or diminished since 1894. In the absence of statistics, and writing only as one whose official position obliges him to keep up a tolerably wide knowledge of the taste of the musical world on the Continent, I should be inclined to think that, instead of growing less, it has latterly become much more marked. As one instance out of many, it may be mentioned that at the Vienna opera, which has always been remarkable for the eclecticism of its taste, during the season lasting from August 1896 to June 1897, of fifty-six operas, given 272 times, forty performances were devoted to nine works by Wagner, while

Smetana's *Verkaufte Braut* was given twenty-one times, Humperdinck's *Hänsel und Gretel* nineteen times, and Goldmark's *Heimchen am Herd* came third with fifteen performances. The Viennese statistics, which have only just been published, are very interesting, as they seem to show exactly the kind of opera-book which the public will accept in the immediate future. For opera in the highest sense of the word Wagner is sufficient; his music dramas have practically made a clean sweep of the works which used to be the mainstay of the lyric stage thirty years ago. After him the only chance of success lies in libretti constructed on avowedly national lines, giving a composer an opportunity of any amount of local colour and the plentiful use of folk-songs.

The earliest work of this description was Glinka's *Life for the Czaar*, which saw the light so long ago as 1836, and was itself founded on an older opera by an obscure Italian composer named Cavos. Glinka's work lived through its strong national colouring, but it was hardly enough known, like most Russian music until recent years, for it to have any distinct influence out of the country of its birth. Bizet's *Carmen*, which was produced the year before the first Bayreuth Festival, really marks the foundation of the new style of opera, and it is noteworthy that it was this work which Friedrich Nietzsche, after he had apostatised from the cult of the Wagnerian School, upheld as the model of what opera should be. It is the fashion to look upon Nietzsche's 'Fall Wagner's' as the product of a diseased brain; exaggerated and bitter as much of that brilliant pamphlet is, it undoubtedly draws attention to the fact that *Carmen* was the one modern work able to hold its own by the side of Wagner's productions, and, as now seems to be the case, to become the point of departure for a new school of opera. The last twenty years have seen an increasing

X

tendency, partly of political origin, to emphasise racial and national differences. The Scandinavian and Sclavonic schools of music are now accepted facts, and there seems every probability that the same causes which have led to their formation will have effect on the development of the opera of the future. The production of Stanford's *Shamus O'Brien* in England is not without significance; it shows that our own musicians and librettists are alive to the conditions which have won success for Smetana, Humperdinck, and the modern Italian school. Unfortunately, the existence of opera in England is much more precarious than it is on the Continent, and the question of language makes it a very difficult thing for an English composer to obtain a hearing at Covent Garden. The late Sir Augustus Harris, with that curious insight he possessed into everything connected with the stage, foresaw that in the future opera would be so much based on national lines that for Covent Garden to retain its place as the focus of the operatic world it would be necessary for performances to take place in French, English, Italian, and German. How this is to be accomplished is a problem which has not yet been solved, even if (as is very doubtful) it is capable of solution. Meanwhile the fact remains that if opera is to live it must be based upon national subjects and seek its inspiration more and more in the music and poetry of the people. Not only is this recognised in Germany, but it is the secret of the rapid rise to celebrity of men like Mascagni and Leoncavallo. The *Cavalleria Rusticana* of the former, and the *Pagliacci* of the latter, undoubtedly owed their extraordinary vogue more to their strong national colouring than to any great musical genius of their composers, and the reason that neither master has succeeded in sustaining the sudden reputation which was achieved in these works is that their subsequent librettos have reverted to subjects which belong to a class of work that no longer has any hold over the public. The same reason explains why France, with all the activity of its operatic stage, has produced nothing of permanent interest during the past few years. César Franck's two operas, musically of the greatest value, have failed owing to the nature of their librettos, and neither the Grand Opéra nor the Opéra-Comique has latterly given birth to any work which has gone the round of the opera-houses of Europe like the best operas of Meyerbeer, Auber, and Adam did in former years. The only composer who seems to have a right idea of what is now required on the operatic stage is M. Bruneau; his *L'Attaque du Moulin* struck the right note, and if its composer were a stronger musician it would be to him that France should look for the reforms that are needed if the French lyrical drama is to maintain the place it has held for so long past. Unfortunately M. Bruneau's dramatic insight and feeling are not enough to atone for the poverty of his musical ideas. His *Requiem* was sufficient to show that he has no claim to be considered a composer of the first, or even the second, rank, and in his *Messidor* he has made the fatal mistake of trying to combine myth, realism, and the conventions of Grand Opera,.ingredients so utterly incompatible that even a strong score—such as the music of *Messidor* is not—could hardly have welded them into a perfect work of art.

Beatrice and Benedict

E. HANSLICK

IT must be remembered that Hercules once spun wool,
and that Samson ground corn, in order to be able to
realise Berlioz as a composer of comic opera. From
studying his musical creations, we know him as a revolutionist, whose spirit is directed towards the highest
passion, and the most fantastically tragic ; by studying
his writings, as a hard ascetic, for whom all entertaining
music—in the broadest and best sense—was an abomination. He especially abhorred comic opera, and used to
designate what appeared to him to be most contemptible
and most worthy of annihilation ' Opéra comique.' Those
who knew personally the man with the unkempt, grey
forest of hair, his gloomy glance and pessimistic contempt
for the whole world, would have expected almost anything else from him than a light comedy-opera. It was
no Delila, but the renowned director from Baden-Baden,
Benazet, who cut the locks of our musical Samson, and
delivered him up to the comic opera. At Benazet's invitation, Berlioz for several years gave annually a grand
concert in Baden-Baden, largely devoted to his own

compositions. Next the King of Baden, as Benazet was called, undertook the building of a new theatre, and commissioned Berlioz to write a comic opera for the opening ceremony. The latter quickly decided to make use of Shakespeare's comedy, *Much Ado about Nothing*, for his work, and to arrange his own libretto from the play. He changed nothing but the title—a dangerous one for composers—and gave his assurance that in *Beatrice et Benedict* 'much ado' should nowhere find a place. The first performance took place on the 9th of August 1862, 'with great success,' as Berlioz writes— 'with very little,' as the German papers state. The second performance followed on the 11th of August, a third did not take place. The very flower of the Paris Opéra Comique was at the disposal of Berlioz : Madame Charton - Demeur, 'une femme d'assez d'esprit,' sang Beatrice ; the excellent tenor, Montaubry, Benedict.

In Shakespeare's *Much Ado about Nothing* two distinct 'actions' are interwoven : one grave—that in which Hero and Claudia's love-affair is disturbed by the intrigues of Don Juan ; and one gay—the 'merry war' between Beatrice and Benedict. Each of these two actions has been used for operatic material : Berton's *Montano et Stephanie* is founded on the grave, Berlioz's *Beatrice* on the merry half of Shakespeare's comedy. Berlioz assumes at once that Hero and Claudia are betrothed, and leaves them blissful in their happiness ; consequently he is all the busier with Beatrice and Benedict—the enemies of matrimony—who provoke one another with not very withering mockery in order that they may eventually marry ! All the remaining personages of the piece group themselves as subordinate figures round these two, to whom they merely have to give the cue, as it were. In all the important scenes Berlioz has retained Shakespeare's text, word for word. The comic episodes he suppressed, and replaced them with others of his own creation. To him alone belongs the comic figure of the bandmaster Somirone, in whom, it is alleged, Berlioz was caricaturing his antagonist Fétis. Let us follow the course of the piece.

The overture makes use of two well-contrasted themes from the opera. The delicate, playful allegretto, merrily sparkling, is taken from the closing duettino; the melancholy andante belongs to Beatrice's aria in the second act. The cheerful motive very easily obtains the upper hand, which it retains to the very last note; unfortunately it is not exactly developed, but is merely wearily repeated. Herr Richard Pohl, the 'farmer-general' of the Berlioz-enthusiasm in Germany, calls this the weakest of all his overtures, a judgment with which I cannot agree. It is no masterpiece, it is true, but it is a genuine comedy-overture, and, in any case, is clearer, more natural, I may say, musically speaking, more seemly than the overtures to *Waverley*, to *Les Francs Juges*, and *Le Corsaire*. The opera opens with an everyday festival chorus.

After this a Sicilienne is danced, which is not so much wanting in grace of form as in light and vigorous colouring. As this dance vanishes without any regular close, so it also disappears, leaving no sign in the mind of the audience. Adolphe Jullien, as a French supporter of his colleague Richard Pohl, declares that this Sicilienne must be envied even by Auber! I presume that M. Jullien has heard the ballet music in *La Muette de Portici*? It appears that Berlioz, who could write no dance music, could not trust himself to write a festival march, for here, at the return of the victorious army, he had a most superb opportunity. Hero remains behind on the stage, in order to give vent to her longing for the expected bridegroom in an aria. The andante sounds tender and dreamy, consequently the more trivial sounds the allegro movement, which, to our astonishment, terminates in a lengthy, tasteless coloratura tail! Don Pedro appears with the knights, and immediately that irritating wordy war between Beatrice and Benedict arises, and develops into a very long duet.

The declamatory first part, where the voices are not retained in the dull, deep register, is really effective; the second and quicker part consists entirely of commonplace, old-fashioned phrases. The best of the following trio of the three friends is its commencement, Benedict's hearty cry: 'Ich, Ehemann? Gott soll bewahren!' which the two basses repeat in thirds, and continue thus. In course of this continuation—and it lasts a very long time—the trio becomes very commonplace and wearisome. Now the conductor Somirone hurries with his singers on to the scene, and commences to rehearse the wedding cantata. As this opens with the following words, 'O die, thou fondest pair,' it belongs to the most doubtful of jokes, as it is written in the form of a double fugue, to the most unpardonable of offences against good taste. Berlioz hated the fugal form, and made it appear ridiculous whenever he had the opportunity. At the same time he himself composed some, it is true, as he states, in a more or less parodic spirit, but—a fugue, nevertheless, remains a fugue. The public does not remark the idea, and is put out of humour; instead of having a comical effect— as was hoped—the piece becomes cumbrous and wearisome to listen to.

The rondo, in which Benedict rejoices over his latest conquest, flows along evenly, and is not without a certain piquant rhythm. Hero and her companion, Ursula, appear hand-in-hand in the garden, and celebrate the summer-like moonlight in a notturno, which, with its pretty successions of thirds, accompanied by a quiet rocking movement, captivates the hearer. It is the best

piece in the entire opera ; the only one which met with
any success at the first performance in Baden-Baden, and,
until now, the only piece which has become familiar to
Parisians through concert performances.

Very original the melody is not, but the number is
expressive and well-sounding. With this duet the first
act closes right happily ; the second has not so much to
offer. In order to freshen it somewhat, Director Jahn in
Vienna introduced the *Ball-Scherzo* from the *Symphonie fantastique* into the first scene. This graceful
number, however, is more effective when independent
than with the dance—which it rather hinders than assists.
A trivial drinking-song of Somirone's, which is only
effective on account of its original accompaniment of
guitars and trumpets, is followed by the most important
and, indeed, the only weighty number in the second act—
Beatrice's aria. The *Andante*, whose theme we recognise
in the overture, is noble in expression, but, unfortunately,
wearisome in its inordinate length. The *Allegro* returns
again to vulgar, old-fashioned phraseology. Beatrice
sings with Hero and Ursula a trio, which has nothing
whatever to do with the action, and which was composed
later by Berlioz. It is an error that this piece should
remind one, both in melody and accompaniment, of the
two-part notturno, whose effectiveness it almost attains.
A curtailment of this painfully long trio seems to me to
be very desirable. An unlawfully simple bridal-song for
chorus, which in its original length would be unbearable,
but which, through the kindness of Jahn, is 'put on half-
pay,' leads to the last and shortest piece in the opera—a
Scherzo-duet between Beatrice and Benedict. It is the
allegretto theme of the overture, which at first was
intended as an orchestral number, and afterwards arranged
in much too scrappy, rhapsodical phrases for the voices.
It might have been very charming had it been written in

a more vocal manner and been better executed. With a sudden outcry on the part of the chorus 'Demain, demain!' the opera closes,—if one can call this informal outburst a close! The nearer one approaches the end, one sees the better how hasty was the composer.

The Berlioz of *Harold*, of *Romeo*, of the *Requiem* is not recognisable in *Beatrice et Benedict*, or, more correctly, only recognisable by those who are most thoroughly in touch with certain rhythmic and harmonic eccentricities of the composer,—with his finer mixture of colour in the orchestra, and with his transitions from strokes of real genius to the most childishly trivial cantilena. In this opera Berlioz entirely laid aside his *rôle* of musical revolutionist; he makes no attempt, or shows no disposition, to reform anything at all of the usual customs of 'Opéra comique'; he abides by the change from song to spoken dialogue, and accommodates himself to the established form of 'morceaux carrés.' Into these old skins he never pours the new wine of his original individuality; on the contrary he returns, rather, to the older forms of expression adopted by past French composers. As a matter of fact, *Beatrice et Benedict* could have been composed before an Auber ever saw the light of day. Only in the detail, and not in the form, nor in the fundamental principles, does he show any sign of modern spirit.

The orchestra is extraordinarily discreetly, almost timidly, handled ; the trombones have half the evening to rest, the noisy instruments the whole. This reserve gives the opera an agreeably graceful, pleasant character, a light, brilliant distinction. The tone of 'comedy' is never disturbed—never developed into the fortissimo of grand opera.

However, there is more of fine grace therein than of healthy, full gaiety or hearty comicality. *Berlioz ne sait pas rire*, once remarked Jules Janin, and he was right. Berlioz's nature was thoroughly earnest and grave, one which must be compelled to be gay, and which, even with very great efforts, never could attain to the comic. How very far beneath the similar scene in the *Czaar und Zimmermann*, or even that in *Don Bucefalo*, stands the ostensibly comic cantata rehearsal of Somirone!

Since Berlioz greeted Shakespeare's *Much Ado about Nothing* as particularly well suited for operatic treatment, it is possible that he overlooked two not unimportant points. Firstly, that the witty railleries between Beatrice and Benedict, which in the comedy follow each other as quick as lightning, and through this quickness gain their power of amusement, do not lend themselves in any way approaching the same degree to musical treatment. Music requires both time and repetition. Secondly, the by-play of Beatrice and Benedict, when extracted from Shakespeare's comedy, is not in itself sufficient for an entire opera. Its dramatic interest is more or less ordinary, and in any case 'short-lived.' Berlioz's original idea of making a one-act opera was evidently the correct one. There is too little action and too little music for an entire evening's entertainment. In order to help in this latter difficulty to some extent, Herr Felix Mottl altered the whole of the spoken dialogue, which occupies a considerable amount of space, into recitative.

These recitatives—at times quite Meistersinger-like— are conspicuous by reason of their pregnant, lively expression, as at times they appear between two numbers of Berlioz's compositions. It is a very singular, and a unique example of precedent, to alter the dialogue of a French comic opera for us Germans, for we are already accustomed to prose even in serious opera. The beauties of Berlioz's operas are elegant and original, but are intermittent and ordinary in their force. *Beatrice et Benedict*

interested all in the Royal Court Opera-house from beginning to end. In order to make a powerful and enduring
effect on the public this fine music must develop at once
a much greater wealth of rich melodious ideas, fresher
colouring, and more lively motion.

Berlioz's latest biographer, Adolphe Jullien, tells us that
Berlioz made no secret of his hatred for Wagner, by
whom, indeed, he was shockingly treated. When Berlioz,
on one occasion, was, in society, speaking very heatedly
against Wagner, a lady timidly ventured to remark that
she considered Berlioz and Wagner very nearly related in
their particular tendencies; Berlioz received this as the
greatest possible insult, rose quickly and at once angrily
quitted the room.

It vexed him sorely when any one spoke of 'Wagner
and Berlioz'; but as German journals introduced the
'trifolium' 'Wagner, Liszt, Berlioz,' his anger must have
been boundless. Jullien, who has also written an enthusiastic book about Wagner, comes out in the affair between
these opponents as well as possible. He might have
declared openly that, though Wagner could not have
written a Symphony like *Romeo and Juliet*, Berlioz was
still more unable to cross swords with Wagner in the
region of opera-writing. Wagner thoroughly well understood how to devote his entire strength exclusively to the
dramatic province which appealed to him, whilst Berlioz
followed a pathway of grievous self-deception when he,
in the ambition of his old age, yoked himself to a gigantic
operatic creation—*Les Troyens*—which, in point of fact,
merely defined the insufficiency of his dramatic gifts.

I do not share the opinion that the future will produce the wished-for laurels for these *Trojans*. Berlioz's
wretched text, dovetailed together from Virgil's *Æneid*,
renders the opera half impossible; the music is conceived
in the widest sense, but is weak, dull, not lively—and this

is not happiness. This does not prevent us blaming French neglect, in that since Berlioz's death—nearly thirty years ago—they had not deemed it worth while to perform one single opera of his. So much respect, or, at any rate, so much curiosity, might one presuppose from Berlioz's countrymen. No Paris theatre dreams of performing *Beatrice* or *Benvenuto Cellini*—two easily represented operas, which are frequently given in Germany, and are full of beauties. Still less do they think of giving again *Les Troyens*. *Beatrice* is now quite unknown in France, as is the first part of *Les Troyens* (the fall of Troy); *Benvenuto Cellini*, having failed fifty years ago, has never been tried again; *Les Troyens en Carthage*, after surviving a few performances in the Théâtre Lyrique in 1863, has vanished for ever. The failure of this latter work was one of the last and hardest blows from which the aged master suffered. As Gounod so expressively remarked, Berlioz fell—like his heroic namesake Hector —under the walls of Troy. So long as the French, who are, musically, still a theatre-going nation, have not paid their fourfold debt of honour—whatever the success may be—so long have they no reason whatever to affect feelings of important superiority because of the posthumous veneration for Berlioz!

Alfred Bruneau and the

Modern Lyric Drama

ARTHUR HERVEY

Une œuvre d'art est un coin de la nature vu à travers un tempéra-ment.—EMILE ZOLA.

IT is scarcely necessary to point out the profound difference existing between the 'musical drama' of the present time and the 'opera' of the past. Imperceptibly, but no less surely, the theories and innovations, musical and dramatic, of Wagner, have been absorbed to a greater or less extent into the systems of all dramatic composers, irrespective of nationality.

The principle of the close union between music and drama, involving as it does the abandonment of vocal acrobatics and all sops to the vanity of the singer or the bad taste of the public, has been generally accepted as sound, while the immense latitude allowed and even imposed upon the composer in his musical methods has furnished him with practically unlimited means wherewith to vary his modes of expression. The spirit of 'routine' is, however, so engrained in the human mind that any departure from the ordinary course is viewed with distrust, and the innovator has to face an opposition as fierce as it is relentless; though, if he be a man of genius, he will find compensation in the enthusiastic admiration and devotion of those who understand him. Time, however, gradually creeps on, and the power and beauty so long denied to certain works finish by asserting their existence; the change in public opinion is as thorough as it is sudden, and the disdain of former days is converted into frenzied admiration. The compositions of Berlioz, Wagner, César Franck, to mention only three, are examples in point. As regards the last, his hour has even yet not arrived, but the gradual awakening of interest in his compositions points to the fact of its not being far distant. The above three masters are those whose influence upon the younger generation of French composers is, at the present moment, perhaps most marked; that of Gounod, so long predominant, being perceptibly on the wane.

Every composer whose individuality is at all pronounced naturally finds scores of imitators, and his mannerisms may be said to pervade the musical atmosphere for the time being until the public become nauseated, and gradually the air is cleared through the admixture of some fresh element. The suave and tender accents of Gounod, the intoxicating and luscious melodies of Massenet, having been inhaled for a long while in France, they have for some time past been tonified by the invigorating breezes of Wagnerism.

In the valiant phalanx of the younger French composers actively engaged in the pursuit of their art, eager to tread new paths and to conquer fresh victories for their country on the lyric stage, there stands one who, by reason of his great individuality, may be set apart from the rest. This is Alfred Bruneau, the gifted and inspired composer of *Le Rêve, L'Attaque du Moulin*, and *Messidor*.

These admirable works, so novel in form, so bold in
their absolute unconventionality, and so profoundly
touching in the sincerity of their strains, have naturally,
by reason of these very qualities, stirred up endless discussions. As Camille Saint-Saëns once wrote, *Oser, en
art, est ce qu'il y a de plus terrible au monde.* People do
not care about being taken out of their habits of routine,
they resent any effort at originality that compels them to
think.

Some there are whose reactionary tendencies cause
them to look with suspicion upon any effort in the
direction of emancipation from traditional formulæ ;
others who, knowing they cannot be far wrong in pinning
their musical faith to universally acknowledged masters,
affect a contemptuous indifference towards all music
unsigned by one of the objects of their exclusive admiration.

At the tail of these follow the *moutons de Panurge*, who,
having no opinions of their own, echo those of the
majority. And so the ball merrily rolls on, and the artist
who has had the courage and the talent to come forward
with something new finds himself the subject of acri-
monious discussion. And yet he can scarcely on that
account be deemed worthy of pity, for the very discussions
provoked by his work are a tribute to his originality and
daring.

Better far to be discussed and to be the object of
heated controversy than to be patronisingly patted on
the back and dismissed with a few words of faint praise.

What strikes one so forcibly in the case of Alfred
Bruneau is the courage and determination with which he
has nailed his colours to the mast at the outset of his
career, when so many artists are swayed hither and
thither, doubtful in their anxiety to make a name, which
course to pursue to the best advantage. With a supreme

indifference to the *qu'en dira-t-on* he has followed his own ideas and has struck out a fresh path in the yet unexplored forests of art.

Ten years have elapsed since *Kérim*, his first opera, was produced in Paris, at the Théâtre du Chateau d'Eau. In this work the system so successfully employed since by the composer, of constructing his work upon a symphonic foundation of representative themes, is already followed, and the score is highly interesting through the richness of its Oriental colouring and the novelty of its harmonic effects.

Kérim may, however, be considered rather as a *ballon d'essai.*

The work which first revealed Bruneau to the musical public was *Le Rêve*, produced in 1891 at the Paris Opéra Comique. In this, and in his subsequent works, *L'Attaque du Moulin* (1894), and *Messidor* (1897), Bruneau has been allied to Emile Zola, and the collaboration, so fruitful in its results, is, happily, like to continue.

And now, in what sense do these works constitute a new departure? Musically they are constructed according to the theories of Wagner, inasmuch as the system of representative themes is rigidly employed throughout. The fact of Bruneau's ability to apply this without in any way lapsing into plagiarism is a proof of his great individuality. Until the appearance of *Le Rêve*, French composers had toyed with the *Leit-motiv* without venturing to break away entirely from traditional operatic forms, with the result that their works, however admirable, too often savoured of a spirit of compromise.

In *Le Rêve* Bruneau went in for innovations wholesale, for not only did he boldly adopt the Wagnerian principle in its entirety, but he showed an absolute independence in his harmonies and modulations which scandalised musicians of reactionary tendencies not a little. In

L'Attaque du Moulin the freshness of the melodic inspiration seems to have disarmed the adversaries of
Bruneau to a certain extent, and the composer was even
taunted with making concessions to the public, which was
far from being the case, the nature of the subject naturally
demanding a different style of treatment to that of the
former work.

With *Messidor* the battle was renewed afresh, and the
fact of the libretto being written in prose furnished matter
for further discussion.

If Bruneau has adopted the Wagnerian system of representative themes, he separates himself from the
Bayreuth master in the choice of his subjects. Only
lately he has expressed his views in the clearest possible
manner in the columns of *La Rivista Musicale Italiana.*

After speaking of the evolution that has taken place in
the lyrical drama owing to the 'magnificent genius of
Wagner,' he propounds, as his opinion, that if the master's
art, 'by its splendour, its nobility, its eloquence, its
humanity, is universal, by its very spirit, it remains
absolutely national, and this is what gives it all its
strength.'

Following this idea, Bruneau comments upon the nature
of Wagner's influence over composers of other countries,
and points out that these, notwithstanding their adherence
to the new creed, have remained national in their style.
He exhorts his compatriots to be true to their country, to
shun the nebulosities of legendary lore, and not to allow
themselves to drift into the current of Wagnerian imitation.

The following words may indeed be taken in a measure
as embodying a profession of faith, and they tersely
explain the ideas that actuate the French composer in
the elaboration of his scores:—'In composing *Le Rêve,*
L'Attaque du Moulin, Messidor, dramas not legendary
but thoroughly contemporaneous, very French in action

Y

and sentiments, I have had the constant and firm desire, singing the tenderness of mystic love, the abomination of unjust wars, the necessity of glorious labour, of being at once French and modern.'

It will be seen, therefore, that Bruneau is not in any way a servile imitator of Wagner, and if he has, in common with all the dramatic composers of the day, profited by the master's wondrous innovations and shared in a glorious inheritance, he has not thereby sacrificed his own independence.

To translate into music the thoughts, feelings, sufferings, and aspirations of human beings, to present stirring pictures of life in its uncompromising realism,—such are his objects.

And how different are his characters to the ordinary puppets of the operatic stage! How thoroughly does his music reflect the spirit of the words and intensify the poignancy of the situations! Then how perfectly original does he prove himself in the turn of his melodies, the novelty of his harmonies, the combination of his themes! For, after all, sincerity of purpose is all very good; unless, though, it is accompanied by great individuality, as in the present instance, it avails but little.

In London we have heard *Le Rêve*, *L'Attaque du Moulin*, and the fine Requiem performed under Professor Villiers Stanford at a Bach Choir Concert last year. When are we to hear *Messidor*, the magnificent prose poem by Emile Zola, set to such wonderful music by Alfred Bruneau, the absolute unconventionality of which puzzled the *habitués* of the Paris Opera this year?

Donner le poème du travail, la nécessité et la beauté de l'effort, la foi en la vie, en la fécondité de la terre, l'espoir aux justes moissons de demain.

These words were penned by Emile Zola in order to explain the lesson *Messidor* is intended to teach.

To say that Bruneau's music admirably realises the sense of the words, intensifies the action of the drama and idealises its sentiments, is to give but a faint idea of its power and beauty. The composer has in the following words expressed his aims in the composition of *Messidor* :

Sur un fond de symphonie, j'ai voulu laisser à son véritable plan, c'est à dire au premier, le drame humain dont je n'ai été que le serviteur. J'ai essayé de traduire de façon aussi simple, aussi nette, aussi fidèle que possible les sentiments des personnages et j'ai désiré que le public ne perde pas une seule des paroles chantées.

Taking these words in connection with those at the head of this article, it will be seen how absolutely fitted to work together for the regeneration of the French operatic stage are the two artists whose names are Emile Zola and Alfred Bruneau.